Briars, Brambles, and Barbed Wire

Kay Haggard Hock

outskirts press

Table of Contents

Special Dedication

TO DANNAH MORRISON PROCTER BAYS - my mentor, inspiration, dearest friend, and generous traveling companion. Without her unrelenting encouragement and faith in me, this collection would never have come to fruition. Blame her.

> *"There is nothing better than a friend, unless it is a friend with chocolate."*

> *-Linda Grayson*

***

TO LARRY SMITH. We miss your intellectual insight, support, and humor every day. May you rest in peace with all knowledge.

> *"There is more stupidity than hydrogen in the universe, and it has a longer shelf life."*

> *-Frank Zappa*

Acknowledgements

TO STEPHANIE, JACE, and JONAH: Half of my heart.

> *"How could a 5-ounce bird possibly carry a 1-pound coconut?"*
>
> *-Castle Guard*

***

TO ANDY and EMILY: The other half of my heart.

> *"I hope you check the plumbing. Had I been drinking out of the toilet, I might have been killed."*
>
> *-Ace Ventura*

***

TO ROBIN RITCHIE, KASSIE, ASHLEA, ETHAN, and FAMILIES:

> *"Beelzebub has a devil put aside for me, for me, for meeee..."*
>
> *-Queen*

***

TO CLASS OF 1974, FAMILY, FRIENDS:

> *"...wherever you go, there you are!"*
>
> *-Mike Brady*

Introduction

I've spent my adult life (almost 50 years, depending on when you define onset of 'adulthood') on eighty acres in rural central Texas. When this fact is revealed my Yankee friends envision a vast prairie with coyotes, longhorns, and cattle roundups; locals think of a cute little "spread" with a decent yard to mow. It's a bit of both.

I explain I don't raise cattle or slop pigs, tend chickens or plant a garden. I don't ride the range on a horse or harvest crops. Their questioning expressions pose "then, what exactly do you do?" I reply, "I shred briars and bramble. I grub mesquite, honey locust, and catclaw trees. I take down old out buildings and barbed wire fences." After considering the response some go away, I assume in search of an old crazy cat lady. The most curious ask, "But, why?"

Forty years ago, I cleared enough briars and brambles for the new husband to back a used trailer house into a spot on the abandoned family farm. The husband has long deserted, but all the other pricks stayed. They remained – through sixteen years of marriage, divorce, and raising two children as a single mother, as I cared for my ailing parents, and as my grandson was born and began his exploration of their thickets and the secret world hidden beyond. They remained through my time as Business Manager of the local 1-A school and as I've entered retirement and settled into a routine - a routine including regular confrontations with briars, bramble, and old rusty barbed wire. Again they ask, "but why do you do it?"

As they might imagine, this eighty doesn't acres doesn't look like much. There are no creeks or streams teeming with fish, no pastoral meadows or lush crops. Most wildlife of my youth have even abandoned this old farm for greener pastures. There is, instead, an old earthen tank that overflows in the heavy spring rains, dries up in the summer droughts, and sustains a healthy growth of green algae the rest of the time. There are sagging, broken fences of rusty barbed wire and rotten cedar posts, the fences stretched in years long past by my Granddad to keep the old Jersey cow and mules out of the peanut fields. There are armadillos and skunks, the wildlife less intimidated by the plethora of fire ants, wasps, and yellow jackets. Most would say this old farm lacks curb appeal and they'd be right.

However, Granny and GrandDad raised three kids (my father, his brother and sister) here during the Depression with no running water, no indoor plumbing, no electricity. Heating and cooking was by wood burning stoves, cooling was by raised windows, refrigeration was by an 'ice box' or lowering a food item into the shallow well. They were self-sufficient- raising peanuts and watermelons for crops, planting and harvesting a garden for food, raising chickens for meat and eggs. Dad returned from WWII and eventually convinced his father to add electricity, propane, and a telephone; he never talked him into a well or indoor plumbing.

My father and his siblings left in due time in the 1940's as they came of age, establishing their lives elsewhere and desiring a better future for their own families. Dad, however, always stayed connected to the farm. We drove from town almost every weekend to visit the grandparents. My older brother would hunt rabbits and explore, my sister and I would make mud pies and spend the night when we could. Occasionally, we'd have family holidays at the farm when my aunt and uncle and their families would make it back. Almost every 4th of July my uncle would return with his old Plymouth packed with fireworks and we would all gather to have homemade ice cream and watch the show over the stock tank. Diminishing health eventually forced the grandparents to abandon their home and spend their days with us in town. Granny was happy and content; GrandDad, however, tried to hitchhike back to his home until he became so weak he could only return in his dementia dreams.

After his parents died, Dad never considered how selling the farm would benefit his life financially or ease his burden. Instead, he started keeping a small herd of Black Angus out here, driving the ten miles at least once a day to check for broken fences, monitor the health of the herd, and enjoy the open spaces. He'd feed hay when needed, break ice on the tank when it froze, haul water from town if the tank went dry.

Mom shared his fondness for this old farm and appreciated the history and stability it represented. She, too, was raised during the Depression. Her family, however, had no roots and she spent her younger life as a vagabond - her father moving them from town to town across Texas as work became available. This old farm represented 'home' to her, too. Home. When Mom and Dad retired they chose to sell out and leave town, moving a used mobile home next to the old, abandoned farmhouse. She said, "People think we're crazy, moving from town to the farm when most people our age are moving from the farm into town. I just tell them if I can't take care of myself on the farm, I can't take care of myself in town...so I'll go as far as I can." And she did.

I look from my house to the north and see where my father was born on the hill. I look from my house to the south and see where Mom and Dad spent their final years after retirement and took their last breaths. Everywhere, I see a lifetime of memories. And briars, bramble, and old barbed wire needing my immediate attention and efforts. Why?

People think I'm a tad odd, spending much of this golden time engaged in a seemingly lost battle. They remind me I have options. I have a degree in Finance, an MBA in economics and business management. I have a decent retirement and savings and could hire much of the work done by others. Or, I could sell this old farm and move anywhere - perhaps a maintenance-free apartment or retirement condo where I could be playing bridge and shuffleboard and sipping sweet iced tea! And it's not like I don't do other things. I travel and read, visit friends in other states, and go to Kansas twice a year to work with a silage chopping crew. I spend time with my family. I solve puzzles -crossword, jigsaw, Sudoku. I do most of my own home maintenance, repairs, and remodels. I grow flowers. I putter. I do stuff.

So, why? I've asked myself that many times and the answers are evasive, yet clear. Experiencing the pangs of an empty nest, I silently vowed to start clearing the land and get the old farm looking good again; I knew Dad would like that. Although I was still working my full time job and caring for the parents as needed, I got busy in my spare time and had made some actual progress. Unfortunately, their health declined steadily after their retirement. Too soon their well-being took priority and I abandoned the work to better see to their needs. I never got back to the task and watched as nature reclaimed any progress I had made. Dad died, never knowing my plan or seeing this old peanut farm looking like much more than abandoned fields and overgrown pastures. In part, I clear the bramble and briars as homage to my father and to fulfill a personal vow.

Additionally, donning old work clothes and boots and sweating in the sunshine suits me. Never a frilly girlie girl, I've always preferred the comfort and utility of jeans and t-shirts. I've never backed away from hard work, appreciating every inch of progress made by my own sweat and efforts. I don't need validation or accolades from others; I just need the personal satisfaction of knowing I made progress and did the best I could do. I postulate all of us are surrounded by an abundance of pricks; I merely have chosen to surround myself with pricks I can actually run over with a shredder.

Working alone suits me fine. Professionally, I spent many years in semi-solitude doing office work. The grinding din of large crowds annoys me and I don't feel I perform well with the small talk required of most casual conversations. I prefer associations with close friends and family as the opportunities arise. Other times, I do quite alright alone with my thoughts. It keeps my mind and hands busy in ways I find constructive and therapeutic.

Finally, I endure the scratches, sweat, fatigue, and frustrations required to face the challenges of clearing the land because this old farm is home. Not only to me but to my family. My sister and her kids and grandkids think of this old farm when they think of home. My children and grandchildren, being raised here, will always consider this their home. I work to ensure the home fires can always be seen above the bramble and briars, that all can return if they need to feel their connection to roots. I've been entrusted with this empire of dirt and appointed the caretaker of its heritage and legacy. And, as Mom once said, "I'll go as far as I can". Or as far as the old Ford tractor will carry me.

Following is a collection of short stories recounting memories, awkward situations, and thoughts on various topics - stories often interwoven through the briars and bramble and barbed wire. The stories are meant to entertain and amuse in a humorous, often self-deprecating manner. Basically, I laugh at myself first and loudest to deny my family the pleasure. It's how I roll.

A Rose by Any Other Name

My Dad would say, "Load up. We're taking a ride to the country!" Robin (my younger sister) and I knew this meant we were going to Granny's and Grand Dad's. We didn't stop to pack our favorite toys. We didn't grab games or balls or books! We were going to the country; nothing else would be needed. There would usually be a quick stop at Earl Weather's Cafe for a bottled 'Coke', perhaps a bar of candy or peanuts, then we would be on our way!

After warm hugs and smiles, we could be found outside in search of entertainment. Making mud pies and searching for garnishments, such as China berries or Redbud blossoms to adorn our culinary creations. Riding the propane tank like horses and playing 'Gunsmoke'. Hiking to the barn and through the woods. Throwing rocks in the tank or looking for frogs and turtles. Watching the jerseys graze or chew their cud. Sitting quietly, listening to the birds or watching the buzzards circling high overhead. Chasing an occasional cottontail or roadrunner. Sometimes, Granny would trust us to carry water from the well and help water her collection of prized potted plants. There was always something to do.

At some point in time, however, we would stop and pick bouquets of wildflowers...one for Mom and one for Granny. The pastures had an abundance of flowers: Indian blankets, phlox of blue and purple and pink, Brown-eyed Susans, Mexican hats, pinkish winecups, yellow Coreopsis, spotted purple bee balm, and the occasional rain lilies. Even the Texas thistles and some weeds were pretty enough to include in our bouquets. (I encouraged Robin, my younger sister, to gather the thistles to complete our surprise. She eventually decided her bouquet was just fine and if I wanted thistles, I could pick them myself.) We would run in the house proudly and bursting with pride to present our bounty! After their obligatory 'ooooooos' and 'ahhhhhhs', we would smile and be off again in search of another adventure.

Gradually, the pastures became less welcoming and no longer dotted with splashes of color. I suppose years of grazing, cultivation, drought, and erosion eventually took a toll on the wildflowers. I don't think Robin and I gathered so many flowers we picked them ALL? Maybe? Whatever the reasons, as an adult living on that farm I was saddened by their absence and decided to stop whining and do something positive. My intentions were never to replenish the vast landscape. Waxing nostalgic, it was my simple desire to recapture a bit of the past and cultivate a wildflower garden within the small confines of my yard fence.

That said, last year I researched wildflower varieties, planting times, and soil types. I prepared the ground. I bought a bag of Wildflower Mix from the seed store. And when the timing and climate were just right per the almanac and instructions, I lovingly sowed my seed. And waited. And watered when needed. And waited. Finally, little plants could be seen dotting the soil. Unable to distinguish between emerging wildflowers and weeds, I waited until I could identify the weeds and then, carefully and methodically removed them while leaving the cherished plantlings undisturbed. It was a tedious process but eventually I had some flowers! True, I was a bit disappointed in the yield and variety. But I did everything possible the past fall to ensure the plant seeds dried and scattered; I anticipated a much better showing this year.

What a beautiful spring it has been! Warm weather! Sunshine! Occasional rains! And big robust plants, most of which had added a green presence and an unexpected hardiness through the winter, have already been blooming and taking over the bare ground recently cleared of henbit and chickweed. "How nice!" you're thinking, "wildflowers have returned to the hill!" Allow me to be more specific. By big robust plants...I mean oenothera speciosa, also known as evening primrose, aka Mexican primrose, aka pink ladies! By taking over the bare ground, I mean spreading and choking the life out of anything within a mile radius of my yard. And by unexpected hardiness, I mean it will be impossible to control this specific flora in a lifetime dedicated solely to its eradication by any available means – herbicides, machetes, lawnmowers, goats, or blood, sweat, and tears! Unbelievable.

Evening primrose. Pinklady. Aren't those lovely names? They hide behind aliases for a reason; beyond those sweet, delicate, pink blossoms beats a heart of stone. Those are the hardy drought-resistant plants you will see growing where all else fails – clinging to rocky cliffs, roadsides, slopes, and highway rock cuts – well, ANYwhere there's full sun and a teaspoon of dirt! And they are breeders! They spread by seed AND runners so they're working the nasty all the time. ALL. THE. TIME. Even as I write this I know they're back at it, shaking their fertile little stamen in the air and all about! And something else you must understand; although they bloom some during the day, they are called 'EVENING' for a reason. Yep. Their prime blooming time is at night, usually closing their delicate pink blossoms in the heat of day. So, instead of sweet blossoms attracting butterflies in the day (as I had hoped) ... I have night bloomers and moths. MOTHS! I have flowers that bloom at night and attract MOTHS! Go me!

Soooooo, I've been on my hands and knees for two days, grubbing the ground like a hog after acorns in an attempt to eradicate what I took such care in nurturing. They must go! Or at least be controlled if possible. Why? 1) My yard was looking like the entrance ramp to a cheap roadside restroom and I expected a knock on the door from some weary traveler wanting to use my facilities. 2) I can't sleep at night, knowing they're out there spreading wide their fleshy pink lady parts for an onslaught of amorous moth hoards! 3) Upon removal, I've discovered a hidden world of tiny seedlings begging for sunshine and a chance to live and fulfill my initial wildflower vision; they must be saved! I've loaded a pickup bed with unearthed evening prim- roses, carefully pulling one and trying to leave the starving plantlings beneath undisturbed. I transplanted a hundred other struggling seed- lings, found clinging to the dirt between the stone walk – the only soil available to tiny seeds looking for a place in a world overrun by eve- ning primroses. I've done all I can do for now.

This is not my first venture into the undergrowth. No. This Primrose experience is reminiscent of the Great Salvia Fiasco of 2006. That's the year I was walking the farm and spied a single salvia beside the trail. It was so pretty, a beautiful butterfly hovering above its vibrant red blooms. I hadn't seen another one anywhere and it reminded me of my Granny. It spoke to me. It was a sign. So, I carefully and lovingly transplanted it to my house. Long story short... I have also removed a pickup load of these in the interim years. They're everywhere now. Everywhere. Who knew I was transplanting what many consider a weed? But at least they're pretty, I think. AND they do attract but- terflies and hummingbirds...NOT moths! I shall consider this one a semi- sort of win!

Mom always said Granny could plant a sucker stick and grow a lollipop! So true! Obviously, I do NOT share my Granny's green thumb - unless cultivating invasive species of weeds counts for something! However, as my Granny did, I will keep marching forward... planting...weeding... cultivating...watering. I will muddle my way through this thistle-laden garden of life, forever attempting to add just a touch of beauty and splash of color to my little empire of dirt. I hope to die in the sunshine, dirt under my nails. And when I die, I've requested to be cremated and spread across the pastures and terraces. I have, however, recently added a clause to the burial plan for my children. They are to mix a heaping helping of my ashes with wildflower seeds (I still have plenty in the bag) and sow us abundantly outside their backdoor! I will be very low maintenance. AND this will ensure my presence forever and ever and ever...amongst the immortal Evening Primroses and moths! Always. They will never be rid of me completely. This should bring them all great comfort - the knowledge Mom will be forever lurking outside their back door ...in the garden...in the dark. I know it brings a smile to my face!

Best Laid Scheme

At the risk of you visualizing a rooster crowing from my headboard and Arnold the pig running wild through my house on a dirt floor...

I was in my dimly lit kitchen last night (dimly-lit for energy conservation and mood-setting purposes, not as by kerosene lantern) and I saw a snake crawl from behind the microwave. It slithered between the toaster and wall and dropped unceremoniously behind the stove before I could identify it (due to aforementioned lowered lighting) or grab it. I got a flashlight and tried to get a visual but it had disappeared. Not in the mood to hold a snake vigil in my kitchen all evening, I simply checked for it occasionally until time for bed. Nothing. Had it gone back from whence it came when I wasn't looking? Or moved to another part of the house? Or was it still enjoying the warmth of the pilot light? I didn't want to consider the possibility of a viper dropping from the ceiling fan as I slept so I decided to consider it still under the stove. I had some sticky traps and made a 'minefield' in my kitchen, reminiscent of that kitchen scene in "Mouse Trap". *That should slow that rascally serpent until I can grab it*, I thought, and went to bed.

Two minutes after stretching out I heard a rustling noise from the kitchen and smirked at the thought of my swift, utter victory! I was horrified when I switched on the light (full power) and saw it...sitting there... all beady-eyes and nasty and icky!! **Insert full-body shudder here**A mouse!! That gross, horrible, flea-bitten creature was in my snake trap! Disgusting! I was pondering how to remove the mouse without having to see it/touch it/acknowledge its existence when I had an epiphany! *Snakes like mice, yes? So, why can't I just leave it there... as snake bait? The snake will come out, eat the mouse, get stuck and unable to crawl away! I'll simply pick up the snake and take it outside in the morning! I'll not have to see the mouse at all or dispose of it! Eureka!* I grabbed the hoe I had in the kitchen (I don't always keep a hoe so conveniently located. I had brought it in earlier for...you know... the snake) and poked around on the mouse to ensure it was soundly and irrevocably STUCK.

The alarm sounded this morning and I jumped up, anxious to bask in the glory of my conquest! ...But, alas...

> *Mousie, thou art no thy lane*
> *In proving foresight may be vain*
> *The best-laid schemes o' mice an' men*
> *Gang aft agley*
> *An' lea'e us nought but grief an' pain*
> *For promis'd joy!..."*

What the heck does that mean? Well, it means my brilliant, foolproof plan wasn't. There was no snake. AND there was no mouse. They were nowhere in sight. The quandary being 1) did the snake eat the mouse and escape, meaning I have a temporarily satiated reptile settled in some dark corner of my home? Or 2) did the nasty rodent rip himself from the glue board, meaning I have a ravenous snake on the prowl for the half-naked rabid mouse running amuck in my house? Either way, it's going to be a very long weekend.

Bigger Is Better

I'm considering starting a cottage business and requesting feedback. This is the initial step of my business plan – a bit of marketing research- and appreciate your honest opinions and suggestions. Thank you in advance. Also, since I'm asking for your advice I thought it only fair to share my thought processes which can only be described as inspired! I apologize if this writing seems rambling and disjointed, but I'm putting these thoughts to paper before I forget. I know if I sleep the inspiration will leave me and I'll have no memory of it by morning. I will be left with only the nagging feeling I had a very important thought ... or at least I think I did... and move on to other endeavors. Moment lost forever.

BACKGROUND INFO: I like wind chimes and have previously re-searched making them as a hobby. I found examples of chimes made of old silverware and wine bottles and bottle caps and just basic recy-clable miscellaneous and sundry scraps of anything that would make a 'clinking' sound in the wind. Some were pretty, I suppose, but most I thought were downright ugly. Nothing appealed to me. Blah...blah... blah... B-O-R-I-N-G. I had googled 'huge wind chimes', however, and was intrigued by the concept. These wind chimes are HUGE – made of 2-inch tubing, dog chains, J-hooks, and ½ inch braided nylon rope; the bell tubes themselves can be any length but the best are around 8 feet long! HUGE! And they sound so cool. Not a 'tinkle tinkle' as much as a melodic 'ding dong'. But not like a doorbell 'ding dong'...more like 'ding DONG'. Actually, I think the sound can be described better as "DONG DONG"! The size is not for enhanced volume ... it's more for enhanced and unique tonal quality.

INSPIRATION: As I worked outside today and enjoyed the little 'tinkle tinkle' of the chimes, my mind returned to the aforementioned hobby research. I then began to wonder if I could actually make them... and SELL them. (I believe that's what I'm supposed to do as a retiree, think of things I can do as a hobby but also generate a little extra income like for food and shelter and stuff). Anyway, I got all excited and my mind started racing with questions and ideas.

First, I reviewed the construction process and feel confident I can make them. And if I can make them, certainly someone else can buy them! So... that's defined as a business. Right? And a business must have a name. Any name with 'chime' seems mundane, even misleading. I need the name to be representative and descriptive! They are big and long...so I need to address the size. And they're not chimes in the traditional sense. The sound is unique and should be a part of what is communicated to a prospective buyer. As I tried to put the ideas of size and sound together in a descriptive way, I remembered a phrase I had heard a long time ago. It was during the hearings to add Clarence Thomas to the Supreme Court. I didn't follow the process closely. However, the phrase 'long dong silver' was in the news several times. I suppose it was some play on the pirate name, Long John Silver? I doubt it was the fish restaurant. Anyway, I thought it might be the perfect name for a business... the chimes are long, silver-colored, and make a 'dong' sound. But, the more I reflected the less I liked it. I think it would be a mistake to start a chime business with a name reminding people of pirates. Or fish.

I abandoned that name and moved on, again seeking a name reflective of the unique size and tone of the chimes. I then remembered a song from my youth, 'Bang the Gong'. Wow...if I named it 'Bang the

Gong' I would already have my own theme song associated with the business. I liked it, but it still wasn't right. 1) It's not actually a gong, although the sound is similar and 2) nothing about its super-size is contained in the title and 3) it implies you have to actually bang on something for it to work. I thought of changing it to 'Bang the Dong'. I admit I like the sound of that. Bang the Dong! However, it still implies you have to bang a dong to get the satisfactory effect.

I returned to square one and broke it down to the elements...size and sound... and after a few more attempts I think I have a name for my new business. MEGA DONGS! Size and sound... most representative of what the product is! And always in capitals. And in a cool font, perhaps the M like the M in Metallica? Score! MEGA DONGS! I like it!

NOTE TO SELF: *Google search MEGA DONGS, trademark requirements

So, I really started serious thinking from that point. I need to determine if there is actually a market for MEGA DONGS! Do any of you have a MEGA DONG or know someone who does? Do you like them? If you could get your hands on one, would it be something you would be interested in having? If I had a MEGA DONG party, would you come and invite your friends? Most of us have the smaller ... regular 6 inch or smaller...hanging out in our homes. Some of you lucky ones may have access to a larger size. I've never had one of those larger ones either but I have touched a few displayed for sale. It provokes disapproving glances in my direction but I think if they don't want people touching them they shouldn't be left hanging out! Anyway, I really like the big ones and believe MEGA DONGS would provide an almost overwhelming sensory experience. I hope you agree.

Next, I thought about how the MEGA DONG works and realized you may see some problems. No blow, no go. No motion and there is no action at all...just a limp banger (that's what the longer hanging-down part is called by those of us in the biz). Conversely, too much motion and it can be simply too much to handle and a little annoying. Who wants a huge banger beating out of control and bumping into everything? It could do some real damage and someone could lose an eye or worse. I needed to address these issues and believe I have successfully problem-solved. If there is too little motion to get the MEGA DONG in action, I will develop some kind of mechanical device ... something to crank manually or perhaps plug in... that would start the banger swinging for a predetermined amount of time. It would eventually wind down, of course, but hopefully it grinds long enough to provide enjoyment for all. Additionally, there will be times someone might need to shut it down completely for a while. I don't want someone getting so frustrated they decide to cut the banger off; it could get to be too much if it goes on and on for days. I will devise a simple procedure for cinching all the moving parts together. Or even move the banger over to the side and tie it down Either way, the consumer isn't left at the mercy of an uncontrolled, beating banger!

I should point out to you MEGA DONGS have another advantage over the smaller varieties. The less substantial ones wear out and/or break rather easily from regular use. They are somewhat fragile and collapse in a heap after a short period of time. At least, that's been my experience. But the MEGA DONG is made of superior and more durable products. As the old Timex commercial says, "it takes a licking and keeps on ticking"! The size alone aids in longevity and should be good for many years of pleasure. Additionally, the modifications I mentioned earlier will keep the MEGA DONG under control and keep the banger from wearing out too soon.

So, that's my MEGA DONG business pitch in a nutshell. I'm really excited and seriously considering this as a viable venture. I think with proper MEGA DONG promotion, it will find its position on top in the marketplace and beat down the competition! I can see the advertisements now: OUR MEGA DONGS ARE HUNG FOR YOUR LASTING PLEASURE. I know the market can expand to accommodate. Look at Starbucks, for example. It created an entire industry around coffee, convincing even non-coffee drinkers it was cool and they had to have it first thing every morning! And that was just a little cup of coffee!

Imagine the possibilities if everyone felt compelled to start each day with the soothing vibrations of a swaying MEGA DONG ringing in their ears!

NOTE TO SELF: **My personal experience with MEGA DONGs is limited to internet videos. Place a personal ad to inquire if anyone in this area has one. If so, offer to pay for the opportunity to see and touch it! It's possible it won't be as impressive up close and I just won't be feeling it. If so, I'll probably turn my back on the MEGA DONG venture, get a headache, and go to sleep.

Again, thank you for feedback concerning this venture. Maybe I'll see you at the party!

Case of the Disappearing Dragonfly

All of us have those moments when an unexpected event, usually trauma, seems to affect the space/time continuum; the universe suddenly switches to slow motion. We leave our bodies and hover, observing ourselves helplessly reacting to intervene and change the chain-of-events we know is inevitable. The more intuitive among us probably experience this phenomenon often. I don't. I'm more the 'Golly, Gee! I didn't see that coming' type of person. But, not today.

The daughter, son in law, grandson and I went for a drive this nice, sunny day to enjoy the warmth and fresh air after an unusually brutal winter. We had been driving for a while, taking in the sights and smells of spring, talking, singing to the radio, and entertaining the two-year-old. However, we agreed it was time to look for a facility of the bathroom variety. Stephanie was getting a bit fidgety when we happened upon a very nice rock structure in the middle of nowhere. How fortuitous - a bathroom, snack bar, and gift shop!

The others ran ahead to the bathroom and to scope out the place. The grandson and I, however, took our own sweet time and leisurely strolled along holding hands, stopping to smell flowers, touching rocks, picking up a few random sticks, and watching ants and bugs do their thing. He's at that magical age when all the world is a wonder and must be touched and experienced; I have the pleasure of seeing the sheer joy of it all through his eyes anew. Sharing an appreciation for nature was a blessed experience I shared with my children and now, the grandchildren. I find it to be one of the greatest pleasures of having small children around. I try to ignore the myriad of less pleasant things.

We finally reached the top of the stairs and discovered the 'building' was actually a roofed, open area. The bathrooms and gift shop were enclosed in respective air-conditioned rooms with doors. The remaining space under the roof was open and offered vending machines, brochure racks, and picnic tables. Exposed beams, trusses, and rafters made for a nice patio ambiance...and shelter to a variety of birds. Their songs were a nice addition to the breezy, open air experience; their other contributions...not so much.

As the two of us stood observing our surroundings, I noticed a dragonfly sitting on the floor. I thought it was dead. After more observation, however, I determined it was alive but grounded, probably nearing death for whatever reason. I didn't know; I'm not an entomologist! Considering this a precious moment to share nature with Jonah, I retrieved it and I held it out for him to inspect closely. He gently touched it, stroking its wings and talking to it. I didn't tell him it was hurt and would probably die. I let him believe I snatched a dragonfly from the sky just for him. At that moment, I was his hero.

After sharing a bonding experience over our dragonfly, I told Jonah it was time to take him outside and let him rest. My plan was to take the injured bug outside to the shade and lay it gently on the grass to die. I would explain to Jonah how the dragonfly looked very tired and hot and needed to rest awhile; I would explain that he would fly away later. That was my plan.

The dragonfly had another agenda. We started toward the entrance, the dragonfly still perched peacefully in my outstretched hand. I walked two steps and that's when my space/time continuum hiccoughed, sputtered and coasted into slow motion. In slow motion, I watched the dragonfly rally and leave my hand. I felt my nerve endings shoot a meandering flare into my brain. I saw my empty hand reaching out toward the direction of the dragonfly and close around nothing but air. I saw a bird tense in the rafters, actually sharing a moment as we stared into each other's eyes with all knowledge of the immediate future. I sneered as I watched a little bird smirk directed at me slowly form on his little bird beak. I watched helplessly as the bird left its perch and began his dive, my mind silently forming the word, "noooooooo!" Then, as abruptly as it began and before the word could leave my lips, my existence suddenly snapped back into real time to play out the remainder of the scenario. He dove directly at the dragonfly, snagged him in his beak in mid-air and flew out the nearest opening.

I was stunned and looked down at Jonah who, in turn, was looking up at me with a most puzzled expression. "Where did he go? Where did he go?" he asked in his two-year-old way. Feeling this was a prime opportunity to impart Grammie wisdom, I considered explaining the circle of life. I considered introducing a treatise on survival of the fittest. I even considered telling him it disappeared because it was a magical dragonfly and that's what they do. Instead, I found myself waving madly toward the rafters, waving and shouting, "Goodbye dragonfly! Good bye! See you later!" as passersby looked upwards hoping to see a dragonfly. Jonah waved, too, as he shouted his goodbyes. Satisfied, his attention was immediately consumed by questions about other things and we moved along.

Considering today's event, I was asking myself if I handled the situation correctly. Could I have been less dramatic in my immediate response?

My daughter certainly thought so. Should I have simply told him the truth - the bird ate him for lunch? Truth is a virtue that can't be taught too soon, but that seems honest to a brutal degree. Should I have told him the truth and taken the opportunity to explain the intricacies of life and death? No, I believe that falls in the domain of his unsuspecting parents and I don't want to relieve them of that golden nugget of parenthood. Besides, kids grow up so fast! They are only this young for such a short time. I think I'll take advantage of that fact and lie every chance I have while I still can. These precious days are numbered and he'll soon see through my lies. I know it won't be long until he'll realize Grammie didn't really pull a dragonfly from the sky just for him! For now, I like being his hero.

Christmas CPR

1950's. My oldest brother came home from school crying. Mom pulled him close and asked why he was so upset. Between sobs he told her, " 'Johnny' told me there is no Santa Claus." She assumed this would be the moment in which she would have to whisper her oft-rehearsed responses to this inevitable question. She was prepared to say, "Santa is the spirit of the holiday, Charles. He's the magic of giving and warmth of sharing. He's the twinkle of the lights and sounds of bells and carols and smells of cookies baking. He's the smiles and laughter" She pulled him close and asked, "but what do you think?" My brother answered, "I told Johnny there is too a Santa Clause because my parents can't afford what I get for Christmas!" And so it was...and so it is...and so it continues.

My parents, children of the Depression era, had been happy with a piece of fresh fruit and assorted exotic nuts in their stockings and ecstatic with a new pair of shoes in which to trudge the two miles to school. But like so many of their generation, they wanted a better life for their children and would go into debt to ensure their children had a 'special' Christmas. They would stress and scrape and save to see those smiles on Christmas morning. I didn't understand financial matters and how illness and doctors and hospitals could drain a bank account. I didn't understand how utterly grueling trying to make a Christmas for three kids would have been under those circumstances especially. I had no inkling of the downside and stress of the holiday. I only knew I would probably get that 'one special thing I really, really, REALLY wanted' and life was good. Knowing what I know now, I wish I hadn't shown my disappointment with panties and a doll.

There was magic in the Christmas air when I was a kid. I suppose some of it was the same notion "my parents can't afford what I hope to get, so it has to come from someplace magical." But it was more. It was seeing Christmas decorations magically appear in the stores AFTER Thanksgiving. It was the banners and lights on the downtown square. It was the Christmas scenes painted by Mrs. Lewellen on the store-fronts. It was driving around the 'rich' neighborhoods to see their artificial silver trees with the light disc that changed their color to blue and green and red and yellow. It was the smell of our scraggly tree and the beauty of the lights and reused tinsel and icicles and mismatched ornaments. It was decorating sugar cookies with my mom and sister. It was the homemade candy Mom, Grandma, and Aunt June only made at Christmas. It was Uncle David telling us he heard something on the roof and making us shriek, 'Santa'! It was hot chocolate and marsh-mallows. The magic was a state of being – contentment and simple joy.

I don't know how I failed to evoke those same emotions in my own children. I don't believe I was as stressed emotionally or strapped fi-nancially as my own parents had been. And I do know I wanted them to 'feel' the same magic. But it was different...times were different. As my generation took the holiday helm, both parents in most families worked to provide. Time was the valuable commodity of which we had little. I seldom made the time to bake cookies or decorate them with my kids. They didn't seem to mind, however, because we could buy cookies already decorated on the fly at Walmart. I would try to recapture the magic of Christmas lights but they weren't impressed; they could watch huge displays on the computer, blinking multi-colored lights dancing in sync to awesome music! Christmas decorations vied for shelf space with back-to-school supplies, so by the time the season actually neared we were already over it. It seemed the older they got, the more it took to actually impress them. This was not my fault or their fault – it's just the way it was. Months of visual/audio bombardment by media and retailers desensitized us and the magic remained at low ebb. We have devolved into a society of 'competitive shopping'… one in which 'to the victor goes the spoils'…one in which spraying chemicals or riots or trampling the weak and fallen for the prize is to be expected. We've had to become vigilant and cautious, knowing the perverts, crazies, cons, and thieves are out seeking prey. We have allowed our expectations and that of our children to spiral into an unrealistic dimension, one in which our reality will most likely leave us full of disappointment and depression.

As the birth of my first grandchild nears, I want to challenge myself – and all young parents (the next generation) – to search their hearts and revive the 'old' spirit of Christmas. It won't be easy. Let's divest ourselves of the stress and economic drain of the season. Let's remove the worry of political correctness and social propriety. Let's remember the days when a smile, a nod, and a friendly "Merry Christmas" exchange was enough among casual friends. Let's find a way to keep Wall Street, Main Street, and Madison Avenue from dictating our wants and needs and 'gotta haves' for the season. Let's stay in closer touch with our families throughout the year. Let's start or continue meaningful traditions. Let's teach our children lessons of service, giving, and gratitude. Let the kids decorate a less than perfect tree with less than perfect ornaments. Let them sloppily wrap a gift given from the heart. Let's go back to the simpler time of fruits and nuts and a good pair of shoes – family time and baked cookies. Maybe, just maybe, we can reconnect with the peace and joy of the season. The attitude adjustment would make the rest of the year much better, too.

This is my Christmas wish for my kids and their kids... as I'm pretty sure the silver Ferrari Spider 360 V-8 I ask for every year...the one with red heated lumbar leather upholstery and lighted spinners... is probably NOT going to be under the tree... AGAIN!! But the point is, I love you anyway!!

Classic 1974

Getting older is similar to trudging up a mountain. It seems to get steeper the closer I get to the crest...footing more unstable, breathing harder, muscles aching, more effort required to conquer less territory, and greater degree of apprehension as to what I will discover as I plant my tiny banner at the top. Sometimes, I stop and sit a spell. Not to rest exactly, but survey where I've been...the steps I've made and the footprints I've left. I don't concern myself about the distance to the top because I'm in no hurry to get there and will arrive soon enough. And I don't worry about the trip down the other side. I know it will be a steep decline, an effortless freefall, and a painless landing. So far, I've had the motivation to get up and continue. I think that means I'm still alive and have more stuff I want to do. That's a good thing, yes?

Wow! There's nothing like a 40-year High School class reunion to get me to dust off the old rearview mirror and wax a bit nostalgic. Looking back at my vision of the future at graduation, 1974, and contemplating where I actually am opposed to where I thought I'd be, I'm perplexed like Bugs Bunny...I must have "taken a left at Albuquerque". My reality is much different than my vision. It's different, not inferior or a disappointment. Different. I understand that now, although it took me forty years to figure it out.

I vowed when I graduated High School no classmates would be seeing me again until I 1) had earned my first million dollars and/or could 2) roar up on a custom Harley behind a black helmet, snuggled against a beefy and ripped pro-athlete or 3) come to a screeching halt behind the wheel of a Lamborghini Espada with my brain surgeon husband donning a flowing scarf and large sunglasses, all mysterious and Audrey Hepburn-like. I wasn't sure which one. What can I say? I'm now convinced (after 40 years) ain't none of it gonna happen, so if I'm going to make a dramatic entrance at a reunion of the class of 1974 there will be no better time than now. I will be content at this point to make a quiet and discreet old-lady entrance...alone...in my white F-150 truck. I will, however, be wearing sunglasses with an air of mystery. Score for me!!!

I do worry I won't be remembered or recognized. I fear meeting with a lot of blank stares and friendly, "oh, yeah...uhmmmm... Sure, I remember you (as they frantically try to discreetly glimpse my name tag). It's Fay, right? How've you been, Fay?" Then, after a brief and polite exchange, they will walk away mumbling amongst themselves, "I don't remember her, do you? Do you think she crashed the party or the class of '65 sent her to spy?"

As a way of circumventing these awkward confrontations, I'm making a list of physical changes they may observe to help identify me tomorrow night; it should help me avoid moments of silent insecurities. I'll distribute copies upon admittance:

1) My hair was long, brown, and flowing. It is now short and graying.

2) My skin was tight, tan, and smooth. It's now loose and flawed.
3) My teeth were sparkling white. They're not quite as pearly and definitely fewer to brush.
4) My boobs were 'perky' Cs. Now, not so much of either.
5) My butt used to be higher, firmer, and rounder. It doesn't leave a trail in the dirt yet, but that's about all I can say in its defense.
6) I wore cool hippie glasses in High School. Then, after graduation, I had lasik surgery and didn't wear glasses for a few years. But, never mind on second thought ... I'm back in glasses again, though they're not cool hippie glasses. They're uncool bifocals.
7) My weight hasn't changed a lot. However, it has been redistributed

to various parts that now flap in the wind like bat wings. Actually, they ARE bat wings! Dang!

8) I had one chin when we graduated. I'm not sure now. Do sagging jowls count as chins?

9) I could hear a pin drop at forty paces. Now, my hearing isn't quite as sharp. I also don't care. Let it drop. I'm not going to pick it up anyway.

10) I glided through space and time with the grace of a ballet dancer in High School...at least, compared to how I hobble and limp and shuffle and creak now.

11) My memory may or may NOT be as keen as it once was. I can't recall.

So, yeah, I'm not the same person I was forty years ago. Thank goodness!! Life has happened and it's been good. And the best thing about getting older? As I sit quietly contemplating atop this mountain, I look around and notice lots of familiar faces. They, too, are looking back in time and remembering the stops along the way. Zigs and zags on the trail we could never have anticipated forty years ago...the jobs and mortgages, defeats and triumphs, kids and grandkids... all marking a specific place in the time defining our lives. We look at each other and give an understanding nod. We know where we've been and are satisfied. We know where we are and are happy and content. We know where we're going and are thankful to still be climbing. And we recognize how lucky we made the fateful left turn at Albuquerque that brought us to this moment! It's all good, silly Wabbit!

Clean Underwear

Mama instructed us to "always wear clean underwear when you leave the house because you never know..." She never finished that thought, what I considered an incomplete directive; I suppose she assumed I was smart enough to fill in the blank. It took a few years, but now I understand.

I try to do everything around the farm in a safe and responsible way. However, occasionally situations arise that fall into a 'no one thinks this is a good idea and tries to talk me out of it and I probably shouldn't but I'm going to do it anyway for expediency sake because it needs to be done NOW category. Such was the case earlier this week when I noticed some acorn-laden branches rubbing against the roof. Normally, I would point and grunt directives and the son would jump to it. But, alas, it was a happenstance everyone would be gone on the ONE day those acorns decided to drag and the branches had to be snipped.

I got the extension ladder in place, collected my gloves and loppers, and prepared to do battle with the oaks on my roof; I had one more thing to do. My sister and I have a safety system for the rare occasions I decide I need to go on the roof or under the house. I notify her of my plans and an estimated time for completion. Since I don't take my phone with me (because, you know, it will only be in the way or get dirty or possibly broken) ... my theory is if she doesn't hear from me in the allotted time she'll at least be able to report my possible GPS coordinates to the men in white who will come and take me away. At least I hope she understands her part of my safety plan. I don't actually think we ever discussed it in detail. Maybe she thinks I'm just telling her about my day. Maybe I should ask. Anyway, it should make everyone feel better knowing I think things through in detail and don't take unnecessary risks. I called to tell her I was initiating PROJECT BODY BAG. She had my back, so it was full steam ahead.

I climbed the ladder and lopped away, cutting and discarding the low branches causing my distress. I noticed the gutters and roof could use some additional attention in the knowledge it would eventually rain again. I had, however, used my allotted time. I texted the control center and told her I was going back up for an additional hour and would be in touch. Again, everything went as planned and I texted 'Major Tom to Ground Control, Old Crow has landed!" She acknowledged with some snarky reply and we signed off.

It was noon as I entered the house, hot and sweaty and seeking a cool place to congratulate myself on the successful completion of the task. I was feeling really good about life in general as I stood at the sink looking out the window, chugging water like a sorority girl at the keg on a Saturday night (a generalization, no offense intended if that doesn't apply to you personally). Slowly, the vision of the branches rubbing against the well house's roof came into conscious focus. I had forgotten those bad boys were also on my agenda! *They must be done! TODAY!*

It was mid-day; I was already hot and tired and began trying to talk myself out of it. I advised myself there were very several good reasons to just walk away and leave it for another day. I advised myself it's always at this point in a project I get in trouble, the point in time when I'm thinking that went well so just one more round on the mower, one more turn of the screw, one climb up the ladder, ad nauseam. It's that 'one more thing' that pushes me over the edge, the point when I destroy something, get hurt, or generally screw up. I veer off-road, crashing my project into a deep ditch and have to claw my way out to daylight. I advised myself to walk away. Myself didn't take the advice.

After moving the equipment to the well house, I further assessed the situation. It's a SMALL metal building with a gable roof, the bottom edge seven feet from the ground rising to a ridge in the middle. I don't know how high the ridge is from the ground because looking up from the ground I swear it disappeared under cloud cover. *I don't remember ever climbing up there. It looks steeper than I remember IF I ever did. But I must have. I know those branches have dragged on that roof at times through the years. I must have done it before. Funny I don't remember.*

I was halfway up the ladder with the loppers when I realized I had failed to initiate the safety plan, Code Name BODY BAG; I forgot to call my sister. I started down, and then hesitated. *I've already pestered her twice today. And it's such a little roof. A few branches. A little project, really. I don't think I'll bother her again. Maybe I should get my phone, though...just in case? No, I don't have a way to carry it and I don't need it. I can do this!* I finished the climb and peered through the ladder rungs. *It's steep, alright! But the ridge is not that far away; that's good. How difficult can this be?* I stepped out on the roof and got a speedy response to that query.

I had tested the traction with my left foot as my right foot remained firmly planted on the extension ladder and deemed it acceptable enough. It seems, however, I totally underestimated how the situation would swiftly deteriorate the moment I had two feet on the roof and no ladder! The shoes immediately started slipping at such a rate I didn't even have time to get back on the ladder, knowing I would only succeed in knocking it over with me if I grabbed it on the way by. Survival instinct dictated going down was not a viable option at that juncture, only up. My legs started pumping in a 'run' toward the ridge, trying desperately to go forward and up faster than I was sliding backward and down! Yikes! After many 'strides' I finally made enough forward progress I believed I could make a lunge and grab the capped ridge. So that's what I did... a forward belly buster lunge, arms outstretched to grab the ridge. Then, with much flailing and flopping I managed to finally get to my knees and pull myself up to sit atop the ridge.

I perched astride the ridge, smiled and congratulated myself on the successful implementation of my plan; I would have patted myself on the back if I wasn't afraid I'd fall off. That's when the realization dawned that I was sort of in a little situation. It seems I had made a plan that didn't get me OFF the roof; my plan had only succeeded in actually getting me farther ON the roof! Ooopsie! What was I thinking? The smile faded. I considered my options from that point, none of which ended well. I played them all out in my mind to fruition and all ended with me in various states of harm and breakage on the ground. So, I did the only thing I could do; I could reach them from my perch... so I pulled the loppers up and cut the pesky branches I blamed for my current situation. I relished every snip but was soon finished and back to the dilemma at hand, getting off the roof!

I replayed all the previous options to extricate myself in case I missed something useful. Nope...they all ended badly. *O.K. So, what if I just sit here until someone comes home. It's noon, so that's only four or five hours. That's not too bad, right?* I pondered that option. *But do I really want them to come home and see me up here like a stranded cat? I know there would be lots of pointing and jokes and pictures. Yeah...the pictures. They'd probably NEVER leave me alone again. They'd never take me seriously again; "remember that time we had to rescue you from the roof?"* I'm wondering, too, HOW would they get me down? *A rope, maybe? No, they would probably call the volunteer fire depart-ment and all my friends there would know. Then, THEY would laugh and point and take pictures, too! Urghhh!*

I reconciled to the notion I would have to swallow a heaping helping of embarrassment with a pride chaser if discovered in this predicament, but I had no other options. I sat there, defeated, surveying my lair from the perch. *Five hours of this? At least it's shaded here under this stupid, leafy tree! But my butt cheeks are already tired from clenching the roof's ridge. My legs will soon start cramping. No food. No water. No breeze. AND it's hot! So hot! I'm so sweaty! I'm sweating like a ... like a..."* And that's when the universe and inspiration took the wheel!

All that was between me and getting to the ladder was traction and I had what I needed to make some traction. *SWEAT! And lots of it! Yes!* I clenched the roof a little tighter with the cheeks and carefully re-moved my shoes and socks. I was disappointed, however, to discover my feet don't sweat to the same degree as the rest of my body. They were barely damp and slipped on the metal as I slid them for a test run. *How can that be? I'm sweating like a pig! My hair is wet. My shirt is wet, my jeans...I'm sweating all over. I bet if I was naked I would stick to this roof like a fly to sh... whatever flies stick to. So, why can't my feet... Whoa! Whoa! Back up there. What did I just say? If I was naked...? Hummmmm...*

So. Yes. Another decision to make. 1) I could stay on the roof for another five hours through the midday heat suffering dehydration, butt ache and leg cramps; I would get the help I need to get down safely but the cost would be an abundance of jokes and snarkiness and pictures for years to come. Or 2) I could strip down to my briefs and hope my knees and legs are sweaty enough to provide the traction needed to get safely to the ladder without sliding off the roof. If I'm successful, no one ever needs to know. If I fail, there will certainly be broken bones, lacerations, and hematomas to explain. Additionally, I might eventually have to explain the whole being found 'unconscious-and-half-naked-behind-the-well–house-thing.' What to do?

I weighed the options and realized the choice was obvious. I began the task of peeling damp jeans clinging to my body after hours of sweat, whilst teetering atop the metal roof and secured only by the depth of the ridge wedgie between my butt cheeks. *If this works* no one ever has to know about this little miscalculation and SNAFU. I nodded. If it doesn't and I fall and get cut and broken, the sympathy factor alone should minimize the jokes and snark. AND they most definitely won't take pictures of me unconscious and in my underwear; that would be so wrong. It's a win either way!

It took time and effort, but I finally wiggled and squirmed my way out of jeans sticking to me like a second skin. *I've got this,* as I tossed my shoes, socks, and jeans over the edge, *it's show time!* I was now committed to getting myself off the roof, one way or another. (The only thing worse than later being found stranded on the roof would be to be found stranded on the roof in my underwear.) I managed to bend and toss and flip until I was again on my knees and holding onto the ridge, white knuckled. I could see the ladder over my shoulder only seven feet away...as the crow flies. So close, yet so far. And nothing between me and it except a metallic slippery slope, sharp edges, and a million sheet metal screws. My bare knees and legs seemed to be holding me in place for now. However, the only way to know for sure would be to release my grasp on the ridge and make a speedy, yet deliberate, dash for the ladder. "TOWANNNNNDA!" I can report the descent to the ladder was a bit tedious and unnerving, yet successful. The sweat and bare skin withstood the trek; I successfully transitioned to the ladder and safely planted my two bare feet on solid ground. *Well, that was certainly interesting*, gathering my clothes and making my way to the house and air conditioning, *I knew it would work, though. I always think things through and have a plan. I love it when a plan comes together!*

Obviously, I made it down safely and no one had to ever know I may have made a slight miscalculation and an error in judgment. I'm sharing this experience in hopes it may help others in similar circumstances. The morals to this story are the following: 1) Don't ignore the inner voices saying, "Uhmmm... STOP! We don't think this is a good idea". They are usually correct. 2)Do the mathematical calculations BEFORE you're sitting naked on a rooftop; it's not the size of the roof that matters, it's the SLOPE. 3) Your safety plan may be outdated if its main function is to report your body is in need of a bag. 4)ALWAYS WEAR CLEAN UNDERWEAR WHEN YOU LEAVE THE HOUSE BECAUSE YOU NEVER KNOW... (Thanks, Mom. I swear they were clean when I left the house that morning. I think that initial slide down the roof, however, may have rendered them less than pristine!)

Interesting footnote: I found a perfectly good pole pruning lopper and a pole pruning saw in my gardening shed a few days AFTER this incident. Seriously? How could I forget having access to the exact equipment required to easily accomplish such a specific job? In my defense, they aren't mine. But they have been in the shed for three years. And I have even used them to cut branches...the branches hanging over the well house...the well house with the steep roof. I KNEW I had never been on that roof. I would have remembered something like that. I WAS RIGHT!

Color Blindness

My thoughts center most recently on my Dad. And black history. And the announcement of a sequel for "To Kill a Mockingbird". And no, my dad wasn't black. However, I have a few experiences and memories related to Erath County black history by virtue of growing up a poor, white girl in the South. I am justified to give a commentary as all history intertwines and influences. I decided to combine an incident involving both my Dad and black history. From my perspective, it pays homage to both the gentle soul of my father and the sweet, peaceful nature of the black community of Erath County circa late 1960s.

Discrimination comes in all shapes and sizes and colors. I'm sure my father was summarily dismissed by some people he met on the street as a redneck, given his Southern drawl and ways, grease-smeared clothes, and the dirt and grime permanently staining his chipped fingernails. His neck was 'red', discolored by years of toil and labor in the sun. He was flawed, as are we all, in appearance and character. He was not perfect. However, anyone guilty of summarizing a person's worth based upon condition of apparel, degree of mental capacity, color of skin, accent of speech, or origin of birth deprive themselves of the richness of depth and breadth. They will remain in a small dark box, a lonely place from which they peer out and angrily judge those passing by based upon superficial 'colors' and not the 'content of character'. My dad taught me that. Those knowing my father knew a man of values and regarded him highly. They knew a man of faith, living and dying by the Word. They knew a man who treated others only as he wanted to be treated (Matt. 7:12) and loved all he met (Matt 22:36-40). He may not have always spoken politically correct by today's standards, but his words and actions never disrespected or devalued anyone.

***

Dad was born in 1925, the son of a poor, dryland farmer. Poor.

Depression poor. They mostly ate what they could grow, raise, catch, or shoot. Anything extra (like proper high-top basketball shoes) was possible only if his mother allowed him to sell eggs and chickens to the country store. His life consisted of working the fields with his father and brother, caring for livestock, chopping wood, etc... with a greatly appreciated break in the day to go to school. After school, it was back to work and chores. He grew up hard. He grew up fast. But he grew up with a compassionate and gentle soul contrasting greatly to the scars and calluses of the hard, manual labor he embraced his entire life.

In my memory, he always had something to do and rarely sat down to rest. No favorite TV shows. No hobbies. No favorite sports. No favorite recliner. His only relaxations, if that's an accurate description, were coon-hunting and caring for his hounds. Almost every Saturday night, right at dusk, he and my grandfather would load up the little trailer with dogs for hours of traipsing through the creek bottoms and heavy brush of the backcountry. Having earned a reputation around the county as a good 'coon man', farmers began approaching him to set traps in corn fields or watermelon patches besieged by the rascally, masked bandits. Dad built some traps and started setting them around the county upon request. Most, but not all, were trapped and released miles from the field to be chased by hounds another day. Most. Not all.

One day, Dad was working in the shop. I was hanging out there (as usual) and 'helping', probably hammering on metal with a ball-peen or pushing the creeper across the hard concrete floor or something equally annoying. My little sister was in the house with momma this day, as most usual, doing whatever it was they did together there. A black man quietly entered the shop. It was not unusual for blacks and Hispanics to visit his little shop for mechanic work. A good number of the poorer of all color came; he was known to be fair and extended credit, allowing them to pay as they could. Dad stopped working and greeted him by name (I wish I could remember who he was). They shook hands and spoke of weather and health and family. The man finally and awkwardly told Dad he was there to ask a favor. Dad assumed it was related to fixing an old car or something similar. However, the man said he had heard Dad trapped coons and wanted to know if he would sell him one. He wanted the biggest, fattest coon he could get...and as soon as possible. Daddy looked perplexed. A few folks had asked for delivery of baby coons to groom as pets. We had one. Most had asked for them to be trapped and taken far away. However, he had never been asked to special deliver a big, fat live one. The man must have assumed his hesitation regarding payment and assured Dad he could pay upon delivery. When Dad told him there would be no charge, the man dropped his shoulders and his eyes filled with tears. With a quivering voice, he explained his mother was very sick. She was not eating but had requested one last taste of coon. Daddy patted him on the shoulder, gave his condolences and promised to deliver as soon as he trapped "the one". They shared another handshake. The man nodded, turned and left the shop. My only thought was, "Ewwwww. Gross!"

I soon forgot about the black man's visit. I had moved on to other things, as is the way of children. Several coons were trapped - and released as usual - over the next few days, perhaps weeks. One day shortly, Dad asked if I wanted to stop 'work' and make a quick run of the traps with him. I never turned down an opportunity to be with him and quickly jumped in the truck. We drove out of town and eventually turned into a lane leading to a huge cornfield. He drove along for a while before stopping the truck. I followed and he soon led us directly to the trap, hidden nicely at the edge of the field. The coon hissed and lunged at us through the wire. 'Oh, yeah", he exclaimed, "that's a nice one". Dad grabbed the chain and dragged the trap to the truck as I scampered ahead. I was excited because after he trapped a coon, we usually took another long ride to release it.

But this time we turned the truck back toward town. "Odd," I thought, silently riding and looking out the window as the town came into view and we made our way down Graham Street, south toward the old square. We turned left onto Tarleton Street and Daddy immediately slowed the truck and pulled off into a grassy area just past Anderson Feed Mill. He parked short of a small, white frame house, the one at the corner of Tarleton and Floral streets facing the old rock building. I remember it as abandoned at the time but would become Grant's Plants and The Dinner Bell in later years. I thought it was a strange place to release the coon, a block from the courthouse and hospital!

The house was surrounded by black men and children. No women, which I thought odd. I don't think I had ever seen so many black people together in one place. The men filled the small porch (half hidden by a green hedge) and spilled into the yard, standing around in small groups and talking. The children were running and playing nearby. Daddy dropped the tailgate and activities immediately ceased. They all - men and children - turned in the direction of our truck and stared as the sound of Daddy dropping the tailgate still echoed through the neighborhood. Silent. Stares. *Were we in trouble? Were they mad? I knew this wasn't a good place to release the coon! They must be mad.*

One of the men on the porch (I recognized him to be the gentleman stopping by the shop a week earlier) stood and started toward the truck, followed by a few more. He yelled something back at the group and they began to smile and nod. I quickly turned in the seat to look out the back glass as the men approached. They shook hands, as men did. And they all (including Daddy) smiled – a contented, victorious smile -as they checked out the contents of the trap sitting on the rusty tailgate. Two of them soon grabbed the cage and started toward the house, followed closely by Daddy. He glanced my way and gave a little wave, his signal to "sit tight and wait in the truck – I'll be right back". The group closed ranks and crowded around the steps as the odd procession passed onto the porch and my Dad disappeared into the house.

I turned my attention to the children. I have no doubt we shared a mutual curiosity of each other in many ways. Hair. Skin. So different. The boys remained focused on the door and quietly waited for a glimpse of the strange white man. The girls in pigtails and dresses seemed much more interested in me as they returned to skipping and hopping, continually glancing in my direction. My eyes darted between them and the door of the house. After only a few brief moments, the door opened and the sea of men and boys separated to make a path for Dad. They smiled and patted him on the back. He grinned warmly, occasionally stopping to speak or shake hands with someone he knew. He said nothing as he closed the door and started the truck, stopping only long enough to pat me on the knee. "The trap, Daddy! You forgot your trap!" He looked straight ahead as he turned the truck for home. "Don't worry about it. They'll bring it back when they're done with it." I looked back over the seat and peered through the back glass. The yard was still full of black smiling faces, waving in our direction. I waved back timidly as we turned the corner and they soon disappeared from view. I felt we had shared a moment, but I didn't know what or how. And that was that.

It was years later I learned what happened inside that little white house on Tarleton Street. A woman lay dying inside that house, too weak to get out of bed. Her last request was the taste of coon on her tongue cooked the way she liked it. News quickly reached her that her coon had been delivered; she insisted on seeing both the coon and the man providing it. Two sons had carried that trap and its hissing, lunging raccoon up the steps and through the house crowded with women busy with meals and other preparations, directly into her bedroom. They held it there in the dim light for her to see and told her Mr. Haggard had brought it. She had smiled and held up her arms, insisting on hugging his neck. Daddy went to her and bent over. With tears in her eyes, she pulled him close and weakly whispered in his ear, "thank you, Mr. Haggard, thank you" ... and kissed him on the cheek.

I often visualize that moment...remember the incident... when thinking of my Dad. I visualize the deep emotion and humility he must have felt. I visualize that sweet black family, first entrusting him with such an important personal mission and so graciously welcoming Daddy into their home at a most private time. I'm presumptuous, perhaps, to compare the events surrounding that day to great drama. Perhaps I'm wrong to compare Daddy's relatively small gestures to grand, life-altering ones – however fictionalized they may be. But when I heard the whole story, although an adult and already holding my father in high regard, I couldn't help but feel like Scout respectfully rising with the others as Atticus passed.

Perhaps the search for 'content of character' should begin within ourselves, before we search for it in others. I'm sure I read that somewhere.

Confetti and Bass Drum

I recently had another epiphany!

I am a new grandmother and it is sheer and ultimate awesomeness! Unfortunately, it's the only thing 'new' about this ol' gal...unless you want to consider the new aches and pains or the new prescriptions. Anyway, I was quietly observing my little man the other day as a rather goofy expression crossed his face. I laughed and gushed, "you're just like your Grammie, aren't you? Yes, you are!" I giggled at the thought and hugged him a little tighter, starting a mental list of the similarities.

My smile began to fade at #3 as realization of the true similarities slowly came to light. We both gum our food, lack stellar bladder control, and display a pitiful level of coordination. We are easily distracted and lose interest in our surroundings, zoning out into a reverie known only to ourselves. I, too, sometimes stare at my hands and feet as if I've never seen them before. Why? I just don't know. We go to bed at the same time and get cranky if our routines are jacked. We drool and make funny noises in our sleep. We can stare at a TV screen as if we're paying close attention but, really, we're only looking at the pretty colors and blurred motions. We look intently at people when they talk to us (even watch their lips move) but don't actually comprehend what they're saying. It's not that I don't comprehend so much as I either zone out, as mentioned previously, or forget the original topic. A dancing shadow can keep us entertained for an extended time. I'm certain if I sat on the floor awhile I would need someone to pick me up, too. The similarities continued ad nauseam.

So, yeah, Jonah... Grammie just realized she is old. The only question in my mind is, 'when did this happen?' I remember as a child viewing life as a west Texas highway -linear, going on for miles and miles with only an occasional break from the monotony and disappearing out of sight way off in the distance.

As I approached adulthood, I viewed life more as the traditional bell curve, human characteristics on the x-axis and ascending years on the y-axis. That meant at some point in the time which was my life (I assumed middle-age) I would triumphantly reach a zenith...an apex... a joyful height representing respectable degrees of self-actualization, victory, peace, and rest. Confetti would rain down from the heavens and I would plant my flag on that mountain-top, marching all the way to the edge beating on a bass drum. I would listen to my joyful shouts returning on the wings of an echo..." I made, made it, made it. I'm here, here, here! Life is great, great, great!" I would pitch my tent on that mountain and live in a blessed Xanadu for several years before making a slow, calculated descent on the other side, tired and prepared for the long sleep.

Well, what the heck happened? Unless I'm going to live to 120 (my kids will intervene before that happens) I'm thinking that bell curve theory was slightly miscalculated. How did I miss it? Where was my triumphant entry and confetti and drum? How did I just wake up one morning over-the-hill with a tiny bladder and sagging body parts and a mind which seems to have a mind of its own and an 'old lady' med dispenser full of pills in my medicine cabinet? Huh?? When exactly did my chest fall down into my drawers? Have I already passed my primus perfecto and didn't even recognize it? I feel like I'm sliding down a rocky cliff with no brakes and heading straight into a pit of broken dreams and mushy, bland food.

But I digress from my aforementioned epiphany, which I now share with my kids and grandkid(s) and anyone caring to take notes:

It doesn't matter what metaphor we choose to describe life...a line, a circle, a bell curve...symphony, tapestry, buffet, or a cinematic production. It only matters how we live it and if we leave a little bit of ourselves behind for posterity. Material things rust and break and fade, but our memory and spirit endure forever.

Therefore, I'm informing you of my plans to be spending your inheritance over the next few years. I've had my eyes on a Harley for quite some time and I think it's time to go get it for an extended ride into the sun. Or perhaps that Alaskan cruise? Or both, because I can. I'm going to learn how to weld huge wind sculptors and rock climb and pilot an ultra-lite. I'll take line dance classes and learn to play the bagpipes. And only to prepare you should the occasion arise, I may wear my underwear outside my pants, go barefoot, burn the bras, and eat ice cream for supper - because I can. I will at various times be a total curmudgeon, crazy eccentric, or only slightly skewed depending on my mood -because I can.

I'm compiling a list and it's a work-in-progress. I'll keep you informed. However, let me leave you with this thought: Life is like a huge bee hive full of golden honey tucked away in a dead stump. I may get stung but Grammie's going in! I only wish there could be confetti and a bass drum! Perhaps I'll add that to the list.

Congrats on Graduation

Today is a day of reflection. I'm starting my twilight years trying life as a migrant farmer, sort of, having followed choppers and trucks to a triticale and alfalfa harvest in Kansas four hundred miles from home. The weather has been much the same here as Texas, intermittent rain keeping us pacing the floors and watching weather forecasts as much as gleaning the fields. I had decided last night I would hang up my farmer boots early and head back to Texas. This morning, however, there is a slim hope of sunshine and the next two days will turn more productive. After reconsideration, I will remain and hope for the best. Which is, after all, my life here or home or anywhere... staying in the trenches and hoping for the best. Sigh.

Then, I was reminded it's graduation time! Wow! It's hard to believe the school year has already ended and another generation of fresh-faced graduates prepare for the passage over. I remember that sweet feeling (class of 1974), believing the world was out there breathlessly awaiting my arrival.

A new graduating class! They, too, feel the liberating relief of final attainment sprinkled with the anticipation of future achievements! A collective sigh hovers over the land, followed by the joyful sounds of sweet victory! They have the world by the tail, they have found the mountaintop, they are prepared for anything and everything, and there is nothing they can't do or achieve. They are being carried aloft on the shoulders of pomp and circumstance, hailed as conquering heroes! The opportunities and possibilities are endless and all things are possible! The world is in the grasp and for the taking! They laugh and dance; birds are singing and the sun is shining as they float on clouds of joy and the hope of tomorrow...

Then, tomorrow comes. And another one. And another one. And stark reality sets in. And the little mirth-makers realize they did not have all the answers after all! There will always be more questions than answers. Always.

They'll quickly lose those smirks and smiles as the rain begins to pour on their parade, leaving their banners twisted and sagging and the glittering confetti washing down the gutter and into the darkness. They will realize the path does not always follow as planned; there will be bumps and dumps and detours. Bridges and roads will sometimes be destroyed by the deluge, leaving retreat as the only option. Their self-assured gait will halt, their steps will falter as their envisioned dreams are left blowing in the wind like so much fodder chewed and spewed forth from a John Deere silage chopper.

They will awaken one day in a strange land surrounded by strange people and not even remember taking that left at Albuquerque. Sooner than they will want to admit, the little snots will find themselves beginning the twilight years sitting alone in a motel room and contemplating life as a migrant farmer. My only prayer and hope for them will be... to meet that day with a smile and the spirit of a conquistador and the realization they would not go back in life and change a thing.

Dear Abby

Dear Abby,

I need some advice regarding my grandson, "Rocky". ("Rocky" is not his real name) Anyway, I've noticed he's developing some odd behaviors which concern me. He has always shown a tendency to put all of his Hot Wheels in a line and organize his Lego Mega Bloks by color.

Most recently, however, he asked to go to the "Red Library" while we were out running errands. The "Red Library" (as he calls it) is actually a local tractor supply store – not to be confused with the "Library" (as he calls it), which is actually a book and sundries store and not "Star Shopping" (as he calls it) which is actually Walmart.

Anyway, the red library sells a variety of farm supplies but also a small number of die-cast toy cars and farm equipment. Rocky is three and likes such things so we went to the red library. He spent thirty minutes admiring the displays and organizing the shelves. Starting with the cars - all were sorted... first by size, then model, then color. Not satisfied, he rearranged them to put the 'families' together; all similar models together while maintaining the size and color groupings. He then moved over to the tractor/farm equipment display and grouped them using the same formula. I believe he would have stayed another hour if I hadn't finally pulled him away with the assurance they were all in order; I admit I bribed him with the purchase of a car.

The next day we were out on a mission and he wanted to go back to the Red Library. I said, "no, we don't have time today." "Please, Meme? Pretty please?" It was difficult but I had to refuse. "No. We will not go to the red library every time we are out. Besides, I got you a nice car yesterday. You don't need another one today!" To which he replied, "But I don't want a car. I just need to pick them up and put the families together. They are all messy and I need to fix them!"

Abby, is this behavior normal? He's only three but I'm worried. It just doesn't seem right, somehow, for him to continue to call Walmart "Star Shopping". That seems weird! It's weird, right? Do you think he needs professional help?

PERPLEXED IN TEXAS

DIY Blues

I hate the Lowe's Home Improvement slogan "Let's build something together" on so many levels. The commercials show a clueless suburban couple deciding to build something themselves – like a landscaped multi-level deck with a gazebo and waterfall stocked with koi. They trudge into Lowe's and have a conference with the first salesperson rushing to greet them at the door, nod their heads with all understanding and enlightenment, and skip out of the store hand-in-hand with their bag of goodies.

The next scene is of them at home midway through the project, casually following what I can only assume are the mental blueprints somehow permanently etched into their memories during the brief encounter with the Lowe's DIY guru a few hours earlier – smiling as they walk around their spotless workspace (void of any construction clutter or tools)- in gardening gloves, clean capris, and sandals.

The final scene shows them relaxing on their new deck nestled among the flowering vines, feeding the koi, clinking their glasses of wine together to toast "a job well done and not a bad way to spend our Saturday". Whut?

My experience with DIYs could not be further removed from that of Lowe's Biff and Barbie. Typically, I have a general plan in my head but lots of questions as to execution. Experience has taught me there is no reason to ask anyone in the store – even if I manage to track one down in the stacks. I'm lucky if the pimply, disinterested employee picking at his wedgie knows the difference between a thingamajig and a whatchamacallit, so I don't ask.

I don't leave with a magic bag containing all I need for my project. It's usually more like a pickup full of sundry items I have to unload before I can even start. If I catch the yard guys on a good day they will probably manage to load all I ordered, but I never get all I need in one trip. I still have multiple trips back over time as I realize I forgot to get something – either due to faulty memory or ignorance- or what I hoped would work doesn't or doesn't fit or breaks or is the wrong size, color, material, etc. If my project is outside it will be sandwiched between the time I come home from work and sunset -on days I have nothing else more pressing to do- and will last until the project is completed.

It also seems no matter how small the project is I tend to unload my complete arsenal of tools. Why? I don't know. I will eventually have tools pulled out from their boxes, the well house, and dark corners and they will be scattered everywhere – underfoot and in my way. My workspace quickly resembles a disaster area and looks like I tossed a grenade in a home improvement store. (There's an idea). And because my Daddy taught me to never leave any implements or machinery out overnight in the weather I start packing them up as the sun starts down – only to drag them all out the next time I have an opportunity to work on the project.

My clothes get grungy and dirty and torn, my nails break, I sweat, I bleed, I make mistakes, and I don't smile a heck of a lot (unlike Biff and Barbie with their pearly whites).

This was basically the scenario yesterday afternoon as I rushed (shut it, family, I said RUSHED) to get two coats of paint on a fence frame before dark: the customary assortment of tools and materials were scattered about, extension cord stretched – saw horses, water hose, paint bucket, post hole diggers, etc... - all effectively turning the yard into a minefield of random opportunities to trip myself.

I was about halfway through the painting and stood up to move, paint-brush in hand, and stepped back squarely and whole-footedly into a basket. Not just a basket – a plastic planting basket with the wires attached along the top rim and coming together to form a hook for hanging. (I had set it aside to plant creeping petunias if I determined the grasshoppers were looking thin and in need of additional nour-ishment). I don't know how I managed to step so squarely into that basket through that mesh of wires, but I did. And those same wires quickly closed rank around my ankle and half my leg to effectively make it impossible to free my tightly-wedged foot. I tried to kick it off but only succeeded in losing my balance. So that was the situation in which I found myself yesterday: my foot fully entrenched in a hanging flower basket, jumping around like spit on a hot skillet, trying not to fall and maneuvering through the obstacle course of tools and various objects – hoping upon hope I could keep my balance until I could get to something solid to grab.

It's always situations like these in which I think, *please don't let me be found like this – petunia basket on my foot and impaled by a random sharp object or petunia basket on my foot and unconscious due to a nasty knock to the head or petunia basket on my foot with a broken hip.* We all have those thoughts, but I digress. Anyway, I successfully managed to hop and jump across the yard without falling and liberated my foot with a bit of persuasion. I smiled... eventually.

I encounter these 'situations' fairly often in my DIY mode but seldom are they repeated or revealed to anyone. I think if they're resolved without broken bones or stitches or fire trucks – no harm, no foul. But that Lowe's Home Improvement commercial struck a nerve and I needed to vent my frustration. It is NOT representative of my DIY experiences.

I hope in years to come if you ever see me wandering through McCoy's Building Supply-tape measure in one hand, level in the other, and muttering incoherently – you will not judge me harshly. You will know I was finally pushed over the DIY edge. You will know why I'm there. You will know I'm looking for Biff and Barbie and I'm there to kick their happy DIY butts! Indeed!

Do You Know the Way to San Jose?

I've been enjoying the warmer weather and must constantly remind myself it's only February, especially since so much is already in bloom. It's not been easy dismissing the impulse to get into full blown Spring mode – such as disconnect heaters, rip insulation off outside water faucets, and plant stuff. I know this time of year we use both the air conditioning AND heater - often on the same day. As we say in Texas, "if you don't like the weather, just wait a few minutes!" It doesn't mean, however, I can't go outside to rake, weed, mow, and generally rearrange the dirt on nicer days.

A few days ago I was enjoying the warm sunshine, immersed in these tasks, when my attention was drawn skyward to a honking skein of geese circling northward...then south...then north again. They seemed most discombobulated by the weather and in disagreement whether to stay and catch a few more rays or head north to beat the encroaching, inevitable heat. Two of the smarter geese particularly (I dubbed Bubba and Beulah May) kept trying unsuccessfully to lead the others back to the south. The geese eventually honked and circled out of sight to the north, confused and never truly committed to moving in that direction.

My thoughts return to the geese this cold, wet, blustery day... wondering if the Yankee snowbirds in the bunch are now wishing they had been less hard-headed and impetuous. Are they convinced they should have listened to the wiser Bubba and Beulah May? I'm thinking, "yes"! But, then, you can't tell those Yankees anything...

Driving Miss Crazy

I'm a relatively even-tempered person. Truly. And it takes a lot to get me riled, especially on the highway; I'm a defensive driver the majority of the time. Really. But an anonymous male driver, that ASSSSSS-inine JERK OFFering to drag race in the flats? Yeah. That shoved me over the line. I immediately transformed from mild-mannered, cookie baking Grammie into Mad Max's Toecutter. It wasn't pretty.

I was travelling at road speed (65 mph) as I prepared to enter the west end of the flats - a long, straight stretch of wide, well-paved county road on which I drive from my house into town. As I topped that last hill before the flats proper, I observed a nondescript older Ford sedan puttering along at 55mph. That's not unusual; there's often old men in pickups or seasonal farm equipment slowing traffic on the highway. Slower traffic is not usually a big deal and rarely moves the needle on my patience gauge...certainly nothing over which to tangle my Fruit of the Looms. As there was nothing but wide, open spaces for the next three miles, I took to the passing lane well before nearing his vehicle and planned to simply make a casual pass. And what does this shiatsu decide to do? Yep...accelerate with me! "What? Are you kidding me?" We continued increasing speed, side by side, for quite some distance; he was unrelenting. I glanced over and observed the driver to be a younger guy, his wry smile betraying his ill-advised intent to NOT back down. Kid, do you seriously want to do this? Here and now? I sat straighter in the seat and popped the tension on my seatbelt. Challenge accepted! *EAT MY DUST*! Nearing the east end of the flats I kicked that F-150 into overdrive and was going 88 mph when I left him sucking tailpipe! "Stupid, silly, little man," I muttered under my breath as I adjusted my rearview mirror. I was even tempted to serve up a heaping helping of a 'California Howdy'. Would that have been so wrong? Yes. Yes, it would have been wrong. I know. But don't mess with Grammie when she's on her way to the Walmart to get her Dr. Peppers! Really.

***

You cute, sweet, adorable little GMC Canyon truck. You had no way of knowing about my less-than-ideal weekend when you pulled out from a side street, opting to cross the first lane and pull in front of me and my F-150 SuperCab to do your hokey-pokey routine. You couldn't hear the thoughts in my head or recognize the momentary urge to increase speed and ram you from behind. You couldn't see my white knuckles or know I evaluated exactly how much damage it would do to my truck as I tried to determine if it would be worth it or not. You don't know how lucky you were I didn't have an optional steel grill/bumper/

cattle guard mounted on front. You don't know how close you were to having a really bad start to your Monday compliments of me. So you just scoot along, now, little fella... and remain oblivious to everyone around you. Please... and you're welcome.

***

I came too close to being 'fatalized' in two separate vehicular events recently. Both times I was in the wrong place at the wrong time and totally innocent. They occurred within a few miles of my home and only hours apart. Strike one. Strike two.

Since these incidents I've been contemplating life...and death...as I anticipate strike three. I've been trying to reconcile my feelings of vulnerability and mortality to the conflicting impulse to barricade myself in the house, boil my water, and eat only food I could grow in a solar-powered room. Perhaps I should wrap myself in a soft yet impenetrable cocoon and only venture out to check my perimeter? I have felt something like a sitting duck. With the third strike I'm outta here! I've considered the philosophical phrases offered to explain and cope with the fragility of our existence. "Today is the first day of the rest of your life" and "live each day as if it's your last". The more hedonistic retort, "eat, drink, and be merry for tomorrow you die" or "grab the gusto!" The spiritually faithful offer "it wasn't your time" or "you must have a Guardian angel watching over you" or "God has other plans for you".

We absolutely have no promise of tomorrow and that's one truth I tried to impart to my children. Some may be thinking, "Gee... what a fatalistic approach to life. Why would you raise your kids to think like that?" Very simply...it's the truth and it's reality. (I also told them they couldn't catch a falling star or fly with a towel 'cape'). I don't believe God actively decides who lives and who dies. I don't believe our lives are assigned a predetermined number and fate. I don't believe those I've loved who've gone on before me are wasting their blessed and promised rest guarding over me. Conversely, the thought of some stranger being assigned the role of my guardian angel is just...well, it's just too creepy to contemplate!

I've concluded I will repeat the same mantra that has led me through life thus far... 'some days you're the windshield, some days you're the bug!" That's it. Simple. And it incorporates all the others into one easy-to-understand truth...I am not in control. Who even wants to think about the number of times each day we may innocently dodge the bullet and never even know? I can only give thanks for each day I've been given and its bountiful blessings. I don't sweat the small stuff and acknowledge MOST OF IT IS SMALL STUFF. I will enjoy life to the fullest each and every day, seeking my part in the 'plan'...just in case. I will control what I can, exercise due caution, and have faith everyone else is doing the same. Because when they don't...BANG! CRUNCH! KAPOW! THUD! It's over... I'll be just a June bug splattered and served on a hot Mazda windshield. Bug Juice Cocktail on the rocks, shaken and not stirred - metaphorically and metaphysically speaking.

Rise and shine, singing and dancing, and hoping for another windshield day! Amen!

***

"Hey, Lady! Oh, yes! Please allow me to wait as you turn that big van around between two rows in the Walmart parking lot. I suppose you missed a spot and don't want to spend your time driving back around like the rest of us. I'm sure your time is much more valuable. It's fine. We'll wait. Hummmmm.... What are you doing? Oh, I see. You're pulling into a 'handicap' spot. My bad. I'm sorry. Now I feel so selfish for thinking anything ill of your actions! No wait! That's not a handicap spot. What are you doing? Oh, I get it! You have your own special parking spot...the one at the end of the row with the yellow hash-marks! I wondered about the purpose of those prime pieces of real estate and now I know! They are special spots for the really, REALLY handicapped. Silly me. I thought they were banned from parking. I thought they were possibly there to provide a line of sight at the end of the row. Boy, was I wrong! I see they're reserved for you, because the empty handicap place next to it would be entirely too far for you to walk. Well, now I just feel bad for thinking you were taking undue advantage. Hummmm…. Interesting. I see you're perfectly capable of walking. Perhaps your passenger …? No, I see she is just as able. She jumped out of the van without a problem. That's odd… I don't see a handicap placard or license plate on your vehicle. Hummm… Oh, I get it! I can tell by your gait and the way you hold your head you are not disabled… just entitled! The hash-marked spaces are for those considering themselves ENTITLED! Well, excuse me! I can also tell you really hope I say something. I won't. I won't give you the satisfaction. I won't say a word. Why? Hummmmm…. Because I don't have the energy for a takedown in the parking lot today. And it's not on my list of things-to-do. And I believe, perhaps naively, Karma is in your future. She always is. I can practically see her now, slapping you up beside your entitled head like the witch she knows you to be. Oh, and have a nice day.

***

Has anyone heard anything regarding a lost cyclist on west FM8? There are cyclists riding on that highway all the time taking advantage of the wide shoulders, sporadic hills, and Bosque Flats. But this is different. There has been a portable neon marquee about two tenths of a mile inside the city limits for four days now. It flashes **"SLOW DOWN. SLOW DOWN. WATCH FOR CYCLIST"** as you're leaving town and heading west.

I try to be cautious and obey all signs although I must say it is becoming more difficult as time passes. They've erected so many signs along our streets and highways it's hard to drive and keep your eyes on the road due to reading all the signs! Don't litter, don't drink, don't text, buckle up, keep it beautiful, don't speed, don't loiter, we can see you speeding from the sky, stand up, sit down, turn around, etc. School zones have warning as you enter, different speeds for different times of the day, watch for kids, watch for buses, watch for kids getting on buses, rules about cell phone, gun, drug, and alcohol usage, arrows and lines and yellow paint...a barrage of information and so little time to process it. Don't they worry that someone could have an accident just trying to read all the signs? I'm thinking the drunk pedophile packing a gun in his pants talking to his drug dealer on the cell phone and speeding through on his way to a drop isn't going to stop to read the signs. Enough with the signs, already! But I digress...

The lost cyclist. I've been wondering about that sign. As I said, I try to obey the signs along life's highway. But there are unanswered questions. For example, **"SLOW DOWN. SLOW DOWN".** Whoever put the sign there obviously thinks I'm going too fast already. However, the 45 mph limit at that juncture does not seem too excessive to me. Does that mean 45 is too fast and I should slow down to say... 40... or 35? And for how far? The sign is positioned just before the speed transitions to 55 and then 70 leaving town. Am I supposed to drive the 8 miles home at 45 just in case I happen to see the cyclist? It's taking me forever to get home going that speed, just sayin'. Coming to town isn't a problem though. They don't seem to think the cyclist will be on that side of the highway. No sign. Unless, of course, it's further west than where I enter the highway. I'm thinking if it's further west and I don't see that SLOW DOWN SLOW DOWN I risk missing the cyclist because I'm going too fast. Should I be coming back into town at 45? Or slower? I just don't know.

"WATCH FOR CYCLIST". Who is this cyclist and what am I supposed to do if I see him/her? I'm thinking that would be helpful information to have on a sign somewhere in that 8-mile stretch. And what they're wearing perhaps. And what kind of bicycle. I assume it's a bicycle, but maybe I should be looking for a scooter or a unicycle or a moped? And instructions regarding what to do if I find the cyclist. Maybe a phone number to call? I might get in trouble if I call 911, but that jurisdiction thing between the deputies and troopers can be a real mess. Should I approach with caution? Soooooo... Now, I'm thinking they need more signs! I've been told I think too much. I think they may be right.

***

A wide paved residential street easily accessible between two major highways is primed to serve as a shortcut for travelers just wanting to pass from here to there; it's only logical. And some of the more impatient and inconsiderate of these interlopers will speed through, unnecessarily putting lives and property at risk. They display great degrees of carelessness, thoughtlessness, and immaturity and should be controlled...stopped...fined...punished.

HOWEVER...

What the H – E – double- hockey sticks are up with the speed bumps on North Dale Street? Really? And I use the terms "speed" and "bumps" loosely. These are speedLESS (in that you are required to practically stop and do a slow roll). Bumps? A rash has bumps. A pimple is a bump. These are more like concrete barricades meant to crack some teeth if you are not speedLESS upon approach. They should be renamed.

Additionally, there are FIVE of these in a half mile of street. FIVE! Overkill, much? The more rebellious drivers immediately began to circumvent the barriers, driving around them on the grassy shoulder. The city's response was the installation of 2 poles, one at each end of the bumps, to prevent that option. Ten poles in total. Oh, and don't get me started on the signage accompanying this homage to traffic engineering and logistics management. Fourteen signs! Fourteen additional signs (I know because I counted them). Bright yellow signs on poles. Signs telling you 'speed bumps' are coming up ahead. Signs pointing them out, "here they are". Signs asking, "Was it good for you?" (I added that one).

I've experimented going 30mph (the posted speed and the speed one should be able to travel) and 25mph...15, 10, and 5. The results? It's impossible to consume beverages of any sort under these conditions. Also, you can't text, FaceTime, apply lip gloss, or load bullets! I've tried! Actually, I consider it fortunate to make it to the other side with all organs intact and no internal hemorrhages. Maybe 'they' should have considered moats stocked with alligators and electrified grids and locked gates. Perhaps some deep pits with spikes or hot, boiling oil. Even a strategically positioned sharpshooter to shoot out the tires of those taking liberty with the posted speed? It would have been more humane for the innocent villagers seeking safe passage through the kingdom...

***

My dad stressed two things as he taught me to drive: 1) drive defensively and 2) "don't do as I do...so as I say do". He had to throw in #2 because he drove like the proverbial bat out of hell...if said bat was rabid and high on meth. Both lessons served me well today as an old multi-toned and mismatched Chevy long bed blew through his stop sign on a residential street. And it wasn't even a four-way! Defensive driving saved my BEEhind though I did have to fight the urgent impulse to run him down and beat out his windshield with my trusty ax handle. Thanks dad.

Earth Angel

My older brother, William Cecil, was born in 1950. He was my big brother by six years, but he didn't help me learn to walk or help me up when I fell. My younger sister understands; she experienced the same fate. He never picked wildflowers with me, helped catch frogs, or chase lightning bugs. He didn't run beside me as I learned to ride a bike. He would never watch Saturday morning cartoons with me or share a good joke. He didn't offer a hug when I was hurt or stand up for me in a dispute. Willie never helped with my homework or told me I did a good job. He didn't sing Happy Birthday, not once... hide Easter eggs, go trick-or-treating, or give me even one simple Christmas present. He never patted me on the back or made me a peanut butter sandwich.

Willie was born severely, totally, and irreversibly brain damaged. He never walked, his brain incapable of telling his legs and body the process. But he continues to influence every step I take. I recognized at a young age it's alright to trip and fall, physically and metaphorically speaking. It may be a bit embarrassing at the moment but the moment will pass. I can get up, brush myself, and keep going. As my aging legs begin to falter, I feel blessed to still be able to stand erect and take one more step. If the time comes I have to set aside my work boots and ballet slippers, it's all good. I have walked numerous trails and hiked paths less taken. I had working legs. It ain't no thang.

He never spoke, imprisoned in a dark place in which thoughts and words (even instincts) would never form. But he taught me an appreciation for the beauty and power of language. Perhaps I get tongue-tied, my words get jumbled occasionally or I totally ruin the punch line to an otherwise good joke. I may forget what I was going to say or the direction my narrative was headed. To this point, however, I've managed to eventually communicate what's inside my mind. Oftentimes, I should have kept the thought to myself. If the passage of time removes that ability and I find myself in that same dark prison in which he spent his life sentence, it's all good. I've pretty much said all I have to say; my family and friends know I love them. I had a voice. It ain't no thang.

He never fed himself; even the simple act of taking a single bite to his lips was well beyond his mental and physical capabilities. He unknowingly depended on others for every morsel of food, every sip of water needed to sustain his life. He ate when he was fed and whatever was put in his mouth. Did it matter what it was? I don't think so; he gave little indication of preferences, only a dislike of English peas. So, when I dribble a bit of pie or sauce on my nice shirt, the cookie crumbs dust my lap, or I knock over the entire contents of a glass it's not a big deal. If the coffee is too strong or the burger comes with mustard instead of mayo it doesn't ruin my day. I had my fill many times of what I knew I wanted. It ain't no thang.

He never had memories of the past, excitement for today, or anticipation for tomorrow. It was all Nothingness, metaphorical white noise and gray walls- day after day after day, year after year. All Nothingness. So, I can have an occasional long, brutal day. I can be disrespected or ignored. It can rain on my parade or the car can have a flat tire. It's all good. I had Something this day. I had color and texture, sweet and sour, soft and hard. I have memories and hope for a better tomorrow. It ain't no thang.

Do not consider my brother a mistake, a worthless vessel, an empty space deserving only pity and sorrow. Mom called him our Earth Angel; we all did. She didn't know why or how he came to us as he was and she anguished deeply with many questions. However, Mom and Dad were determined we should look for the Something beyond the Nothing. In doing so, he 'talked' to us daily by his mere presence. Our smallest pleasures were intensified, our deepest hurts and disappointments came with the smoother edges. His presence filled us with patience, compassion, gratitude, and peace and lifted us to a higher plane.

Willie's life here influenced us in breadths and depths not understood in this earthly realm. Perhaps the questions will be answered in another place and time, a spiritual realm in which we are finally reunited. If so I imagine him running to greet me, his beautiful eyes looking directly into mine. He will recognize me. He will know me. He will see me. He will smile and give me a hug. A smile and a hug. That's all I ever really wanted, all I asked for. He gifted me with a lifetime of so much more and I'm thankful.

He was here. He was loved. He was somebody. He was my brother.

William Cecil
1950-2009

Eat Your Heart Out, Martha Stewart

Thanksgiving morning began smoothly and I was on task. The alarm sounded and I jumped to it, quickly stuffing the ham into the roasting pan and into the oven. I had planned everything so well and was excited to execute and experience culinary victory! I had all the baking time calculations in my head. I had the roasting pan out and ready. I had premixed and panned the sweet potato casserole the previous evening. My vision- all planned and to be a ballet of well-orchestrated perfection! Ham out of the oven, sweet potatoes in, carve ham, sweet potatoes out- DONE! BOOM! - and with time to spare! The timing and organization were destined to be poetry in motion. Yeah, in someone else's ideal universe far, far away.

The timer for the ham buzzed and I was feeling really good about things. That honkin' hunk of meat was picture-perfect and smelled absolutely divine. *My ham-loving family is in for a real treat with this big boy,* I thought, setting it aside to cool for carving. I put the sweet potatoes in the oven and started preparing the brown sugar topping.

This is when things started to go somewhat awry. I have always melted the butter and brown sugar and other goodies together until they reached the correct consistency, similar to a thick caramel glaze. I would pour this glaze atop the casserole and THEN sprinkle the entire concoction with a generous helping of chopped pecans. For whatever reason, I know not why, I started the melting process and added the pecans to the pan at that stage of the process. I realized right away it was not a good idea. I couldn't judge the consistency of the gooey glob of goo. Was the brown sugar melting correctly? I stirred and stirred but couldn't determine because those pecans were a real game-changer. I couldn't seem to get the texture right (or as I remembered it from the umpteen times I've made this dish) but decided it was time to go with what I had – right or wrong. It was wrong. I should have been pouring a nice, hot sugary glaze. Instead, I was spooning and plopping a thick, sticky mass atop a warm, soft surface – and trying to spread it consistently. It was impossible to spread so I did the next best thing-the only thing, actually. Spoon and plop, spoon and plop. *It's fine*, I assured myself. *It will all melt together in its final time in the oven. It's all good!* So, it was back in the oven with the casserole. *No harm, no foul!*

I was on schedule and moved on to carving the ham. I had examined the ham the previous evening and determined a plan of action to ensure the finished product was like those sliced hams I've seen in pictures. I had sketched a schematic, having calculated weight, mass, and area ratios. Obviously, given the shape and circumference with which I was dealing, I had to bisect at center point and traverse laterally at approximately a 90-degree angle.

I went to the utensil drawer for a 'meat' knife, or what I assume to be a meat knife- the one with the pointy, stabby things on the end. It was nowhere to be found. *Not a problem*, I thought, *I have a drawer full of knives. How difficult can it be?* Very.

I tried knife after knife, determined to follow my diagram for the perfectly sliced ham. The fourth one was serrated and I was certain it would cut-and it did- not the ham, though, but the end of my little finger. (I now know which knife to get if the occasion calls for sawing through ***raw*** meat). I was beginning to lag behind my schedule; I quickly washed the blood and ham juice off my hands, tore a paper towel and wrapped the finger to stop the bleeding.

That's when I noticed the marshmallows Stephanie (my daughter) had requested be put on the casserole. I opened the oven door and pulled out the rack, determined to put marshmallows on right where it sat to save time. *Gee whiz*, I thought, *this is going to be a really full dish now with the marshmallows on top.* I carefully placed them and it was going alright. Then, they started to fall off the dish and roll into the hot oven. The NEW, CLEAN and hot oven. I don't know why I didn't lift the dish from the oven onto the counter at that point in time for the task. I just didn't. Instead, I went in time after time to retrieve errant marshmallows from inside the oven, off the door, out of the broiler- in an attempt to keep from getting the nice, new oven dirty. I only got a few burns but managed to keep the puffs collected before they melted. *Whew. That was close!* I pushed the dish and rack back and closed the door.

Back to the ham. I found a serrated cleaver to try next and soon discovered a major flaw in my calculation. Upon examining the ham the previous evening, I had observed the bone and concluded it was one bone, tapered through the middle. My schematic was based on the assumption the bone was cone-shaped, starting a point A and straight through to point B. It was logical. Imagine my surprise when I finally found a knife to cut, only to have it hit bone barely three inches in! *What the... what?* I tried to adjust my delicate incision-this way, that way- but everywhere I tried to cut I was hitting bone. Who knew tucked inside a nice ham was this massive conglomeration of bones? Practically another pig is tucked away in there. Enough bones to keep a pack of wild wolves gnawing contentedly for weeks!

I wrestled that piece of pork all over the counter, desperately wanting to follow my plan to fruition. But it simply wasn't working for me anymore and the glamour was long gone. Ever the pragmatist, I rationalized, *Hey! They want ham. This is ham. If ham is what they want, ham is what they'll get... and be happy with it!*

I was just getting ready to get down to business, juice dripping off my elbows and still trying to contain the blood from the cut finger when I noticed the house filling with smoke. It was billowing from the oven. *Cripey!* I opened the oven door and smoke poured out, sticky glaze and melted marshmallow oozing down the sides of the dish and dripping onto the oven floor. *Well, Golly Gee! That's certainly going to make a mess of things!* I determined that stupid casserole had baked long enough and pulled the molten, bubbly dish from the oven. It wasn't pretty, at least not as pretty as I had imagined. *Edible! Good enough!*

I left it to cool and went back to my meat slicing. I chopped and hacked and sawed and finally had my platter loaded. It wasn't pretty, at least not as pretty as I had imagined. *Edible! Good enough! And cooked with all the freakin' love I can muster, dang it!*

I was off my schedule when I arrived, but no one really seemed to notice. But as I unveiled my sweet yam casserole (the worst of the nastiness and stickiness of the dish strategically covered by foil and duct tape) I thought of my dear, sweet Mom. She would have looked at that mess and smiled, eyes shining and biting her lip to not say anything. But curiosity would have gotten the best of her and she would have finally had to ask me what happened. I would have related my culinary mishaps and she would laugh as only she could laugh and the jokes would start. My Dad would have then intervened, "It's a mighty poor cook that has to apologize for her cooking. The mistakes taste best. It doesn't matter what it looks like...it's all going to the same place for the same reason." And then he would have offered a prayer for the meal at the appropriate time...giving thanks for the 'repaired' food. We would all have glanced at each other and snickered.

We missed them at the table this year, as always. But, I suppose they are never far away- especially on the occasions we are all gathered together. I'm giving thanks tonight for a wonderful day with my family, "health as good as it is", a warm shelter, and a full stomach. The important things.

My finger will heal. My oven will be clean again (I can hope). And I'll eventually get the ham juice off the ceiling and light fixtures. Mostly, I'm giving thanks for my sweet Momma and Daddy who taught me about important things. Happy day.

Even the Lone Ranger Wore a Mask

Being in Texas and watching the COVID debacle play out on social media was like watching Forrest Gump play a championship ping pong match. It was only intensified through the lens of a Trump election year droning in the background. There were arguments for/against the very existence of COVID, wearing masks, the perceived levels of danger, protocols, need for shelter in place and quarantine, levels of vigilance required in schools and churches, and, well, the list continued. Every issue was subject to arguments. It was frustrating, at times embarrassing, to witness.

At its onset, I naively expected Texans would unite and pull together, whip COVID butt and do a well-deserved victory dance. However, it soon became apparent that wasn't to be. Even the simple courtesy and precaution of masks proved too much to ask of our hardy and freedom-loving range riders. Too many refused, insisting masks were uncomfortable and infringed on their rights. I assumed the logic that wearing masks would help protect people like me would be sufficient. I was wrong. Every time I made eye contact with one of those champions of open face, I felt disrespected and devalued in their world and unworthy of the sacrifice they were asked to make.

Then, people started dying and the statistics calculated and published. I watched as national and state-level politicians, friends and neighbors started arguing about which deaths should/should not be included as a COVID death statistic. How cold is that? According to some politicians and arm-chair doctors if I contract COVID from one of these non-masked Yahoos, spend time on a respirator but eventually die of a heart attack or stroke, they don't want me tallied as a COVID death! They insist it falsely inflates the COVID death statistics and that's not good! They insist I am old anyway, and have 'issues'. Really?

I address this inane and ludicrous argument with the following scenario:

I'm an older person, retired, and decided to enjoy the sunshine and a leisurely stroll in the park. My meandering route soon led me to a trail beside the river. The birds were singing and the outstretched tree branches provided a nice shade. Lost in thought and enjoying nature,

I didn't pay much attention to the footsteps rushing behind me and nearing at a fast pace. If so, maybe I would have prepared for the slight nudge as he (Mr. No Mask) sped past - a nudge with just enough force to send me down the steep slope and into the river below(COVID). A stronger, younger person would have had no problems - the water wasn't that deep, not over my head. However, the current was fairly strong and I'm a weak swimmer. I was soon fighting to stay afloat on the slippery rocks, struggling to keep my feet secured and my head above water as I attempted to return to the riverbank. I supposed it was the exertion...maybe the stress...but my chest and arms began to cramp and I realized I was having another heart attack. I was helpless against the current, no longer able to fight and slowly submerged beneath the surface of the murky water. Drained of strength and pained from the heart, unable to stand or swim, water began to fill my lungs until I could no longer breathe or fight. I drowned and died after being nudged off the trail into the river.

SCREEEEEECH! HALT, THERE! No. Wait! Wait just a minute! You did NOT drown - you were old and had an underlying medical condition. Haven't you heard of comorbidity or multi-morbidity? I know about this stuff.

You possibly - PROBABLY - most certainly would NOT have drowned if you didn't have a weak heart, so you can't blame drowning. And, if you can't blame drowning, you can't blame the person who knocked you off the path into the water. Bubba was young and in a hurry - can't be expected to be inconvenienced by every old and sick person he meets. It's not like he pushed you hard or maliciously. Besides, why should Bubba be expected or required to go around and step out of the shade into the sun; he has the right to be in the shade. He pays his taxes! It wasn't his fault you were old, couldn't swim, and had heart problems... or respiratory problems or compromised immunity or kidney disease or any other disease or malady. It's not his fault...not his problem. And how could he know you couldn't swim? He's a good swimmer. I mean, really - educate yourself.

Well, sure...that makes sense. NOT! But that's how it looks from the other side. That's how it looks to us older folks when so many refuse to wear masks, then additionally refuse to take any responsibility for the results. Either way, I'm just as dead unnecessarily. Just sayin'.

I'm taking another well-deserved break from social media. I'm going insane.

Fences

I'm content most of the time (probably 99.9%) with my position in life. Or lack thereof. But nothing makes me evaluate my life's choices more than a pleasant ride through the countryside and seeing a fence costing more than I will ever be worth, dead or alive. A fence!

Most of you know the kind of fence I'm talking about... miles of artisan metalwork or rockwork or imaginative use of thousands of big cedar posts. And I don't know if these are actually functional, working fences; I never see any cows or horses or sheep or pigs to keep inside. I suppose they're showpieces? Status symbols? Or perhaps just barriers meant to keep insignificant peasants like me on the outside?

Anyway, I observed a fence such as this today and immediately the jaws tensed and I tightened the grip on the steering wheel. *Urghhhh!* I presumed to estimate its value as I passed and suddenly had a Green Eyed monster as my copilot. He whispered all the 'could haves, would haves, should haves' in my ear, pushing me closer and closer to his 'feelings' quagmire of frustration and failure. I'll admit he dunked me in the green slime a few times.

But before he could drag me under his cesspool of envy and self-pity, I was saved by two things. (1) I didn't have to drive very far before seeing an old trailer house in need of major repairs, yard overgrown with weeds, porch rotted and broken. Its downed fence and gate askew and off its hinges served to remind me things could be a lot worse. My peasant life is actually blessed in many ways and that thought made me feel a little better. (2) As for all you fancy fence folks... I know in my heart... IF I had the money...I would totally build a fancy fence, too! Absolutely! And it would be TALLER AND LONGER AND BETTER than yours. I might even have it dipped in gold or gem-encrusted. I would have to hire someone just to keep it polished! Or maybe it would move around the perimeter on a conveyor belt, changing colors and playing rock music. Maybe dancing laser lights or sprinkled with real moon dust! People would drive for miles just to have their picture taken with my fence. Me and my fence would be on the cover of Texas Monthly, maybe People Magazine. So, you are the one who needs to count your blessings; I could have made your fence seem very ordinary. Indeed. And that thought made me feel a lot better!

Now, I need to go out and mend my rusted, old barbed wire fence. I'll probably even think about the blessings I have and hum a happy tune. It's all good!

First Day of School

Oh, yeah! Finally! The first day of school tomorrow! The beginning of a new year teeming with the promise of opportunities for learning and personal growth on the path to self-actualization.

But, they won't sleep well tonight...maybe not at all. Their minds will continue to whirl in twisted anticipation of the morning. "What should I wear? I hope I'm not late! Will they like me? What if they don't like me? Do I have all my supplies? I wonder if I should take my lunch? What if I get lost or miss a class?" Any dreams will be fitful visions of everything that could go wrong to ruin the first day. Counting down the hours through the long night. *I don't think I'm ready!*

They will enter the halls full of apprehension and self-doubt, unsure if they are truly worthy of the challenges ahead. They will meet and greet each other in hushed tones, uneasily scanning the group for friendly faces and allies.

Yes, they will most certainly approach the day with mixed emotions, a great degree of excitement mixed with nervousness and a tinge of fear. And that's just the teachers! Bless their hearts – all of them.

When you see a teacher tomorrow, consider these things:

Teachers initially enter four years of college after making a 'personal choice' to sacrifice their time, effort, and financial credit for a low-paying, labor-intensive service career. So, yeah...they know what to expect...and do it anyway.

Unlike popular thought, they do not get paid for the summer months. They are only paid for the school year and that amount is paid over twelve months so they will not have to go without pay during the summer. In other words, they are only getting the money they have already earned – not getting paid for time off.

Summers are full of preparation for the following year and getting additional required training, mostly on their own time and at their own personal expense.

Their sacrifices continue, quietly spending money from their shallow pockets to buy classroom supplies because they don't want to ask for funds from school budgets they know are already tight.

Their day begins well before the first bell and extends well beyond the last. There are always lessons to plan/grade/review. There are students to support in afterschool activities and sports, either as a cheering voice or sponsor. There are teacher meetings and parent meetings and community functions and fund-raising and mentoring and tutoring. There is ever-changing classroom technology to learn and the expectations they should 'already know this stuff'.

Teachers get a lot of colds and illnesses from operating in close proximity to so many children over the course of a year but often go to work not feeling well. They believe what is on the lesson plan for the day is too important to miss or require of a substitute. They will save their own sick days only for emergencies, usually for the care and keeping of their own ailing child at home.

They enter the school year feeling pressured, realizing the goal has already been set for the end of the year. Regardless of all the factors beyond their control affecting student performance and the limited resources available to accomplish the task, the mark is unrelenting and etched in black and white.

There is not enough time... there is not enough money... there is not enough support. There is never enough.

Our mandate to them as teachers is to 'simply' maintain and hopefully enhance the very foundation of a progressive society – the educating and molding of youth into the productive adults/leaders of tomorrow. Educating alone should be enough. This alone should indicate their importance and ensure them an esteemed place of honor.

However, the scope of this mandate has expanded well beyond simply filling the minds of our children with knowledge. Educators are expected to fulfill their obligation while accepting responsibility for the physical, emotional, psychological, and social development of our children – once considered the responsibilities of parents, churches, and community activities beyond the school house walls. (I realize this is a general statement and some may question what I specifically mean. However, I will step off the soap box at this juncture for professional considerations.) Suffice it to say, the scope and breadth of expectations heaped upon teachers and the educational system by society goes well beyond their perceived role and is sadly oversimplified and under-rated.

The unseen and truly unsung heroes tomorrow will be the support staff. Who will notice the shiny and spotless floors, scrubbed bathrooms, and sparkling window glass? Who will pay any attention to the freshly-painted walls and replaced light fixtures? Who even knew this was repaired or that was fixed or what was hauled to storage? Why would anyone consider the hours required to copy handbooks or policy manuals or organize the workroom? Who would have reason to think of the student data input and record keeping and reporting necessary to start a new year and maintain the operation? Who will consider an aide, working beside a teacher in a supporting role - helping both teachers and students with total dedication and little pay? Who would wonder how the groceries were ordered and appeared and the menus developed and posted and breakfast ready at the appointed time? Who knows the bus driver's name – that person in which you entrust your child for safe transport to and from school? Does anyone think about all the computers and networks and programs necessary to conduct school and who is behind the scenes making it work?

So, tomorrow is the first day of a new school year. Students will rush in, excited to see friends and show off new clothes and school supplies. Parents will heave a collective sigh of relief! And teachers will be standing there as always... their quick smiles and controlled manner successfully covering the apprehension and dark circles under their eyes.

If you see a teacher...today...or tomorrow...or any time in the future... know you are looking at a person worthy of your respect and appreciation. A simple "thank you" and commitment of continued support would mean a great deal, and I promise, brighten a day!

And while you're in the spirit, do the same for a custodian or a maintenance person or the office staff or the techie guy or a lunchroom worker or a classroom aide or a bus driver. They are all worthy of a little recognition and a 'thank you' on occasion. As the saying goes... "It takes a village..."

Administrators are the exception. We all know 1) principals only walk around the campus and try to look important, 2) counselors only hand out unpopular tests occasionally and advise students to go to college 3) business managers only pay the bills, 4) superintendents only come out of their offices for photo ops or donuts in the break room and 5) school board members only sit around and talk about everybody else. Administrators' cushy jobs are their own reward. Still, I'm certain a few words of gratitude at times would be appreciated and encourage them to continue doing whatever it is they do. Maybe it's important.

Flight of Fancy

Today's nasty sleet storm has brought to mind my recent winter trip to Boston. This particular visit deposited me in the first wave of what would come to be known as the "Great Blizzard of 2015." I left Boston for home when there were ONLY three feet of snow on the ground, drifts and piles of shoveled snow nearing five feet in places. This Texan thought it was awesome, though the natives were beginning to grumble a bit. Boston has continued to get slammed again and again and again. At the time of this writing, the snow total is approaching 100 inches! Although I know the air is filled with cursings and fist-pumpings and piles of snow as mountains, they seem to have kept remnants of their humor and characteristic 'hardiness' intact. Please, no offense to anyone, but I'm glad I got out when I did! I know I would have enjoyed observing and being a continued part of this historic event but will remain content to sit out this Texas ice storm in my home and reminisce about my trip.

***

I was certain everyone boarding the flight from DFW to Boston was having thoughts similar to mine. As I breathlessly passed security and stopped to redress, *I was in such a hurry! Did I get everything? Purse? Carryon? Plastic baggie with chap stick? Wallet and watch? Coat?*

Does the TSA use rubber gloves? I hope so. Ticket? Where did I put my ticket and ID this time?" I mentally take inventory and organize my belongings in some semblance of order and find my way to the gate, stopping along the way for a coffee to go as my gate seems to always be a mile trek and the last one in the terminal.

I finally arrive at the gate and survey the area, looking for the best seat. As I review my personal criteria for sitting next to someone, *O.K. Not travelling with screaming kids of any age. Not talking on the phone. Not a group speaking a foreign language. Not two or more businessmen talking shop. Not two teenagers 'in love'. Certainly, not two middle-agers 'in love'. Not a couple in a domestic dispute...*). Soooo, finding no suitable seating companion I stand huddled in a corner alone and re-view the previous inventory of possessions AGAIN. *Where's my ticket and ID?* Sipping my coffee, *Did I remember to lock the truck as I parked it? And the doors? What about the doors at home? Did I lock them? Did I even close the door as I left home? Did I leave the iron on?* I toss the coffee cup. *Where's the nearest bathroom? Oh, yeah... half a mile back toward the entrance. Do I really have to go that badly? Do I have time? It's now or use the one in the plane. Uhmmm....yeah...I have time.*"

I return as the flight and group are being announced and slowly get in line for my walk down the plank, imagining this is how a cow feels walking down the slaughterhouse chute. *What are the chances today of being on THE flight... THE ONE FLIGHT taken down by a goose? Or friendly fire? Or a terrorist? Or a freak wind shear? Or just a freak?* Passing the cockpit and observing the pilot and attendants are people just like me. *I hope the pilot is in a good mood and got plenty of sleep. Too old? Too young? Does he have a drug dealer on speed dial? He seems OK, but would it be rude to ask to see his flight school grades? They go to school, right? I hope he passed with 'flying' colors. Hehehe. Joke. Seriously, does he have a diploma in the cockpit I can examine?*

I walk the narrow corridor toward my seat. Perhaps it's not the politically correct thing to do but I'll admit it; I take mental notes of people as I pass their seats. There, I said it! I check my control at the door but still think it's important to know my surroundings and potential problems aboard. *I'll be keeping my eyes on a few of you! What language is that? It's not Spanish or French. And YOU! And YOU! And... what? Come on, lady! That carryon is much too big and will not fit above, no matter how long you stand there and pound on it! Oh, great. Now we have to have a line-stopping discussion with the attendant before she pulls the bag for checking!* *sigh*

As my seat nears, I know I have no choice but to sit where I'm told and do as instructed; it's the luck of the draw and no personal criteria allowed here. But I can still think. *Oh, please, not that one! NO! Whew, thank goodness. Oh, NO! Whew, dodged another bullet! NO! NO! O.K. Good. Good. Keep moving, you, cougher-with-the-plague. Oh, there's already someone seated in my row. Hello, big sweaty guy on the aisle in the Hawaiian shirt. Is that a pastrami sub with extra onions you're already munching?* *Sigh*

I easily stow my carryon in the overhead, *Hey, Lady back there with the entirely- too-big bag? Are you watching?* and squeeze past Don Ho, settling into my seat for the long flight. We exchange basic pleasantries, the smell of pastrami hanging heavily in the air between us. I fasten the seatbelt and glance his way again. *Oh, good. He's gonna be a sleeper. I can tell. I don't care if you snore, mister, just please keep your pastrami drool and gas on your side of the invisible line separating our personal space!*

It's as I sit there during the awkward span of time between seat belt fastening and the taxi, I review the events of the morning. It hasn't been an easy task, getting ready for an extended winter trip. Besides the obvious packing, last minute cleaning, refrigerator review, and emptying trash I had to ensure all was winterized and able to withstand an extended freezing spell while I was away. Although inclement weather was not in the immediate forecast, it's Texas! Who knows?

The flight was scheduled for 11:10 a.m. Normally this would require a four-hour window from home to take-off, but that allows little time for contingencies. Knowing I would be in rush hour, regardless, I added another hour and would leave at 6:00. Satisfied all was ready except carting the overloaded bags to the truck, I laid down at 2:00 for a little sleep. *I wish I wasn't so worried about that traffic, though. Will 6:00 be early enough?*

The alarm jolted me from a restless slumber but I jumped up, wide-awake and ready to go! I started the morning dressing and brushing my teeth and gathering last minute items. It was then I noticed time on the clock. *What? 3:30? Is the clock broken? Have I overslept? What time IS it?"* After a panicked check of my cell phone, all the clocks in the house, and TV I was satisfied it was, in fact, 3:30 in the morning. *But I heard the alarm! I turned it off!* I then noticed the alarm was undisturbed, still set for 5:30. *I only dreamed I had heard it! Hahaha. Seriously? I slept an hour? Who the heck dreams of ringing alarm clocks? Really!* There was no way I could go back to sleep. *Is this possibly a sign I shouldn't travel today?* I pondered for a moment. *NO! Don't be silly!* I opted to use the extra time to double-check the house and leisurely leave earlier than planned. *This is better! I'll beat the traffic after all and can nap at the airport later. It's all good!*

On a last run-through, I realized I hadn't unloaded the dishwasher. I don't use the dishwasher as a rule but had done so the previous evening thinking it would be a good idea to run it, clear the lines, and drain any water. Unfortunately, that plan backfired and there was now water standing in the bottom. It had run through the cycles but not drained properly. *It's alright. I have time".* I ran it through the cycles, hoping it would miraculously drain this time. It didn't. *There's NO way I'm leaving water in here to stagnate. That's gross!* I began baling the dishwasher, one little Dixie cup at a time. *Is this a sign? An omen of impending doom?*

After one final walk-through I was convinced all was well and carted the bags out to the truck. *Alright! 4:15! Excellent.* I put the key in the ignition and turned... or tried to turn it. It wouldn't budge. I pulled the key to make sure I was using the right one. I was. *O.K. Don't panic! Check the steering wheel. Give it a little turn.* I turned the steering wheel to the left, then the right. The key still wouldn't turn. Repeated. Repeated. I began to consider my options IF I couldn't get the truck started. *Let me think... It's 4:20 in the morning and I won't call anyone I know. They can't help me with this.* I continued alternating between turning the wheel, then the key. *All garages are closed. AAA? What would they do? Tow? No. Will the old farm truck make a trip to DFW? I don't think so. I don't trust it. So, the worst case... I don't make my flight. I can get another one, though... later...."* Suddenly, the key turned and the engine started. *But was that a sign? No! It started, so no! It's all good!*

I was finally on my way! I tuned the radio and headed out. I had driven seven miles and was approaching the city limits. Suddenly, *What's that weird thumping sound? Have they paved this strip of highway or something?"* I quieted the volume on the radio and rolled down some windows. *What IS that sound? I haven't heard that before.* And then, *Uhmmm... OK. Is the truck vibrating? It is! Sheesh!* It wasn't a little quiver; it was a full blown rattle-my-teeth vibration. *Oh, dang it! Is this a sign? Surely this is a sign I shouldn't go?*

I slowed and limped into the 24-hour store conveniently located a short distance up the road. *So, that doesn't look good!* The rear driver tire had blown out, frayed rubber hanging off like hot, seared skin. *O.K. It's 4:40. I'm still alright with the time. I'm fine.* I went inside to get a large coffee. *Think! Think! AAA? No. I need a new tire and don't know what they will do. Probably want to tow... that seems to be their thing. I don't have time to talk to them about it. Uhmmmm... OK. Suck it up, Buttercup, and call Andy's Tire.* I called the 24 hour answering service, gave their service all the info for a new tire and directions to my location, and waited. And waited. And checked the clock. *Is this a sign?* I finished drinking the coffee and waited some more. I was beginning to think of options when I finally saw the repair truck. *5:30? OK. I'm still good...provided he had a tire in stock...AND he remembered to bring it with him. Please! PLEASE!*

He pulled up beside me. We exchanged greetings and he immediately busied himself with tire removal. *That's a good sign for a 'change'. Hehehe. Joke.* I took his coffee order and returned shortly with a cup in each hand. He hadn't made a LOT of progress but was working hard. I delivered his coffee and opted to wait it out in the truck. I sat there sipping coffee and checking my time, watching the action in the rear-view. *Why does he keep hesitating? He seems... unsure... not sure what to do. Am I his first remote repair? What are the chances of that? But, really...what if he doesn't do it right? What if he forgets to tighten the lug nuts or something? Uhmmm.... Is that him coughing? Yes! He's doubled over and sounds like he's coughing up a lung! Poor guy. Is he going to faint? He must be sick. Maybe that's why he keeps hesitating. I wonder if he's running a fever? Maybe he has the flu. The flu? What if he gives me the flu and I spend the next two weeks 1800 miles away on my deathbed with the flu?* He coughed and gagged. I grabbed my hand sanitizer for self-treatment, as if that would help, and checked the time. *5:50. YIKES! I'm getting a bit worried here, fella. Can you speed it up? Just a little!* Finally, I heard the impact wrench, signaling he was almost finished. I felt uneasy about the tire, not knowing if he was very sick or just new to remote repair... or, as I suspected... BOTH. Was that a sign?

As I pulled onto the highway after the truck repair and payment, I checked the clock. *6:00a.m. That should deposit me directly into the pulsating bowels of rush hour! Really? All my good intentions and I've only managed to get 7 miles and leave on my original schedule? Except now I have to wonder if the lug nuts are tightened and if I'm carrying the flu to Boston.* As I finally left town behind and started the long drive to the airport, *and if the flu doesn't kill me... I know someone in Southie who has a friend who has a cousin that knows a mechanic who will!* Was that a sign?

I eventually relaxed about the workmanship on the new tire and forgot about the flu. I had to concentrate fully on the highway, no time to dawdle. Although traffic on the interstate had been moving fairly well, I remained uneasy about what the city traffic would hold in store for me. I approached the Pilot Store in Weatherford, my usual stop for coffee and a restroom break. I checked the clock for the umpteenth time. *OK. Decision time. I have an old lady bladder bulging with approximately 76 ounces of coffee. Do I have time for a bathroom break? Do I chance it?* I had to make a decision NOW! *Do you feel lucky, Punk? Do you?* I drove past. *Yesssss. Yes, I do! I can do this! I can hold it for another hour or so!"* Was that a sign?

Fortunately, I had made the remainder of the drive (and the bathroom) with little interference. Traffic was wicked, as usual, and I caught the flight with precious little time to spare. So now, as I sit on the tarmac and the plane engines start to rev all the morning incidents have begun to frantically whirl about my mind. *Were all those pesky inconveniences really signs this trip isn't a good idea? But I don't believe in signs and premonitions. Do I? No. But, still..."*

Suddenly, I had a memory of something I had heard years before...one of those odd tidbits lying dormant in a cerebral wrinkle until it decides it's an appropriate opportunity to give the memory a little poke:

A flood was coming and an emergency vehicle stopped to warn a man sitting on his porch to evacuate. He refused to get in the rescue car because he believed God would save him. The water started to rise and a neighbor in a canoe floated by, offering a ride to safety. He refused because he believed God would save him. As the water rose higher and began to spill inside the house, a motorboat stopped to offer aid. He refused. The flood waters soon began to rage and the man climbed to his roof. A helicopter hovered and dropped a ladder. Stubbornly, he waved it away, believing God would save him. He drowned in the flood and went to Heaven. "God, I put all my trust in you! Why didn't you save me?" And God answered, "I sent a car and a canoe and a motorboat and a helicopter. What more did you need?"

It was then I felt I had put it all together. My pulse started to race, my knuckles turned a whitish tint. *OMG!" THAT'S IT! WE'RE ALL GONNA DIE! HE TRIED TO WARN ME AND I WAS TOO BLIND TO SEE! I SEE NOW, GOD! TRULY! YOU'VE BEEN TRYING TO WARN ME ALL MORNING! YOU'RE TELLING ME WE'RE ALL GOING DOWN... AND IT WILL BE IN THE WATER, RIGHT? A LAKE OR THE ATLANTIC? DOESN'T MATTER, I SUPPOSE. I WISH I HAD GIVEN MORE ATTENTION WHEN THE STEWARD TOLD US HOW TO EVACUATE BUT MY MIND WANDERED TO THAT SCENE IN TOMMY BOY! TOO FUNNY! DO I PULL THE CORD FIRST? OR PUT ON OXYGEN? WHERE IS THAT EMERGENCY FLOTATION DEVICE? DID I TURN OFF THE IRON..."*?

Just then I felt a jolt. I grimaced, vowing to meet my doom with courage and grace. Then, I realized I had been so lost in thought we had already taxied and were lifting off. *Oh, clouds... how nice...* As I said, I checked my control at the door. Also, I have these same thoughts every time and have always made it fine. I settled back to enjoy the flight and hope for the best. "Now, if I can just get Mr. Pastrami to turn his head and snore in the other direction... There you go, big fella. Good. Sleep." And thus began my trip into the 'Great Blizzard of 2015. I actually think of the blizzard as rather uneventful, considering how it began.

Goin' Off Road

I admit I'm not much of a daredevil. I'm also not a wimpy girl, exactly, but certainly I don't take as many unnecessary risks since I've gotten older and less bouncy. Experience dictates I should possibly avoid motorcycles and sharp objects; they've proven to be a tad risky for me. Good judgment, planning, and common sense have always served me well with most other things. I've backed away from few tasks in my life and never been easily intimidated by much.

However, nothing shouts "SPHINCTERS ENGAGE!" like loading or unloading the ATV into the back of the farm truck. The moment it's determined I'll have to take it in for service, my first thought is *YIKES!...I'll have to load that stupid thing UP THE RAMP and into the truck!* This is immediately followed by the horrid thought of *YIKES! ...and after it's fixed, I'll have to BACK IT DOWN THE RAMP when I get it home!* The whole ordeal makes me sore and sweaty...and that's just thinking about it. The anxiety hasn't eased with experience or time, last week hosting the most recent wrestling bout with my Polaris.

Loading the disabled ATV has been a process learned over time after careful planning and trial and error; I take every safety precaution and avoid taking any risky shortcuts. I use the lawnmower and chain to drag it to my favorite loading berm, which serves to decrease the incline of the ramp from 39 degrees to approximately 12 degrees. I set the ramp...check for alignment with the wheels and adjust for angles...reset...check for alignment...until I'm satisfied it is perfectly set in the correct position for loading. I take the added precaution of securing the ramp to the truck with the appropriate stress and weight-tested straps and hooks. Then, ascending the ramp takes various combinations of pulleys, a come-along, chain, straps...and a lot of patience. I'm chewing nails the entire time it's on the ramp and constantly vigilant to ensure everything stays together and works as it should. The only thing worse are the few occasions I have had to load the ATV for transport and it is actually working. Driving it up the ramp with the engine running is even more tense. Fortunately, that rarely happens. I will make sure of it.

After it was finally loaded, I prepared the vehicle for transport. I put the ATV in park, set the emergency brake, AND strapped it. I checked it all multiple times before starting the truck. Then, I proceeded to drive to town like an old lady...slowly...slowly and close the shoulder...slow and easy turns...slow and easy braking...slow and easy acceleration... slow and easy, constantly checking the rearview mirror to calm my anxiety about losing it on the highway. I'm thinking the tailgate MIGHT fall open and the strap MIGHT come unclamped and the two brakes MIGHT disengage. All MIGHT happen simultaneously, leaving the ATV to roll out the back. That would totally ruin my day, although (on the bright side) I wouldn't have to unload it.

It was such a relief to arrive safely and finally hand over the responsibility to professionals; they told me where to park the truck to wait for someone to unload it. *YES! SOMEONE WILL UNLOAD IT!* I always love to hear those four words! A service tech eventually rushed out from the shop, overworked and out of breath. The poor guy seemed amused to find the ATV strapped in the truck. Or maybe he was just irritated he had to burn daylight removing them? I couldn't tell. Anyway, he grabbed some ramps, slapped them against the tailgate, jumped astride the disabled ATV, pushed off with his feet and a grunt... and rolled down that 76-degree ramp backwards like a boss! *What? No tedious ramp placement? No straps? No nuthin?* I was left standing like an idiot, mouth agape and fists tightly clamped, as he rushed it off toward the shop in stride, waving me off and leaving me in clouds of dust and feelings of inadequacy. Every time. Every time I take it in, I leave feeling like such a... wimp...an overly cautious and fraidy-cat... old woman.

I got the call in a couple of days it was ready to pick up and the immediate dread of unloading it at home began to weigh heavily. After payment in the service office, I drove the truck to the yard and waited for additional directions. I soon heard the ATV roaring around the corner- a young, strapping lad at the helm. The caliche and dust were flying as he skidded to a stop. Before I could say anything, he crudely and unceremoniously leaned some ramps to the tailgate, jumped on the ATV, revved the engine, and rode that ATV up the ramp like a cowboy leaving the chute on a bucking bronc! *YIKES! Are you crazy?* I was visualizing all the ways that could go wrong as the dust settled and he quietly sauntered off toward the shop. *Urghhhhh.* I was left standing, feeling like the kind of person who would take a shower with floaties... or sleep in a lumbar support belt...strain my vegetable soup...

I pride myself on planning and taking proper precautions- most of the time. Of course, I don't want to get hurt due to carelessness as I work to maintain my space. Absolutely, I don't want to be out the expense of replacing equipment I could damage due to impetuous actions. But mostly, I don't want to hear my family say, " I told you so"..."why were you doing that?"..."I knew that was going to happen"..."that was a stupid thing to do"..."we think it's time to get you a keeper". However, the worst is feeling like a wimp – the overly cautious person taking entirely too much time and preparation to do a rather simple task. The memory of those techs going up and down that ramp with such ease replayed in my mind all the way home and as I backed up to the berm. *If they can do it, so can I! I'm not as heavy and that should be to my advantage. Right? Right? I have long legs. That should be good. Right? And the incline will definitely be less! I ain't no chicken! I can do it!* I slammed that truck door, determined to toss caution to the wind and step up my game!

I unloaded the ramp and nonchalantly propped it into an approximate position. *Eh….close enough.* No unnecessary straps. *What a waste of time those obviously are!* I climbed into the truck, boarded the Polaris, and started the engine. *O.K! So far, so good!* My white-knuckled hand gripped the gear shift and put her in reverse. I looked over my shoulder and glared at the ramp –jaws clinched and fire in my eyes as my hand slowly released the hand brake. It was time to give it the gas and back it out; the defining moment of truth was upon me! "COWABUNGA! GOD BLESS AMERICA!"

I hit the gas and…! Nope. Sorry. I meant to say I THOUGHT about hitting the gas! But, not that time. Not ever. SPHINCTERS ENGAGE! The ramp looked like a poorly stretched tight rope to me. That 18-degree slope looked like descending the treacherous Pikes Peak Highway. That distance to the ground looked like the gaping jaws of hell, waiting to claim yet another impetuous soul. "Pride cometh before the fall," I whispered repeatedly, "pride cometh before the fall!" So, yeah; I wimped out. I admit it. I stopped everything in its tracks and took all the precautions, per usual, to set the ramp and secure it to the truck with hooks and straps. I slowly descended, still feeling much like a Wallenda walking the wire with no net. And I kissed the ground!! But only after all the wheels were clear...and I put the ATV in park...and turned off the engine.

I've never claimed to be a daredevil. I have exorcised the demons, although I'm sure I will have the same feelings of envy and injured pride the next time I watch those service guys do their voodoo they do so well. Perhaps I am overly cautious and irrationally fearful of some things. Perhaps. But I'm alive. And that's more than Karl Wallenda can say!

Grrrrrrass Burrs

Some of you got a little rain yesterday, huh? Magical droplets of water from the sky? How nice for you! And I sat here watching the dark clouds swirl all around me, cool wind blowing out of every direction imaginable with rain on its breath... but nary a drop? Zilch. Nada. I have only two words for you (in the words of Sister Mary Clarence) ... BLESS YOU!

I've been grubbing grass burrs in my spare time. I don't mean daintily flicking a few cute little plants out of an otherwise well-manicured yard with a spoon as I sip iced tea and listen to arias. I mean digging plants with two foot stems supporting multiple heads of angry, Tasmanian devil, circular-saw, chew-you-up-and-spit-you-out burrs! Huge, honkin' burrs. Digging with a shovel. In a pasture. In a dry pasture. And sweating like a pig on a spit. Thus, my previous lament for lack of rain. I'm currently required to stomp and stomp on the shovel to get just enough bite under the plants to partially pry them from the hard pan soil. I've never worked and sweated so hard for six inches in my life. And I can honestly say I'd be grateful for less than six inches if I thought it would be enough to satisfy my desire to get this done. Perhaps some rain would help?

You may be wondering why I spend my less than ample leisure time in this way? First, I hate grass burrs...almost more than grasshoppers. I've never been able to determine a redeeming value for either. Sometimes, I imagine a cloud of grasshoppers jumping/flying across the pasture on their way to pillage the Caroline Jasmine in my yard. They are gloriously impaled atop grass burr plants and die slow, agonizing deaths under the burning sun. Their decaying exoskeletons release substances toxic to grass burr plants and the entire crop is infected with a botanical mutant virus and it wilts to the ground! But then I face the reality that ain't never gonna happen but in my sweetest reveries. So, I grab the shovel and start digging.

Second, we've never had burrs in this pasture. It was cultivated this spring and I'm beginning to suspect JP Farms threw some burrs out the cab of the tractor as it made its rounds plowing. If so, tell Eric he didn't do a great job because the burrs seem to be relegated to one quarter acre spot north of my house. No pre-emergent was applied, of course, as there's never been a problem. I can't shred the weeds out there with those buggers waving at me across the fence...mocking me...daring me to spread their prickly pestilence. I can ignore and do nothing. Or I can leave them and shred right over them. Either way, they win and I can't let that happen! So, I grub and stuff them in a black body bag! I consider each individual burr I remove in this way (including the ones I find later stuck to my clothes and arms and boots) a victory for my posterity, not theirs.

Third, speaking of posterity, I've been left the keys to this empire of dirt called the family farm. As such, I try to take care of things like my Dad or Grandad would have done. I'm not a farmer (and bless them all). But I can't scratch out subsistence on dry land or sell a chicken for money to buy flour and shoes like my grandparents. I can't plow with mules and a harrow or grow peanuts and Black Diamonds like my

Granddad. I can't grow a garden or raise cattle or string miles of fence like my Dad. But I can try to take care of this patch of earth upon which they toiled and sweated. I know they would not like those burrs out there and would have done something. But what? I wish they could advise. For now, I do the best I can with what I have.

So, I returned to my grass burr eradication task this morning to take advantage of the cooler air. Ha! There was barely even a breeze and the humidity gauge was registering slightly in the 'yuck' zone, the one between 'gross' and 'Help me, I'm melting'. But it was nicer than under the afternoon sun an hour before dark, when I've customarily had the time to go out and dig a few. I eventually stopped for a rest and leaned against the shovel, realizing the patches of burrs waving in the air were definitely fewer and farther between. Progress indeed! I'll admit it... I was feeling all proud and somewhat puffed up! But real life never waits too long before rubbing my face in a heaping helping of humble pie! As I stood there, perhaps even smirking a little, the morning sun illuminated all the smaller plants hiding among the weeds I need so desperately to shred. Billions of them...most not yet developing burrs, but many full of burrs and not six inches off the ground... just hiding and watching and waiting.

Grrrrrrr! This task suddenly changed colors and may have approached the realm of impossibilities. Wiping at the humble pie dripping from my face and puddling at my feet I had a vision of my Dad and Granddad, standing there and watching. I don't know how long they had been there, but long enough to get a sense of what I'm trying to do. Granddad's pale blue eyes trailed from me to the shovel to the pasture. Then, he spit out a mouthful of snuff before stuffing his hands in his pockets and sauntering toward the barn. Dad took longer to survey the situation, which was his way. After a bit, he smiled and adjusted his hair under his cap and turned to follow his dad. My eyes followed them, hoping for more advice or guidance. Dad suddenly stopped and turned in my direction, making one of many gestures he had developed to replace talking. Sometimes Mom would get so frustrated with trying to decipher his hand signals she would look at him directly and say, "Talk mouth, butt can't". I thought there would be a killing at times he had her trying to back a trailer as he guided her. He would stand behind the trailer and have both hands in the air working together or independently, a barrage of random gestures to indicate left or right or stop or go or pull up and try again. More times than not she would get out and slam the door, yelling at him to "back it yourself and I'll stand back there and wave my hands around like a crazy person."

But, this day he made the gesture I knew well from a child. He owned/operated an auto repair business next to our house when I was a kid. Sometimes he would draft me to help...pump breaks (he had gestures for pump, hold, foot off, foot on, stop) as he added fluid, be a gofer for tools, activate all the lights one at a time in sequence (he had gestures for that process, too) as he checked them from the outside, etc. If he was adjusting a carburetor, my job was to sit behind the wheel, engine running, and wait for his signals. He would then disappear under the hood as he explored or tightened or adjusted. I'd watch intently for his signals as his hand would stick out at the edge of the hood with instructions to 'give it some gas...a little or lot...slowly or take the pedal to the floor...foot off'. Eventually, he would stand up, peer around the hood where I could see him, and give me the signal to turn off the engine. He used this gesture with me many times over the years in different situations. Sometimes, he even added the words, "Kill 'er" or "knock 'er in the head". Regardless of where or when or how, this gesture always meant only one thing. "The job is done. It's finished. Turn off the engine and go home for now. Ship the saddle home." This was the gesture he made this morning before disappearing down the hill.

Wow! Crazy, right? I don't believe in dreams or visions. I realize this was only a figment of an imagination fueled by complication, frustration, perhaps a touch of dehydration. However, I can't help but think Dad was trying to tell me something. What? I'm not sure what but maybe I'll figure it out soon...right after I remove a few more of these burrs! I could really use some rain here...

Great Cluster Buster of 2020

Quarantine seemed much too clinical a term, a word indicating the choice was not mine but forced upon me because I was unclean and tainted. Shelter in Place or Shelter at Home had a nicer ring, indicating I was voluntarily taking responsibility for my health and the health of the village by seeking refuge in my own home. Personally, I consider it the Great Cluster Buster because...well...it's self- explanatory. Ending week 6 seems as good a time as any to take a break from my very busy schedule for reflection of the most recent days of my life dedicated to what is currently referred to as the Corona Reduction Assistance Project.

I started this C.R.A.P. with thoughts of approaching it with the casual consideration given an unanticipated road trip. I was apprehensive, certainly, with what I admit to be a tinge of excitement for the unexplored adventure. I would do a little reading, tiptoe through the tulips, smell the roses, sit back and enjoy the ride. I'd commune with the other passengers and enjoy a bit of quiet self-reflective mental yoga; it would be fine. Full tank...check. Snacks...check. Reading materials... check. Electronics for communication and occasional entertainment... check. Coffee mug...check. We loaded in the 'vehicle' rarin' to go! Let the C.R.A.P. begin!

Road trip? Road trip! Yeah...like a road trip that starts off all nice and relaxed, the first several miles filled with casual conversation and enjoying the sights of the countryside...THEN... the seat begins to get uncomfortable and your backside starts to ache and your vehicle starts to sputter and lose forward momentum and you fear it may not make it to the destination and that's when you remember you don't even know your destination or how it is exactly you are going to get there and you can't stop and ask because no one else out there knows where you are headed either so you keep trying to get somewhere you don't know where...and keep going...but then everything outside the windows starts to look blurry and out-of-focus and you do believe you have developed diarrhea and really need to stop the ride but you can't because the vehicle could stall out and you really would be in trouble... besides, big mess and no toilet paper due to hoarding... so you turn on the radio...big mistake...because you now know the evil Corona Gang has broken out of prison and are in some unknown location near you so you have to suck it up because you can't stop the vehicle and now know you can't even pull over at a truck stop because you might find yourself with explosive diarrhea against the wall in a truck stop bathroom surrounded by the Corona Gang in the middle of a real cluster... so you keep going...and you can't go off road or leave the beaten path but discover you are actually in a loop and have gone past the same dancing flamingo, the same ice-skating clown, the same buffalo in a sombrero, and Donald Trump caricatures like 6 times already...but you keep going... and the seat is really, really, REALLY uncomfortable and the diarrhea is ready to explode and it begins to storm outside the vehicle, the wind howling and rain pelting the windshield making it almost impossible to see in front of you which almost doesn't even matter anymore because you still don't know where you're trying to go but looking in the rearview mirror you see another vehicle, black and menacing... a steamroller with a rocket launcher mounted on top pointing at you and closing in fast and you read CORONA emblazoned in red on the hood so you know it's the Corona Gang on your tail and may launch a rocket if you don't continue evasive action and they get in range or if you stop they will roll over you and anything in the path so you... keep going... keep going....and you finally realize it's going to be necessary to tighten down on the sphincter, adjust the uncomfortable seat as much as possible, ration the snacks, settle back for several more laps around the clown...and keep going...because the alternative is much worse than the road trip. Corona Reduction Assistance Project! Green Light. Sputter...Sputter...or crash and burn!

We will survive the C.R.A.P. I am, however, growing more concerned about surviving the Sequestered Home Induced Trauma Syndrome.

The others are showing symptoms of developing the S.H.I.T.S. - the accompanying sarcasm, loss of humor, eye-rolling, tongue and nail biting, walking on eggshells, shoulder shrugs, and a marked increase in idle (?) threats of bodily harm - most of which are directed at me. It's alright, though. I know they aren't well in the head and I'm the only sane one remaining. I'm caring for them as best I can. Hopefully, I'll continue well and strong. But, for now, I have a window to lick and baskets to weave.

Here's to hope for better tomorrows. Be safe and take care!

Hot Mama

Ladies, I was wondering if this has ever happened to you? I was shooting my Glock 9mm automatic pistol, taking professional rapid-fire target instruction on a shooting range and flanked by two male friends engaged in the same training. Suddenly, one of the smoking HOT brass casings ejected and went straight down my shirt, lodging in my bra between the massive breasts.

I hesitated, wondering if I should ignore and continue with the exercise or stop and remove the flaming metal jacket. I also wondered how exactly does one nonchalantly and with a touch of elegance go fishing blindly down one's shirt to extract an errant projectile? Should I go down from the top or up from the bottom? Should I quietly leave the course or stand my ground and simply turn my back on the guys? Would only a wuss stop shooting to minimize the burn or does protocol dictate I grit my teeth and power through this minor inconvenience?

My sense of propriety (and pride) was soon overshadowed by the smell of searing flesh. At that point in time I neither left the course in search of privacy NOR turned my back. I grabbed a handful of shirt and bra and started vigorously shaking and pulling and hunkering! "Sorry, guys, but I have a little problem here!" I don't know at what point in time the case was dislodged. I just know 1) it wasn't there when I pulled out the shirt collar and prodded for an extended search and 2) it was there long enough to leave a nice, big blister on Thing One.

Perhaps I over-thought the situation and spent too much time analyzing my options? I'm certain it would have burned anyway, but still I will consider reacting in a timelier manner for future reference. I also must consider my reaction should the occasion arise and a hot, molten casing find its way down the front of my cohorts' trousers. It could happen. At this point in time I'm thinking I would gladly stomp until I was certain the fire was extinguished. Sorry, guys. Perhaps if you had reacted with a bit more sympathy and a tad less amusement?

Howdy from Kansas

Retirement can become monotonous (boring) if you don't remain busy. I vary the tasks, occasionally making changes to the routine. I maintain my home. I continue to deal with the briars, brambles, and barbed wire and have my special projects. I also spontaneously spend time with family and friends, read, write, or otherwise chill. I'm blessed and able to travel, having explored to some extent New England, Hawaii, Ireland, Colorado, Wisconsin, and the Pacific northwest. Life remains good!

Not long after retirement, dear friends owning/operating a local large-scale harvesting business asked me to accompany them to Kansas as a moisture tester. Although I would have liked to learn to drive the big rigs or huge chopper things, they assured me they needed me as a moisture tester only. Oh well. It seemed like an opportunity to do something new, the bonus being some extra money to finance my geriatric drug habit. And I hadn't explored Kansas. So, I went. To Kansas. Five hundred miles away. In a slow-moving caravan hauling large harvesting equipment. To stay in a hotel (only to sleep or pass rain days) when I wasn't testing on the dairy (working 12-hour days). To maintain my physique on junk food and coffee.

Following is a fictionalized sarcastic and snarky "letter" home to the family.

***

Dear family,

I made it to Kansas just fine. No problem. It was a long drive but plenty of talk and new sights to keep me engaged for the most part. I'm not exactly sure when we left God's country and passed the last uncultivated tree heading north. Maybe the Texas border? There are some trees around the houses but they seem to have been purposely planted in some strategic manner, perhaps to keep the dirt from blowing into their beds and food? Cedar and cottonwood seem to be the trees of choice. Why? I don't know. We cut them down in Texas and they plant them here. Funny, huh?

The weather has been an odd mixture of clouds and sun and rain. Sometimes all happening at the same time. I can put on a jacket because I'm too cold and remove it because I'm too hot...all in the same walk across a parking lot. Good weather days, they let us work all day and well into the night. If it rains, they let us sit in the hotel and watch Rural TV, local crop reports, and Petticoat Junction reruns all day. And they let us stay in our room for days and days if the rain doesn't stop! The only constant is the wind. Do you remember Forrest Gump...his description of the jungle rain in Viet Nam? "We been through every kind of rain there is. Little bitty stingin' rain; and big ol' fat rain; rain that flew in sideways; and sometimes rain seemed to come straight up from underneath. Shoot, it even rained at night..." Yeah. Like that... but wind. Maybe this is a test. I know I'll be stronger for my endurance IF I don't blow into an adjoining state... God only knows which one it would be. I'm hoping for Colorado but concerned it will be Nebraska. If so, I surmise I would eventually blow back into Kansas. I can hope?

Life as a migrant farmer has been an adjustment, to say the least. I no longer have to plan my days or independently make decisions. That's good! I just go where I'm hauled and do what I'm told, with a dim hope they will not forget where they dumped me on the plains. I'm told where and when to sleep, to eat, to be ready for work. I no longer ask why; I don't want to know the answer. I suppose I checked my autonomy at the border? But I comply; they promised to return me to Texas one day if I do.

They speak a different language here; words don't have the same meanings. Circle, tower, pivot, header, and pit...to name a few. I found the conversations foreign and confusing when I first got stranded here. Talk of laying it down, chopping it, bagging it, and dumping it in the pit were disconcerting. But I think I know what it all means now and no longer have horror movie nightmares when I'm permitted to sleep. Seldom, anyway. I wish I hadn't watched that program about white slavery and people being stolen away for work, never to be heard from again. If I come up missing, have the police trace the pings from my cell phone. (I learned about pings watching ID TV at the motel.) They haven't confiscated my phone...yet.

But seriously, the Big Bosses treat me well. They are kind and respectful and seem genuinely concerned about my comfort. They even got me a pot to boil hot water and a pillow of my own! I think they like me. And they provide us a very hearty breakfast most days...eggs, pancakes, bacon, etc...the works! I graciously declined the first few days, opting to sip on my coffee and wait for the butt crack of dawn. It only took me a few days to figure out breakfast was to be the ONLY meal served. It's all good, though. I have discovered I can store it in my stomach and make it last ALL DAY and into the night! Who knew? I have no complaints!

As for my job here: Control Central (where I base my operations) is basically four walls protecting me from the wind and dirt. But I have my scientific equipment and a coffee pot and need little else to conduct business. I don't operate any of the big equipment or do the hardest manual labor. I don't concern myself with the scheduling or complicated logistics of this major operation. I don't even have to take phone calls or keep up with pesky billing and payroll. You will be proud to know, however, I have the most important job. It's much too scientific and complicated to explain here. Suffice it to say, it involves precise measuring and calculations...grams and percentages and stuff. And the entire thing rests upon the results of my detailed assessment. All is halted until I'm finished and decide when the big rigs roll. There are a few others trained to do the same work but I'm the senior member of the crew. It's a lot of responsibility but I'm handling it well. You'd be proud!

The people I work with are very nice. Most of them are *much* younger, or more precisely, have yet to reach my advanced level of maturity. We nod and smile, pretending to understand each other. I don't. But they are all hard working and diligent, working well together and in whatever capacity they are assigned. We all work hard in hopes we have a ride back home when this is over; no one wants to be left behind. No one.

I hate to be so brief with the correspondence but the TRAIL BOSS has indicated I've used all my minutes. It's time to turn off the light and sleep. (She's coming! I have to hurry!) I just wanted to say I miss and love you all and...

***

NOTE: Actually, I had such a positive experience I've continued to return for three to six week stints every spring and fall for the last five years. Good times with good people; isn't that what retirement is all about? That, and the fact I always have the option to say 'no'...because I can. I'm retired.

It's All Good

What's my status? Well, there's good news and bad news and good news. Given my current employment status (or lack thereof, due to retirement):

1. I finally have time to do a little yard work. Since I'm operating on a shoestring, I broadcast some flower seeds I have accumulated over the years. The good news is there are tiny plants finally waving in the breeze due to my diligent care, watering, and beautiful sunshine! The bad news is I don't know if it's the wildflowers or seed from the pickup load of weeds I cleared. What? But it's OK...at least it's something to watch grow and benefit from my labors.

2. I don't have to wake up to a pesky alarm clock and that's good! However, I'm evidently conditioned/predisposed to rise and shine and get busy. Which means all those years I spent waking before the alarm sounded so I could turn it off faster were wasted time and effort. I wake up anyway. And it doesn't even matter how much sleep I actually got. But it's OK... I don't HAVE to get up if I don't want to, alarm or not! I'm retired.

3. My days are busy and I'm tired when it's time for bed. Good! However, I'm not always sleepy. Bad. But it's OK... I can enjoy green tea on the deck at 2:00a.m.

4. I can also demo and remove cracked ceramic tile steps at 3:00a.m. for no reason other than they bother me. Good! Unfortunately, I realized as the sun came up I have no way to actually fix or replace them. Bad! But, it's OK... another challenging project!

5. And I can make lists at 4:00 a.m. Which I did. A list of projects for the next day, the weekend, next week, next month, next

year, and a five-year plan. I prioritized the list, with sub-lists of materials I have, materials I will need, costs, schematics and plans for optimal project completion, and a system of one to five stars denoting a personal satisfaction scale. I cross-referenced these lists with optional backup lists in cases of inclement weather days...hot days, rainy days, windy days, and cold days...respectively.

Good! Unfortunately, I didn't actually write any of this information down at 4:00 a.m. I thought about it, though. I finally fell asleep and this morning I'm back at ground zero. Square one. I've got nothing. Nada. But it's OK... I let the seedlings out to go to the bathroom, sprinkled water on the dog, and am wondering what happened to the ceramic tiles on the steps. I'm fairly certain the information was on those lists somewhere. Maybe the coffee will help! It's all good!

It Takes a Village

- To those women having endured the throes of childbirth and stared death in the eye to bring a screaming, squirming unde-fined blob of unmolded human to life... and have continued to face the daily challenges of keeping it safe, loved, secure, and nourished with the goal to transform it into a well-adjusted, kind, and productive individual;

- To those women and men having lost a child, enduring each day with a hole in their life and heart that no words or actions or another person can ever fill;

- To those men and women with the depth and breadth of com-passion to (through fostering or adoption) voluntarily accept the challenges heaped upon them to nourish a damaged life and heart to health and happiness...with no promises;

- To those men and women joining DNA in a moment of passion and embracing the subsequent consequences of their actions, moving beyond the unexpected disruption in their lives and making the conscious, mutual decision to do whatever is best for the child - to either establish a solid family unit or give others more capable and ready the opportunity;

- To those men and women considered extensions, embracing little ones entering their families with open arms, regardless of the reasons or circumstances, and accepting them as their own;

- To those random men and women of the village never too busy to help the children...with a smile, kind word, assistance, vigilant eyes, listening ears, support, or pat on the back;

- To those men and women training for careers to help the children to develop into strong and productive adults - teachers, medical professionals, counselors, ministers, coaches, social workers, etc.;

- To those older among us, men and women offering the wisdom of experience to help guide younger guardians as they navigate the difficult, unfamiliar terrain of parenthood and

- To those younger parents willing to open their minds and hearts to the guidance and wisdom offered by the older, more experienced among us...

Thank you.

It takes a village to raise a child. I believe that ideal motivation is more relevant in today's world than ever before. Thanks to all forming a circle around our younger and most vulnerable, clasping hands and working together to keep the howling hyenas at bay. Our children need all the help and guidance they can get. Blessings today and every day!

Karma Requires Effort

"Karma (car-ma) ...refers to the spiritual principle of cause and effect where intent and actions of an individual (cause) influence the future of that individual (effect)...." Wikipedia

It was 8:00 pm on a Thursday and all I needed was a nice pot of mums. Simple. And the parking lot looked almost inviting, sparsely populated but for the Hitchcockian collection of Great-tailed Grackles. *Creepy!* When I see those huge, congregated flocks around town I always think of the movie scene when a benign collection of birds suddenly turn deadly and attack Tippi Hedron as she seeks refuge in a phone booth. (Does anyone besides me entertain that thought and avoid the phone booth? Never mind; I actually don't remember the last time I saw a phone booth). Anyway, there were numerous parking spaces close to the door at the end of the building housing the Garden Center. *SCORE!* I was ecstatic because CONVENIENT PARKING SPOT + ADVANTAGEOUS ENTRANCE + LIMITED OTHER SHOPPERS= LESS TORTUOUS WALMART EXPERIENCE! Psyched was I? Yes!

You may also note I was practically giddy when I entered the wrought iron gates at the Garden Center and beheld a nice selection of 'just what I was looking for' laid out right there before me! Right there, I say! I smiled triumphantly at my serendipitous fortune and quickly selected the pot of mums I wanted... a huge bunch of lavender-tinted mums in a rustic, wooden tub! It was perfect. I strained and grunted as I picked it up to haul it to the checkout a short distance just inside the doors. *Uhmmm. That's a little heavier than I expected* and immediately set it back down. *I'll have to load it in a cart.*

There are always empty, unattended carts stranded all over the Walmart store and parking lot, right? Wrong. There were no empty, unattended carts stranded within a two mile radius of Walmart last night! My enthusiasm was beginning to wane just a tad. To haul it in a cart meant I would have to hike halfway across the store to retrieve the stupid cart... then back again to load the plant and roll it through checkout. I shuddered at the thought, not due to an extreme degree of laziness on my part but for the mere inefficient use of time and energy with such a maneuver. *There must be another option. Think outside the box! Think*, as I paced back and forth. Suddenly, as in a whispered revelation from Sam Walton himself, I knew exactly what to do. My hand was practically shaking with delight as I reached down and simply peeled that little sticker off the side of the tub... the sticker with the BARCODE on it! *Genius! I'll just pop through those doors right there, she'll scan the label, and I'll be on my merry way!"*

It was a good plan. It was! Except for the fact there was no one checking out at the registers in the Garden Center. They were closed. Which meant that hike I didn't want to take to go get a cart? The one I was attempting to avoid? Yeah... I had to do it anyway. *It's alright,* trying hard to salvage my shopping experience. *At least I'm not hauling that huge tub of dirt and flowers around...just this little piece of paper."*

So I smiled inside as I trudged onward...past the toiletries... past the Pharmacy... past the cosmetics and jewelry. My inward smile quickly turned into an outward grimace as the checkout row came into view. *No self-service registers open on this end of the store? Huh?* The first register light ON was halfway to the end of the store and only a limited number were open! *What the ... what?* I began picking up speed, fueled by frustration and a pang of anger.

I walked and walked and eventually approached the first register with its ON light and sped past - it housed two full carts and a hundred-year-old cashier. I also sped past the second register- a lady with a full cart and waving a fistful of coupons. I had my eye on the next opening and was almost there when someone rushed in ahead of me. *URGHHHHhhhhh! No! It's alright. Stay calm.* I reasoned, *how would they know I was checking out? All I have is a stupid sticky piece of paper with stupid bar code on it! Stupid!*

I evaluated each open register as I sped past and all would have basically been occupied for an extended time. I finally found myself at the self-service registers on the totally opposite side of the store from where my journey had begun. And from where it would end, too, due to the fact THAT other end of the store was where my basket of flowers sat and THAT was where my truck was parked.

Fortunately for everyone in Walmart last night that self-check register read and recognized the bar code without fussing at me -making demands, flashing lights and sounding alarms before totally shutting down until 'Associate' can come to my rescue to 'reset' without so much as a smile or a 'howdy do'. I hate when that happens! And it's especially fortunate that the self-check register didn't yell at me in that haughty tone to "please deposit your item in the bagging area". I swear I would have jumped up on that little bagging area platform, squatted, and absolutely complied with its demand. "Here! I have your deposit right here!" And It would NOT have been nice. Or pretty. It would have shut that register down indefinitely (perhaps even Walmart!) The register even accepted my payment without a fuss! Things were looking better.

My hike back across the vast expanse of the store was actually quite calming and allowed me time to rationalize. *I needed the exercise, I'm sure. Actually, I can consider it an added bonus I received free of charge. All in all, I shall consider this a very productive time at Walmart.* I felt even better as I heaved my heavy prized tub o' mums onto the tailgate and wrestled them in the truck. *Excellent!* And my greatest victory, my crowning moment... the fading squawks of the Great-tailed Grackles (I personally believe to be the carnivorous evil guardians of this portal to Hell) and Walmart in my rearview mirror! I escaped once more, yet the tub o' mum's journey had just begun.

The mums were to be my donation to the fourth grade's Garden Basket as part of our rural community school's annual fundraiser, the Halloween carnival. Parents, businesses, and interested parties make donations to build various baskets; the classes then sell chances for a week, the festivities culminating at a carnival of games and food. I delivered the mums to the school Friday morning, where my daughter (the fourth grade teacher) asked to borrow the truck later that afternoon to move all the donated items from her classroom to the gym in preparation for Saturday's carnival. So, I returned that afternoon and we proceeded to make trip after trip, eventually loading the truck for the trek across campus. The donations we unloaded to her booth were quite impressive, vast collection of sundries for working in an outside garden - a shovel and hoe, bird feeders, vegetable seed, bird seed, soil, fertilizer, gloves, coupons for two trees, a wheelbarrow... the list went on and on. Oh, and of course, my donated tub o'mums.

Do you want to guess who won the fourth grade's Garden Basket? Huh? Yeah! THIS PERSON RIGHT HERE! I rarely win anything, so to win something as appropriately matched to my lifestyle was unexpectedly awesome! Who knew Saturday nights could be so festive? Not me! I was excited and overwhelmed, perhaps less so as I returned to the school...AGAIN... to load that ton of stuff ...AGAIN...haul it home and unload it in the garden shed. It was an impressive bounty and all it cost me was $20.00 worth of chances, that trip to Walmart, three trips to school, and a few sore muscles.

Taking inventory of my stash, I stopped to enjoy the beauty of that gorgeous tub of purple mums. I smiled as I retraced its circuitous trail to my patio: Thursday, we trekked the expanse of Walmart and it spent the night at my house. Friday, I unloaded it at her classroom and later moved it across campus to the gym. Saturday, I loaded it back into the truck and returned it to my house. That's karma by definition, I tell you! It's karma in a good way! Karma doesn't usually find me, so it's fantastic wrapped in awesomeness and I couldn't be happier! Well, perhaps if the shopping, hauling, and lifting could have been avoided. Had I known I would win I could have simply hauled them home. But, then, I suppose it would no longer have been karma. It would have just been me buying a tub of mums at the Walmart. I like karma better, I think. I'm not that fond of purple, though. Or mums.

Keep Yer Powder Dry

My memories of GrandDad are of a silent, even tempered, slow-motioned old man. Although he supported his family growing peanuts on this same sandy soil with a 'gooseneck', plow, and a team of mules, he was well beyond that time. His days were spent sitting on his stool on the 'gallery', interspersed with walking excursions to scatter the tiny strips of newspaper he had sat and shredded with his sharply-honed 'Old-Timer'. We would find odd trinkets in the woods he had left on other such strolls - cans, bottles, and 'snakes' whittled from rubber hoses left hanging from fence posts or tree limbs. An odd man, silently sitting and whittling.

I don't recall ever seeing him engaged in a conversation, certainly never had a conversation with him. This is a regret I have, though I doubt it is anything I could have evoked from him as a child. Still, I would like to have knowledge of his experiences, memories, and thoughts. I never saw him display any great emotion - good or bad, raise his voice, give a hug or speak of love or concern. Dad said that was just his way, always had been.

Sometimes when we had visited and were leaving he'd look up from his stool and quietly say, "keep yer powder dry." He'd immediately look down and resume his whittling. I puzzled over what he meant for years. At that time, I was familiar with two types of powder: 1) we would often smooth baby powder on my brother, Willie, when we changed his diapers and 2)Mom would 'powder her nose' with face powder as the finishing touch of dressing for Sunday church or a special event. I thought for a time he had been telling us to not wet our pants. However, I eventually decided he was telling us to be happy, to not cry to keep our face powder dry. I thought of it as his most affectionate way of saying goodbye. I liked it.

Sometime later after I was older and he had passed away, I remembered his odd salutation and pondered its meaning again. In the process, I suddenly realized there was another powder I hadn't considered when I was a kid - gunpowder. Trying to fit the word 'gunpowder' into a sweet and kind salutation was not an easy task. I knew, however, the meaning had to be there; I was determined to unlock the mystery without losing the affection I had always hoped he was expressing. I had always held onto that thought as the only real connection I had with GrandDad on an emotional level. I didn't want to lose that.

I finally decided GrandDad was telling us to be prepared, be vigilant - to keep our gunpowder dry in the event we encountered danger and needed to load our muskets. He wasn't telling us to be happy or he loved us. He was simply saying, "y'all be careful and stay ready to shoot." He was admonishing us to be responsible and take care of our weapons!

I admit I was a little disappointed when I couldn't seem to make its meaning more affectionate and loving. I've tried to embellish it through the years and was eventually able to conclude he was also reminding us to protect ourselves and our gunpowder from the 'rain that may fall'' and 'rivers' we may have to cross -anything which could get us or our gunpowder wet.

Keep yer powder dry! I've finally concluded after years of thought it's logical to believe GrandDad, in his own odd way, was telling us:

"My wish for you is nothing but smooth sailing and clear skies. I also admonish you to take greatest precautions and remain vigilant in the event you encounter difficulties along the way. Be careful and return safely until we meet again. I love you."

Nothing says goodbye like, "Keep yer powder dry". Thanks, GrandDad! Same to you.

Killer Butterfly

I had an interesting experience this past weekend aside from attending a most tastefully orchestrated 'nerd' wedding in Waco. I didn't know what to expect of a Star Wars/Star Trek/Hobbit -themed wedding, but they managed to make it work in an extremely nerdy and unique way! Well played! Anyway, after most of the post-wedding festivities (during which time I escorted my two-year-old grandson on an extended walk for playtime at a nearby park to burn excess energy – his, not mine) we rejoined his parents and a group on the balcony to enjoy the breeze and chat before the trip home.

Jonah was no longer exclusively in my care, though I was keeping my Grammie eye on him as he continued to scamper about and explore. He settled in a corner of the balcony and seemed content to look at the lake for a time. My attention was briefly drawn from him to a rather large yellow butterfly caught in the downdraft of a ceiling fan, suspended about seven feet off the floor. It was so beautiful, hovering there in all its glory. My thoughts were immediately Jonah-centric. I would 1) catch the butterfly as it was trapped in the odd air flow and 2) share the sight of it up close, allow him to gently stroke its beautiful gossamer wings, then 3) share the experience of setting it free to fly away on the breeze.

My sweet reverie was suddenly shattered by a blood-curdling scream! This was not a little scream or a pansy scream or a frilly-girly scream. Oh, no...this was a deep guttural screech that ripped through the air like a jagged sword, the kind of wail which dictated all action STOP NOW – butterfly watching or sipping punch or laughing at a joke or talking... even breathing! A CEASE EVERYTHING NOW AND SAVE ME kind of scream! We all stood there for a moment, frozen in place and terrified as to what would have predicated such an anguished alarm. "Where's that coming from?" "Who?" "What?" "Why?" In that short amount of time maternal mode engaged as I prepared to jump between Jonah and 'whatever'. I'd wrestle 'whatever' over that balcony railing and beat it into the ground! I prepared for a fight to the death!

"Where's Jonah?" I frantically looked to the last place I had seen him only seconds earlier and he was still there...thankfully! Only now he was hunkered over (or was it cowered?), fists clenched tightly, red-faced, jugulars pounding...and screaming like a Banshee! I couldn't actually believe that extreme volume and amount of scream could physically be contained in such a small body. As I rushed toward him checking for blood or guts or protruding bones, I noticed his eyes were fixated at one spot toward the ceiling. And it was as I approached him I realized the source of this utter terror. It was the butterfly.

Yes, I said butterfly. My grandson was terrified, paralyzed, mortified, and sissified by a butterfly. Not a FIREfly or HORSEfly or BLOWfly or DRAGONfly ... none of the flies with at least a hint of menace in their names. BUTTERfly...as in named after something smooth and creamy you spread on a warm biscuit or piece of cornbread. I could have related to fear of a biting tsetse fly... or even a fruit fly. Even a pant's fly has teeth and can pinch you! But a butterfly? Really?

Needless to say, the entire balcony erupted in laughter. Some of it was just the relief of knowing all was well. But I'm thinking most of it was at the spectacle. Either way, I'm seeing lots of butterfly jokes in the boy's future. He's never demonstrated fear of anything before this time, so we're not certain why he displayed such a dramatic reaction. He's never been attacked by a marauding horde of menacing monarchs to our knowledge, and I 'm certain none of the books to which he's been exposed have pictures of viscous, carnivorous butterflies feasting on the flesh of little boys and girls. It remains a mystery.

I'm certain, however, my little guy will soon discover butterflies are of a gentle nature and nothing to be feared. Grammie will teach him. I will impart my wisdom and experience. I will instill in him a strong sense of confidence. He will know his Grammie will protect him always, and he is secure in my care. I will assure him the "only thing to ever fear is fear itself" ...as embodied in the form of the disgusting mouse. Now, that's a beast having the ability to gnaw off your face and fingers in your sleep and spread diseases and germs capable of eradicating entire civilizations and leaving behind nothing but death, destruction and defecation in its wake! Now that, my dear Jonah, is a freak of nature worthy of such a gut-wrenching scream!

And just so you know...should we ever encounter one on our future expeditions through nature... you're on your own. Fight or flight. Sink or swim! Catch me if you can!

Knick Knack, Paddy Whack

Spring Break is practically over and the original 'to do' list is a pathetic underachiever; I completed few of the items. Therefore, I shall make a new list of what I actually did, taking care to draw a big red check beside each item indicating my accomplishment! Back up and punt. Sometimes it's the only thing!

***

Trying to take care of some pesky insurance business over the phone today. I was on hold 20 minutes the first call and 25 minutes the second. Both times I had to endure the most excruciating Muzak ever, interspersed with a maddening canned sales pitch on a 45 second loop. Do you know how many times I listened to that? My teeth were grinding, head splitting, fists clenching. And at the end of each cycle the voice would say "(clicking noise)-ck you!" Now I like to look for the best in situations, give the benefit of a doubt when due. But the longer I listened and the more aggravated I became, I became convinced the partial message was NOT saying "thank you". I'm absolutely sure it was saying "**ck you"! What else would accompany the torture? **ck me? No, **ck YOU! Not cool.

***

"I stand corrected" is only one of several positions I assume for chastisement. I usually nod and smile, quietly receiving the crow being stuffed down my throat. I accept the correction graciously because 1) the contentious point is simply not that important and 2) I know in my heart and mind I am totally correct and they are wrong, which is all the validation I need. It's easy to honestly feign humility when I know I'm right.

***

So, I did some channel surfing earlier this evening and stopped at a movie titled "When a Stranger Calls". Score! It was about 30 minutes in and I like suspense. The babysitter was obviously being stalked, breathing hard in fear as she slowly walked through the dark house searching shadowy corners and behind closed doors for the intruder. However, I was soon bored with her scared look and porno-esque gasping and moved on to other entertainment. I checked back in an hour and the babysitter was... breathing hard in fear as she slowly walked through the dark house searching shadowy corners and behind closed doors for the intruder. Huh? And I thought "Under the Tuscan Sun" was monotonous.

***

I seem to be getting mixed messages on how best to protest perceived racial injustices. The choices seem to be as follows: Protest injustice by breaking out storefront windows of stores and shops in my hometown and simply loot what I want and trash the rest. Or protest injustice by blocking entry to prevent regular paying customers from entering stores, thus bankrupting the business. Both are presented as justified means to an end but seem to be contradictory to the worthy cause. Whatever. I would appreciate an answer soon; I want to join the fight! Besides, I could really use a big screen TV and some socks. Maybe some jerky and Pringles!

***

I like Christmas as much as the next person. Well, assuming the next person resents ostentatious commercialization and gratuitous gifting, disdains gluttony, and has an apparent innate desire to take an ax to anything broadcasting Christmas music. AND I totally loathe walking past lighted Christmas trees and wrapping paper featuring snowflakes or Snoopy in a Santa cap on my way to the Halloween candy aisle! That's just not cool. I prefer to delay my inevitable loathing wrapped in apathy, tied with a ribbon of disdain until at least after Thanksgiving.

***

Today, I accidently cut my thumb with a pill splitter- the type where the blade is tucked deep inside and encased behind a thick layer of double reinforced polymer. They really should improve the design; it's obviously NOT foolproof!

***

I was listening to the news earlier today as I worked on a tax worksheet.

(Let me interject: I was told as a child that when I was an adult I would be able to do whatever I wanted; didn't happen. Then, I assumed I would be able to do whatever I wanted when my kids left home; it didn't happen. Most recently, it was implied I would be able to do whatever I wanted after I retired. It didn't happen or I would never be spending precious time figuring on a tax worksheet. It's like those times I've talked myself into getting dressed and going to some event because I was told there would be cake...only to find NO CAKE!! Where's the cake? I really thought there would be cake?) I digress. I'm sorry. Tax worksheets do that to me.

Anyway, the newscaster was commenting on a major news story from yesterday.... a viral video on the internet of two runaway lamas.

LAMAS ON THE LOOSE! What? It certainly piqued my attention and I ran immediately to the T V to check it out. (Evidently, I use any excuse to leave the tax table). THIS I HAD TO SEE!! Imagine my disappointment. I was expecting to see two escaped lamas- bald monks in white robes running around like crazy and disrupting traffic, being chased by a frantic crowd of concerned citizens with ropes and carrots intent on capturing them and returning them to their monastery. Instead, they were showing two llamas. Barnyard llamas. Like you see grazing in a pasture, occasionally a zoo. Llamas.

Seriously? Llamas? What could possibly be so captivating about livestock running amuck? Personally, I don't consider my day complete until I've dodged at least one cow or goat or wild hog on the road! Call me when you have runaway Lamas... now, that's a video I would watch!!

***

I've discovered I have a talent for sniffing gasoline. I mean sniffing gasoline prices on their way down. I noticed a small price drop a couple of weeks ago. Although I had 3/4 tank, I filled my tank to the brim and felt like a real fiscal kingpin as I pulled away from the pump. The next day the price dropped $.04. O.K. Thanks, universe, for keeping me humble. So, this time I drove until I had only 1/4 tank waiting for the price to drop again. I decided the price was holding steady for a while and pulled in to fill 'er up, again, to the brim... and the next day the price dropped another $.04. Urghhhhhh. I'll let you know next time I decide to get gas. You're welcome.

***

Another first without my Dad...attaching the shredder to the tractor without his guidance. Detaching it a few weeks ago to try and get the truck unstuck wasn't such the thang. However, I knew putting it back would try my patience. It wasn't pretty. It wasn't speedy. It wasn't efficient. It was, however, effectively successful. In my mind, I would walk up to him and calmly and quietly say, "I did it, Pop. I got the shredder back on the tractor". And his slow, even, deadpan reply would be... "yeah, boy" ... That's all. Just "yeah, boy". which is the highest praise! Straight As... new vehicle.... birth of baby... "yeah, boy" would be his response. We all knew pride and love of the highest degree came with those two words and they meant the world. I miss hearing them. Yeah, boy...

***

Went to Abilene today. It's comforting to know no matter which direction or how deep and dark the hole, I will never be alone if I have a radio. I will always be within frequency of Spanish speaking stations, preaching stations, Spanish-speaking preaching stations, bad country and hip hop stations, droning talk shows, commodities reports, and infomercials for colon cleansers. How do they do that??

***

Just spotted a visual paradox - a hummer pulling a work trailer. That's like a man in a three-piece suit jumping off a trash truck to grab the garbage cans off the curb.

***

Is this irony? As an advocate of efficient and effective communication I've always said "Happy Holidays" as my Christmas salutation. This, as encompassing the entire season in two brief words and as opposed to "Merry Christmas and Happy New Year". Now, however, when I say it I feel I'm being judged as one of those "anti-Christmas" radicals and feel compelled to correct myself. Am I now being politically correct? Or am I correcting my political correctness? Or is my political correctness wrong? Or is my lack of political correctness right? I can't tell anymore...

***

Ladies, I know this has happened to you: You're getting somewhat dressed up for an occasion somewhat more formal than the usual. After a final mirror check you realize you forgot some nice earrings to add to the ensemble and in your haste proceed to stab a pointed post into your cheek. And it bleeds! No? Anyone? Well, me neither. But it could happen. (One time I appreciated wearing a face mask).

***

What is commitment? Using a dark porta potty in Kansas at 11:30 at night after refraining too long from its service in hopes of making it to a classier one (one with light and a handle) but your bladder is holding two pots of coffee because the work day was longer than anticipated so you finally relent and halfway down to assuming the go position the flashlight app on your phone goes out. Yeah. Commitment.

***

Torture is ...getting into the shower with the radio blasting one of my favorite songs and just as soon as I'm soaked and lathered the reception changes to static and THEN KC and the Sunshine Band. Yep. That's The Way I Like It NOT! Shortest shower ever!

***

I loved Johnny Weissmuller Tarzan movies when I was a kid, especially scenes of the elephant graveyard behind the waterfall. It was where old elephants went to lay down and die. I thought it was amazing and cool, sort of romantic (for elephants). I don't think that any more...

***

If I attacked 'life' with the same spirited tenacity in which I approach some tasks I would have already purchased a first class ticket to Tanzania to base jump Kilimanjaro in a wingsuit. Unfortunately, I'm too lazy to climb and too afraid of heights to jump. I may seem boring, static, and weird on the outside...but inside my head...I truly rock in a groovy and far out way!

***

Clearing these tremendously dense patch of briars and brambles suits me: it leaves a very clear line of progress as I go, a distinct visual aid making it easier to remember where I was and what I was doing before my coffee break. That's helpful most days.

***

How to Sabotage Major News

1) Get an attractive young female with a flowing mane of blond hair to anchor. 2) Put an oversized pair of black glasses on her to substantiate intelligence. 3) Display her on a split screen with 'experts' (minimum of 2, maximum only limited by screen space), with opposing views regarding a major breaking news story. 4) Allow the 'experts' to drone on incessantly without guidance and parameters. 5) Instruct the anchor to sit quietly, occasionally nodding or shaking her blond mane. 6) Convolute the process with a visual onslaught of scrolling tickers and flashing boxes touting totally unrelated information. 7) Ensure entire screen is at 100% occupancy at all times, even if you have to make up something. 8) "Experts" must all be at odds, sarcastic, willing to argue, toss insults, and talk over the others. 9) Allow the anchor to speak occasionally, removing any doubt about her 'qualifications'. 10) At some point, break into this Breaking News with the latest Breaking News via video and/or voiceover, returning just before the break. 11) Ensure viewers leave confused and uninformed, yet under the illusion of full knowledge of something... just uncertain of what exactly...but something.

Fade to laxative commercial and cut.

DISCLAIMER: Before I'm cited as being sexist and/or prejudiced against blonds, I'll say in my defense I doubt she's a real blond... just a really dumb brunette with a dye job. Is the casting couch still a thing?

***

I have to wonder what's wrong with people these days. I would think the safest place to be during city morning rush hour traffic is sitting in a Starbuck's drive-through with like-minded workforce minions in a line creeping forward slowly like a bad pair of Speedos! That sounds relatively stress-free and the last place to expect a bad case of road rage; they're not even moving, for goodness sake! But, it happened. One lady was in the drive-through line when another lady exited an access road and cut in front of her and almost clipped her car. Words and fingers were exchanged. Then, the woman in the encroaching car got out and beat on the first woman through her open window, pulling hair and punching her face and almost running her down...before driving away. Are they crazy? It was reported neither one waited around afterwards to get their coffee! Really? They left without the coffee? What were they thinking? I really have to wonder about people sometimes...

***

I often lock the front door, walk halfway to my vehicle before remembering I forgot something in the house. Sooooo... I have to turn around, walk back to the house and fumble with the keys to open the door. Sometimes, by the time I unlock the door I forget why I returned in the first place and wander aimlessly for a time trying to remember what exactly I forgot.

Helpful Hint: I've found it beneficial to simply not lock the door the first (possibly second) time I attempt to leave. For example, if I remember I forgot to remember something, I can turn back and return to an unlocked door. This simple solution saves me the time and effort it takes to find the key and unlock the door; the result is less aggravation, enhanced efficiency, and better recall of the reason I returned. Usually, but not always. I think about 50% of the time I forget I left the door unlocked and use the key anyway. And I think 40% of the time I return home after leaving and find the door unlocked because I didn't remember I forgot something so I didn't go back in the house. I suppose that means 10% of the time it proves successful. I LOVE IT WHEN A PLAN COMES TOGETHER! You're welcome!

***

Are you familiar with those 'time wheels' on your phone or computer, the ones where you spin little cylinders to report a date? You spin one for a month, one for day, and one for year?

Anyway, I had to use one recently and thought it was the neatest thing as I started spinning it to report my birth year! Cool! It sounds like a roulette wheel! I continued spinning. I wonder how do they do that? Software technology is truly amazing! I wish I understood it better! Maybe I …. HEY! Is this thing working correctly? I stopped it briefly to verify I was spinning in the correct direction- backwards. TAP. TAP. TAP Yes, that's right. 1970? *sigh*It shouldn't be long now! And resumed spinning …and spinning…! Click. Click. Click. Click.

I don't obsess much over the tap dance Father Time has done on my body and (I'll admit it) mind over the past few years. But that wheel and its incessant noise got on my last nerve! Click. Click. Click. Click. I didn't appreciate its inane accompaniment to the March of Time! Eventually, I was giving it big spins, much like an over-zealous housewife spinning the "Wheel of Fortune" as Pat Sajac drones on about the big prize for which she's spinning! It was practically whistling as it spun backwards. Finally, it arrived at my birth year. There was no big jackpot for me, though. Nothing. I admit that bothered me a bit. There should have been a prize!

It's bad enough I have to do mathematics to figure out my animal zodiac sign on Golden China's place mats; the list doesn't go back far enough to include my birth year, so I have to figure which box is mine! But, at least I can have an egg roll and some Chow Mein afterwards. And a fortune cookie! And that's something!

***

The armadillo is a fascinating critter. I find him interesting to observe as he quietly and peacefully strolls about, oblivious to everything but the bugs and worms for which he's grubbing. I imagine him running with the dinosaurs, poking about amongst the leaves and roots of an ancient primordial forest floor. He doesn't seem to notice the mighty pterodactyl screeches piercing the night air. He raises his head only briefly as the huge flying reptile flaps through the shadows, branches snapping as the rhythmic sound of its massive beating wings shatter the forest's silence. I understand the pterodactyl's crushing disappointment as he swoops down to snatch that armadillo in its mighty claws, only to have its dinner plans thwarted as the wily armadillo sidesteps at the last minute, scampers away and disappears into the deepest jungle brush. Safe. Safe and free to return and dig again!

But tonight, dear armadillo, I will become your worst nightmare. You have ignored all my pleas to vacate these premises. I've begged, reasoned, and tried numerous intimidation tactics to no avail. I've reminded you of the many acres beyond this yard fence, yet you insist on claiming this as your own happy hunting ground. Be warned: If I see you tonight digging another cavernous tunnel under my shrubs, I vow to send you to the hell I can only assume by your tenacious digging you are desperately trying to reach as I don't think there are armadillos in China. So, good luck as I prepare to go all primeval on your ancient, armored butt.

It's too bad the pterodactyl didn't have a 12-gauge double barrel shotgun; it might not be extinct.

Last Cheeto and Testament

So, my Pop called and asked me to come 'take care' of a skunk in the trap at his house. He said he had everything ready. When I showed up a bit later he handed me a shotgun, a shell ...and 3 Cheetos! "What's that?" I asked, eyeing the Cheetos as I loaded the gun. "I thought you might wanna feed him a Cheeto through the wire and shoot him as he's distracted and chewing." I considered the various endings for that scenario. I would be kneeling less than two feet from Mr. Le Pew (who's already peeved and primed) extending a junk food peace offering in one hand and a loaded shotgun in the other? Is it possible he would see the Cheeto as a friendly gesture and simply drop his guard (and tail) and stroll amicably toward me? And would I feel better about performing the dirty deed knowing he died with an orange tongue and Cheeto Puffs stuck to his teeth?

Or is it more likely Pepe would wait for me to kneel, innately sensing my lack of agility to spring and flee, then adroitly spin and spray in my face blinding me and causing me to shoot myself in the process and when they come to haul me away they insist on dragging me aside for a few days to "air" and finally no one comes to my funeral because in spite of all the air and sun and Febreze and tomato juice and hanging pine trees in my coffin I still smell like a skunk and no one likes the smell of a skunk. I declined the Cheetos.

Dad shrugged his shoulders and casually walked away - nonchalantly munching on aforementioned CHEETOS. Personally, I think the old man was setting me up.

Life in the Fast Lane

After a particularly busy day at work (one we all have in which we feel pulled in umpteen different directions, stomping fires, plugging holes, and chasing our tails), I stepped up on a sidewalk just as a Texas Spotted Whiptail lizard came from behind the short wall three feet in front of me. In one rapid-fire motion the little guy whipped out his tongue to catch a bug out of the air, turn and scamper down the sidewalk ahead of me like a flash - bug booty still hanging out the corners of its mouth.

I was fascinated and oddly amused. I've seen lots of those lizards in my life but never that particular culinary process. He cracked me up, frantically running down the walk ahead of me, quickly glancing back on occasion to see if I was still following and intending to snatch lunch from his clenched jaws! Those lizards are always comical when they run. Watching from behind -waddle...waddle...waddle- butt working it from side to side, awkward and not that graceful.

I smiled as I watched him scurry along the length of the sidewalk, lunch in tow. My first thoughts were how wonderful nature is. *Isn't it the grandest thing?* I admired the lizard's instinctual talent, speed, and meticulous timing required to accomplish such a feat. *Excellent!* He darted triumphantly into the bushes to digest and I was suddenly sad. I realized I had a greater amount of empathy on this day for the bug and less for the lizard. Poor little bug. He was just flying merrily along and minding his own business, trying to make a life and survive. Then, without notice or fanfare, SLURP and GULP and it was lights out for him. He ceased to be. He was no more.

The bug and I both ventured out this fine morning with only one goal... to make it through another day. It simply wasn't meant to be for him, as I bear witness. My fate, however, is still undecided. I'm thinking I'll make it. I'm hoping I'll make it. But do we ever truly know? I suppose that philosophical saying is true: some days you are the bug; some days you are the lizard. Hopefully like the bug, I'll be flying high and humming a ditty when WHAM! BAM - I'm taken out in the blink of an eye! I won't know what hit me. Like the bug, gone in an instant! I only hope it's NOT by the flick with the tongue of a giant lizard! I can't relate to that!

Locked and Loaded

Sometimes you just know it's going to be a good day! I had extra time before work this fine morning, so I grabbed my coffee and headed to the well house to check for grasshopper spray. I usually lock this side door on my way out, because I seldom return through that particular portal. As soon as I heard the click I thought to myself, *Self, the reason you had extra time this morning is because you didn't go out the <u>back</u> door to sit on the deck with your coffee OR go out the <u>front</u> door to call the cat in to eat. You just locked yourself out of the house! Duh!* I hate when I talk sarcastically to myself, even when I know I'm right. I continued to the well house to complete the fact-finding mission (of course, no spray) before addressing the more immediate issue - regaining access to my house.

I didn't panic. I knew I had been occasionally raising windows for the nice spring breezes so it wasn't like I was really locked out. Not technically, anyway. Oddly enough, washing the windows was on my to-do list for the afternoon. I had already gathered the supplies and step ladder and.... *Ladder? Oh, yeah... the ladder.* I thought of the windows, their sills set at five feet and towering skyward from there. *Climbing through a window, especially from a step ladder, was NOT on my to-do list today.* After considering the options, I decided the best place to begin the reentry process would be to first check the other doors. *Maybe I misinformed myself previously. Maybe I HAVE been outside already this morning and just forgot. It happens.* However, a quick rattling of the doorknobs verified that it was, in fact, correct information; they were both still locked. *Why am I always right at the least fortuitous times?* I was disappointed but not surprised; walking through an open door would have been entirely too easy. I seldom do 'easy'.

I seldom do 'easy'... however, I occasionally do 'easier'. I remembered the windows on the sunporch were not nearly as high as all the others; entry there would not require a step ladder. *Go me!* A small gardening spade on the porch made easy work of removing the screen and a little push proved the window was open! *Yes! I knew it!* I was feeling somewhat confident, although I took notice the window seemed higher from the floor than originally thought. Also, smaller. *Wow. I hope I can squeeze my giant tatas through there unscathed.* I smiled at the reference. Giant, I mean; not, tatas. *These A cup bras aren't constructed of wire, ya know!* Humor is the best weapon during challenging times; it works for me, anyway.

I stood before the open window, realizing I had absolutely no idea how to climb through it. Unfortunately for me, I had no misspent youth experiences which included Breaking and Entering. *Dang it! I should have spent less time studying and more time on the streets! I knew it!* I evaluated my options. *Should I try and get both feet through first?* That would require a window facing or ledge or something solid on which to grab... by just my fingertips... while lifting and swinging my entire mass mid-air through the opening. *I should have spent less time in the office and more time in the gym! I knew it!* There wasn't any such support, but I honestly wasn't disappointed. *Perhaps, the best way would be one foot at a time - one foot in and one foot out?* I briefly contemplated that option but neither could I casually (or by design) throw a foot up that high nor contort my 6-foot torso in such a way it could be gracefully threaded through the opening. *I doubt I'd be single if I could do either one! Hehehe!* I'd get stuck and have to wait for rescue, found in that position. I visualized my kids, cameras in hand, and decided to not give them the satisfaction.

Desperation started to get a grip; I had spent my excess leisure time and really needed to get ready for work. I briefly considered the agony of defeat, having to go beg for a spare key from some of the family or break in a door or call a locksmith. *No, don't give up! Breathe! I haven't yet considered 'head first' entry.* I deliberated the logistics and geometry of such a maneuver, basically if it could be achieved with minimal lacerations or contusions. *Yes! It can be done, I believe, for the price of a little skin and a pound of pride! Go for it!*

I pulled a water bucket over to gain the extra height required, then poked my head and shoulders through before propelling myself the rest of the way- Rambo-style. *Yes! I'm halfway there!* I was in the window, balanced high-center with arms and legs outstretched; I looked like a see-saw when there's a big kid on each end - horizontal and going nowhere fast. It was then I realized I didn't know how to proceed. Rambo usually made it all the way through the window in one leap. *Yeah, in the movies! Duh!*

I had just lost all patience with my sassy self when thankfully, divine intervention in the form of gravity made intercession on my behalf. Luckily, the end with the arms and giant tatas won; I teetered over until my hands touched the floor and my legs stretched for the sky. *Only four more feet of body and legs to drag over that brutal metal sill.* I walked on my hands (like a cheap circus act) and continued to wriggle my way through; if I could get just one leg on the same side of the window as the majority of my body the landing wouldn't be as severe. I continued, an inch at a time, until I could finally bend my right leg through and into the room! After some additional acrobatics, the left foot crossed the sill and I plopped unceremoniously to the floor. Inside! Minimal bodily harm to remain unexplained. Finally. *BOO-YAH!* I got to my feet and danced a little jig. *I did it! Now, no one has to know about this little SNAFU!*

As I said, sometimes you just know it's going to be a good day! It would have been nice, however, to remember the spare key hidden for such occasions!

Melatonin, Straight. Make It a Double

I should Be sleeping but...

Someone (as yet unidentified) among this locale's Shelter in Place has finally cracked; I just found a gallon of milk in the pantry! I don't know who. It could be Stephanie (who just spent thirty minutes securing a dog in her lap while holding a red blanket for a backdrop, posing the dog for a picture), or Jace (the cameraman, barking poses, feeding doggie treats, and taking the 'doggie portrait'), or Jonah (roaming the house, carrying a homemade cardboard shield, the accompanying sword tucked snugly down the back of his shirt and begging for someone to cross the moat into his kingdom and fight). I'm fairly certain it was NOT me...at least, I don't think it was me. Maybe? Whatever...I'm sleeping with one eye open!

****

Pop. What kind of name is that for a music genre? Pop. What pops? Bubbles, balloons, and blisters pop. Bubble gum pops. An irritating, tasteless cereal pops but only after it snaps and crackles. And don't forget pop goes the weasel, which I don't even care to ponder. Pop. That's just wrong.

****

I saw this sign in a hospital restroom today: *1,000,000,000,000 germs can live in one gram of poop.*

1) Ewwwwwww... Poop...
2) This can't be the same for everyone's poop because I know some people whose poop MUST be a lot more germy than the norm. Therefore,
3) This must be an average number of germs per gram of poop which means
4) Someone had to poke around in numerous random grams of sample poop and do math.
5) How does one even count to 1,000,000,000,000 whilst prodding poop? Certainly not on their fingers?
6) Or perhaps the poop is on their fingers so technically... yeah, they would count on their fingers.
7) They must have been glad they weren't told to count germs per pound of poop.
8) Ewwwww...poop...

****

I had two small jobs done by others at my home today, jobs outside the zone in which I felt qualified or competent to tackle myself. And in both cases I felt like I was forced to grab my ankles, smile, and pretend I liked it! *Thank you, sir. I suppose dinner first is not an option...*

****

Evidently, there's a significant number among us 1) believing if they use enough toilet paper they may ignore that pesky pandemic "WASH YOUR HANDS" suggestion and/or 2) they are confused about where the coronavirus enters the body. Ignorance may be a bigger problem than the virus.

****

So, this weather? Storms? Heat? Cold? Hail? And now it seems mice are trying to escape the heat and flies are trying to escape the cold. It's alright, Moses. I've got this situation under control. I'll call you when the grasshoppers descend.

****

I inadvertently got two fire ant bites just below my right eye. Don't ask. Perhaps I should reconsider how I forage for food.

****

I saw a promo for the extended version of 'Batman v Superman; Dawn of Justice". Thirty extra minutes of never-seen footage. Seriously? I saw the original 'short' version. My thoughts were if they want to sell those things they should've cut at least thirty minutes *off*.

****

I watched a new Oreo commercial with a politically correct, touchy-feely theme... wonder-filled...or something like that. At the risk of sounding like an old curmudgeon, what was wrong with 'well to do it, just unscrew it'?

****

I support anything someone may do to improve themselves and position in life. I'm not sure, however, how much I trust an institute claiming it can train someone for a laser medical career in ONLY TWO WEEKS! Really? It takes longer to train a new haircut! I don't want someone shooting an intense beam of light in my eye that can double as a weapon if it's amped up a notch.

****

I just saw a disheveled and besmeared man with a backpack walking down the street. He was carrying a sign, "QUIT THE WORLD, FOLLOW JESUS". I wondered where they were going.

****

Getting older has its perks. It's expected you might forget your pants, dribble coffee down your front, or pee yourself occasionally. I actually find this quite liberating and one could say I'm living the dream.

****

I was watching CSI Miami and a cell phone was found in a fire ant bed near the scene of a murder investigation. The CSI said, "check the hospitals. Maybe the murderer checked in for treatment of insect bites." They did... and he had! He was a beefy, hunky guy but evidently couldn't handle a few ants. Really? Seriously? I've been the victim of multiple fire ant bites many times and never once considered seeking medical help. I just brush them off and continue with the task at hand. Actually, I don't know of anyone (Texan) that would go to an ER with a bite but for a severe allergic reaction. Is it possible Floridian fire ants are meaner and more painful than Texas fire ants? Or does it mean Floridians are really soft weenies? Another mystery.

****

During a haircut I heard an Asian woman with a heavy Tai accent make a frantic call to a customer service department. I found this extremely amusing given my experiences with customer service reps unable to understand/speak English. They seemed to be having a problem communicating. These are the times that make me smile.

****

I looked out my window this cold, dreary morning and saw a skunk-nose down and tail up. It was too far away to take a pot shot with the .22 (AND I didn't want to stomp around in the cold and rain). I decided to keep an eye on it and only take action if it started making progress toward the house. I'd look out the window periodically and noticed it wasn't going anywhere...just sitting in the same spot and pose. Thirty minutes passed. Was it rabid? Dead? If so, that was another whole set of problems! I started formulating a plan... overalls, boots, load .22, approach to get the advantage. I looked out and it still hadn't moved. *O.K. This just isn't right! I better grab the gun and go check on it.* I then had the brilliant idea to grab the binoculars and do some reconnaissance before venturing forth. Imagine my relief as a black bucket came into focus! No skunk! A bucket! I'm so smart! Imagine how silly I would have felt had I dressed for the cold and rain and gone out to stalk a bucket! That would have made me feel really, REALLY dumb.

****

When I was a kid I wished I could be a ventriloquist and throw my voice out of weird and unexpected places. I don't know, why but I revisit that idea every year as I sit in this little room waiting to assume the stirrup position for the doctor to perform the annual 'wellness' exam. The voice wouldn't be conversational like Lamb Chops or Akmed the Terrorist. It would say just a little something to ease the tension. Perhaps "Ahhhhhhhh", like when I get my throat checked. Or "Hey, Doc. Nice to see you again!" Anyway... if I could, I would. Really. I would. Maybe next year...

****

Candy companies are starting to irk me in a major way, especially since they stopped taking my calls. I was content with regular-sized bars and ecstatic with King-sized bars. But then they had to use valuable shelf space with "fun size", "bite size", and "minis"? Really? Which genius thought these were good ideas? The same genius thinking it was a good idea to individually wrap Kisses in foil with a paper string? At least they are finally implementing my suggestions to remove those time-wasting wrappers and sell in bulk. Now, only if they would listen to me and make UNWRAPPED KING-SIZED IN TEN POUND BAGS! Is that too much to ask?

****

It's been too long since we spent quality time together. You must know how much I anticipate your visits and our time together. I heard you coming and ran to the door, anxiously awaiting your arrival. I could see you in the distance and smiled, happy to know you hadn't forgotten me. I felt the electricity in the air and was breathless as I heard your deep, booming voice. You were so close...so close I could smell the rain on your breath. Then, you passed as if you didn't even know me. How long must I wait? Whose garden are you watering tonight? Whose tank are you filling? I promise they don't appreciate you more than I do and can't need you more than I do. You only treat me this way because you know I'll be waiting for as long as it takes. I'll be waiting. It's you. Only you. I'll wash the truck and leave a window open.

****

What's that you say? ...an hour wait for an oil change? I can't sit for an hour for an oil change! I have places to be and things to do! I thought this as the information was relayed to the person in front of me in line. I turned and left to come back another time. I wonder if this action was 1) a reflection of a new-found freedom to come and go as I wish now that I'm retired or 2) has retirement brought a sense of numbered days too precious to sit in a crowded waiting room chatting with other old people having nothing better to do than sit in a crowded waiting room chatting with other old people?

Metal Rope

I have a confession to make. It's past time for me to come out to my extended family and casual friends. I'm 65 years old (that's not the confession) and ready to move forward honestly and openly with my life. No more hiding in the closet! No more pretending I'm something I'm not and feigning interest in areas that don't excite me and never did. This will be a shock to all but my closest family and friends. Perhaps I will no longer be welcome in homes or invited to events. I'm willing to take that chance and hope my honesty will be met with open minds and hearts and willingness to accept me as I am. So, here goes. I'm 65 years old and love... METALLICA! METALLICA still rules and will always have a special place in my heart!

Shocked, right? However, most crossing my path in the past 20 years know this, or at least suspect it to be true. I've actually been fairly open with my infatuation, the sounds of metal rocking my office, my pickup, my home. I've been asked, 'why?' many times throughout the years. "Why Metallica?" I've usually made some lame excuse or dismissed the question. However, as part of this public confession, I will now reveal the truth: Metallica threw me a lifeline when I was drowning and needed it most.

I was left single with two kids to raise in 1996, X leaving me unexpectedly for greener pastures - though I doubted the carpet matched the drapes. I'll admit, it was a hard time for all of us. I had to make some quick decisions about how to react to the situation, how to present myself, and what was needed to protect and guide the kids. I purposed in my heart I would not be a victim in their eyes - of another, of circumstance, of life. I worked diligently to ensure they perceived me as strong, independent, and capable of protecting and nurturing them. I would not allow myself to become a bitter, angry woman. I would, instead, set our course on the high road in search of positivity and healing. There would be no harsh words or accusations, no name calling or put downs. It became *my* show when that door closed behind him, and I was determined to direct it in a way that would best serve the kids. This was not considered self-sacrifice; it was considered the only path to healing and happiness. For all of us.

The caveat of such a noble endeavor, however, was it required anger, hurt, humiliation, and fear to be tamped down and hidden deep inside - so deep and hidden they could never escape. Most of the time was spent fully functioning and those emotions remained still and silent in their hiding place. Occasionally, however, I felt them stir and feared those demons might conspire to explode the barrier in a mighty meltdown and blaze of glory. I didn't want anyone to get hurt should that happen, so I would go for a walk or drive alone until I had them settle down again. I prayed for help and guidance. *I could use a little help here!*

On one such occasion I jumped in the truck and went on a drive to town. As the negativity and rage bubbled and gurgled beneath the surface intent on destroying my resolve, I scrolled through radio stations looking for - what? I didn't know what but just kept right on scrolling, irritation increasing as the lame lyrics and empty fluff of the music and pleasant banter heaped more anger on my raw emotions.

Suddenly, I found it. I felt it. 'Battery' was blasting through my speakers and I felt the weight inexplicable begin to lift. I wasn't alone and felt stronger, empowered. Windows rolled down, wind blowing through my hair, screaming lyrics and beating down the rage and hurt - one blessed note at a time. It was then I knew I would be alright. I had an outlet for the pain and angst. I had a way to scream and vent and rage and it was acceptable. I found comfort.

Metallica was my release valve for controlled negativity. The music and lyrics gave me the strength I needed to occasionally regain my footing and navigate through the new and unexplored territories of Anger and Uncertainty and Hurt. I had never tread so deeply into those unfamiliar, uncharted places. It was dark and cold and I was alone. Alone only because I refused to pull anyone I loved along on that ugly journey. I knew all I had to do was ask for help and an army would appear, boots and weapons donned and ready. But it was my war to fight alone and I had to win the battle for those territories alone; domination by my own terms was necessary for total victory.

I give Metallica credit for giving me survival tools most often reserved for hormonal, angry, and insecure teenagers. It's said God answers prayers in mysterious ways, often obscure or unseen. No, I don't think God's best answer was Metallica. He possibly sent all manner of help my way and I missed them all. Maybe I was too blind to see. Maybe I ignored them. Or maybe, just maybe...they simply weren't loud enough!

Metallica, on the other hand, I heard. They came through loud and clear! They could never know how their music functioned as metal rope tossed to a middle-aged woman in Texas. I'm thinking if this was publicized it could totally tank their cred, so I keep that tidbit to myself. I still listen to Metallica (and by proxy, Godsmack, Disturbed, Korn, etc.) and relive the Gory Days. I don't always crank up to full volume and seldom scream through rage and hurt anymore; fortunately, it's no longer a necessity. Now, I listen because...well...the truth is I listen because I want to. I like their music. I like the lyrics. And they're still my sweethearts!

Our family and friends closed the circle and enveloped us with love and support we needed at that time; we are forever grateful. We stood up, brushed ourselves off, slapped on some bandaids and rejoined the race. My children grew into compassionate, highly- educated, and well-rounded adults. I'm very proud of them both and the spouses they've chosen to share their lives. And unbeknownst to them all, some of the credit has to go to James, Lars, Kirk, and Tru/Jason). Thanks, Boys! ROCK ON!

I must say it feels good to be out of the closet. If this goes well, I have another bit of news to share.

Meteor Bust

There is a high tower east of my house with a flashing white strobe on top. There is a high tower north of my house with a flashing white strobe on top. They are both about a mile away as the crow flies and the flashing is synchronized. I hate those towers.

***

I've spent the entire night outside watching the sky for meteors from the highly touted Perseid meteor shower. I backed the pickup down into the yard, threw a small mattress atop the truck bed cover, and I waited. Crazy, huh? I suppose. But a funny thing about approaching the 'twilight' years – it often makes people do things which may seem odd to the younger, less time-sensitive set. Some twilighters want to grab a last bit of gusto - sell their possessions and purchase a humongous house on wheels and hit the road into the wide, open spaces or seek adventure in new hobbies - like sky-diving or with the purchase of a Harley. Others try to recapture youth: Face-lifts. Cougars. Hair plugs. And some may spend an entire night outside, watching the sky for meteors...just because. And thinking. And remembering.

I live on the same land on which my paternal grandparents raised my father. My sister and I spent many nights at their tiny house, listening to Grannie's ever-changing bedtime renditions of Chicken Little, the Three Bears, and Little Red Riding Hood. And when it was lights out... it was as if it were lights out all over the world. There were no security lights scattered across the view, no dairies with their huge lamps to illuminate the night-time milking, and no towers with white strobes on top. (Did I stop; it was sometimes hours between vehicles and headlights. Unless the moon was well above crescent it was dark and quiet, like peering into a deep, dark cave full of lightning bugs. And I loved it. I loved the millions of stars I could see so clearly defined across the ebon sky. It was magical.

I positioned myself tonight for the best view of the northeastern sky. I watched and waited. It's amazing how bright it still is at night – even with no moon. The lights from the neighboring towns cast a glow across their respective horizons. Security lights illuminate the surrounding landscape in all directions and dairy lights rip through the darkness for miles. I developed a dull headache, my eyes pulsating with the rhythm of the tower strobes reflecting off the trees and house and carport. I missed the darkness of my childhood as I sat and waited, scanning the sky for the meteor show!

Have you ever seen a shooting star that seemed to blaze across half the sky, leaving a long streak of brilliant light trailing behind during its descent? I have, too! But not tonight. I suppose my expectations were too high based on my interpretation of the hype? Or perhaps astronomers tend toward the hyperbole? I expected to see hundreds of meteors, streaking through the sky in all directions for hours. What I actually saw was a few an hour. And they burned extremely fast, a short tail trailing behind and disappearing in a flash. Was I greatly disappointed? No. How could I be? I spent the night under an only slightly imperfect sky (due to no fault of its own), a nice cool breeze, and no mosquitoes. It was great!

Well, actually, there was one disappointment. I made a hundred wishes on falling stars tonight and none of them came true... those %##&@ strobes didn't explode and collapse in a heap on the ground; they're still flashing away! So much for that myth. And no more coins in the fountains! I bet that's a crock, too! Thank goodness I still have birthday candles!

I wanted to share this now (before I sleep) for a few reasons:

1. I was excited to immediately report a bit of the experience; I'm proud of my spontaneity.

2. I may not remember these details so well after a nap, if at all.

3. When I go back outside later, well after the sun comes up, I

may need reminding as to why the truck is backed into the yard facing northeast and why my grandson's baby bed mattress is outside on top of the truck. I don't want to be running around in circles screaming hysterically, "Dingo got my baby! The dingo got my baby!"

Now... THAT would be weird!

Miracles Are Non-Refundable

Perhaps it was the fully leaded coffee, perhaps it was spring fever and the whirl of activities looping for a place in my mind's queue... but whatever... I found myself wide awake. After exhausting the reruns of 'My 600-Pound Life' and 'Hoarders' I finally reached the train wreck dimension of infomercials – wrinkle creams made from Andean goat urine, robotic floor sweepers, blenders capable of pureeing bicycle parts, and turbo-lax colonic cleanses. It was difficult to watch but I couldn't turn away... I might miss a phone number or website address!

It was in this sleep-deprived stupor of channel surfing dementia I first saw the smiling faces of people touting testimonials of their newfound wealth. This piqued my interest as I had just moments before maxed out my credit card. *Was this an omen of pending doom in need of spiritual intervention?* It was simply too fortuitous to ignore; I put the phone down and tuned in.

It seemed this new wealth came in a variety of forms – forgiven debts, unexpected mortgage payoffs, lottery/casino wins, gifts, angelic delivery via the breeze, and even unmarked postal deliveries containing cash and mysterious bank deposits! Whut? Yeah! And it was all due to the vial of FREE miracle spring water they ordered from the program. *Seriously*, I said to myself, *a vial of miracle water?* They all replied in unison..."YES! Miracle SPRING water!"

I moved closer to the screen. It was then I got my glimpse of the benefactor behind the abundance. A televangelist(prophet) in his sixties…I think…but it was hard to tell with the black hair and white teeth…sitting on the edge of his wingback chair, hands flailing for emphasis, and the animated 'preachy' voice one would expect from a mere mortal on such a magnanimous mission mandated of God! Seated to his left was the wife, equally difficult to be age-specific due to artificial hair and boob enhancements paid by God, no doubt, to ensure camera-friendliness and more effectively read additional testimonials.

I admit I was a bit skeptical; I had my doubts about Miracle Spring Water delivering me a financial windfall. *How is that possible? But… what if? No, it's not really miracle water. It's probably a scam… water from a faucet or bottle or toilet.* Shudder. I dismissed the idea and reached for the remote at the exact moment the preacher's name was emblazoned across the screen and the announcer's voice introduced the mysterious man in black. PETER POPOFF! *Who?* PETER POPOFF! *Is that for real?* I grabbed the phone and credit card. I mean… who was I to question someone on a mission from God with a name like PETER POPOFF? *No legitimate scam artist or snake oil salesman would tag himself with that moniker! Right? It's a name only a porn star would choose to have. It must be real!* And it's fun to say…PETER POPOFF.

So… I'm here with my face besmeared with green goat urine chasing the robotic sweeper from room to room and trusting the colon cleanse I whipped up in the new blender doesn't activate before my miracle SPRING water comes in the mail! It's all good! Or will be, if I can just drag myself to the mailbox!

Mistaken Identity

No one has to tell me I'm old and getting older. I've noticed the parts of me that should be thick are thinning, tight are sagging, sharp are dulling, hot are cooling, limber are stiffening, and perky are... well, not-so-perky. Although during the past few years I'm starting to feel 'it', I like to think I've held up fairly well and have a few good jigs left in me. I can hope.

I was seated in an office today to finalize some business. The office manager whirled into the room as she was looking over my records, plopped down in her chair, and excitedly exclaimed, "I see here you are Robin's mother." It was one of those moments when your life force suddenly gets ripped from your body unexpectedly and is ricocheting off the walls and floor and ceiling like a pinball – BOING – BOING- BOING- and you hope no one can hear the bells and whistles exploding in your head and your eyes are darting about the room following the bouncing ball and you feel your head sort of bobbing and weaving to dodge it so it doesn't hit you directly between the eyes but you're still hoping to catch it and put it back before anyone notices it is gone and that they are actually talking to an empty body sitting in a chair with all the life totally sucked out of it. You know the kind of moment.

I knew she continued speaking because her mouth was moving. My mind, however, had totally checked out and moved on to damage control and planning the rest of my life. *"Whut? Robin's mother? (Robin is my sister. YOUNGER sister) Is this woman serious? She's not laughing so...yeah...she seriously thinks I look old enough to be Robin's mother. Must be the lights in here? Oh, wait... maybe she thinks Robin looks young enough she could be my daughter? No, that doesn't make the situation better. But, she does look pretty good for her age. Maybe she hasn't seen Robin in like... 15 or 20 years. I need to get to the gym. And drink more water. Should I color my hair? Avocados are good. And almonds. What is that Lifelift Debbie Boone is always selling on TV? I knew I should write down that number. I should probably wear a hat. And sunscreen. It's probably too late. I'm going to die, now..."*

I felt like I made an audible gasp as the spirit reentered my body at that moment and I was able to breathe again. My ears quit ringing and I heard the lady ask, "What's she doing these days?" Still dazed, all I could manage to say was, "uhmmm.... Doing?" She looked at me oddly before adding, "I remember her from the weight-lifting days. She was really good!" *HALLELUJAH!* I was very, VERY quick to point out that she was referring to her daughter, Ashlea. "I'm not Robin's mother. I'm her sister. Robin is my SISTER. Ashlea is my NIECE. MY NIECE WAS THE WEIGHTLIFTER! My SISTER, Robin, is HER mother!" I may have repeated and clarified perhaps a few too many times as I answered her question. She apologized for the mistake and we quickly concluded our business. However, I seriously doubt she will make that mistake again.

The first thing I did when I got to the truck was take a deep cleansing breath... and check myself out in the mirror. *Not too bad,* I thought. *Not GREAT...but not too bad.* I put the truck in reverse and was thinking, *Robin actually does look fantastic for her age. Really good! Pretty! She probably even looks younger for her age than I do.* And as I pulled forward to exit the parking lot I added, *And why wouldn't she? She's had a much easier and better life than I have! I mean, look who SHE'S had for a sister!* That made me smile. *SCORE!*

Mocking Bird

I entered a long hall at school today and noticed a mockingbird had come into the building through the open doors. It was frantically fluttering at the glass transom at the opposite end, trapped and unable to find its way back to freedom. I love mockingbirds and wanted to ensure it made it out safely and was free to sing another day!

As I approached, it launched over my head and darted at several ceiling lights before settling on the transom on the other end of the hall. We played this stupid tag back and forth for a while. It would wait for me to come near and almost touch it, then take off and dart around before perching on the ledge at the opposite end. And again. And again.

And again. I was glad the students and faculty were in classes at the time because I looked quite ridiculous, talking to the bird as I walked the hall and waved my arms. "Come on, little fella," I would say softly, "you're going to hurt yourself if you're not careful. Let me help you."

And then... it happened. It suddenly flew head-first into the transom glass and immediately folded its wings and crumpled to the floor. It hit with a muffled 'thud' and I knew it must be dead. I ran to it and fell to my knees, cradling its limp, lifeless body in my hands. I detected no signs of life. Nothing. As tears welled in my eyes, I felt the crushing weight of guilt grip my heart. *Did I cause this in my lame attempt to help?"* I felt such anguish kneeling there and stroking the lifeless bird. *Perhaps the waving of my arms or the sound of my voice frightened it too much? Maybe I was getting too close? Maybe if I'd just been more patient or ...?*

Suddenly, I felt a tiny flutter in my hand. Had I only imagined it by my selfish, wishful thinking? But I felt it again... the beating of a little heart in a little bird's chest! I was hesitant to be too optimistic lest the beating cease as quickly as it started. But, suddenly its eyes opened - clear and focused and totally bright. "It's alive! It's alive," I exclaimed to myself (in my best Dr. Frankenshteen imitation)! "How awesome is this?" My heart and soul were singing their own sweet song. I felt metaphysically and spiritually one with the mockingbird. I knew I could soon share its winged flight to the treetop near the playground. I would share in its song. "I will come by and visit you every day, Little Fella... maybe bring some seed or fruit or popcorn for a treat... "

At that very moment the ungrateful bird made the conscious decision to reach over and peck my hand! My instinctual reaction was quick and precise. It was a visceral 'survival of the fittest' reflex to its most primal degree. My fist reflexively tightened around the ravenous bird's throat, before hurling it unceremoniously with all my might into the stone wall. I shook my throbbing hand and checked for bleeding. I wondered if I could get Bird Flu from a bird bite and if so, do I wear a surgical mask now or later? Or do I have to be Japanese to get it? I looked at the bird's lifeless body with disdain and couldn't help but wonder if Atticus Finch was right and "...it's bad luck to kill a mockingbird." Is it? Is it really? Even when you're the target of such unprovoked savagery? Even when you know it has the ability, with one little whistle of its bird beak, to summon the minions to attack and rip the flesh from your bones and peck out your eyeballs? I don't *think* so!

Oh, I hear the horrified gasps. I feel the judgments raining down upon my head. To which I reply, 'do not judge me'. Not until you've been in the grasp of an evil, carnivorous condor from hell and had your translucent old-person skin in its vise-like mandibles and being ripped apart by its razor-sharp talons! Is it bad luck to kill a mockingbird? Perhaps. But today my luck was obviously much better than the bird's!

NOTE: I didn't really kill a mockingbird. Really. I was just kidding. The bird actually did reanimate just as I indicated, but it didn't bite me. I stroked its sweet little head and feathers and spoke soothing words in soft, encouraging tones. I checked its wings and legs for breaks. After a time and determining its degree of activity and alertness warranted its release, I took it outside and lifted it to the heavens. Its maiden flight was beautiful to behold— high into the bright, blue sky before settling in its rightful and customary place in the treetops near the playground. It will hopefully live to serenade the children at play and passers-by on the sidewalk for years to come.

I didn't really kill a mockingbird. I couldn't. I wouldn't. Well? Maybe? Maybe, if it bit me on the hand!

Mom's Parting Gift

Sitting here this cold, sunny morning and remembering my mother. I sit here thinking on the anniversary of her death and want to convey how special she was. I suppose, in my mind, sharing will in some small way bring her closer. Probably not, but I want you to know what a blessing she was in the lives of everyone she touched. I want you to hear her laugh and touch her spirit. But my mind is awhirl with adjectives and images of moments and emotions too numerous to sort in any way that makes sense. I think of her last week on this earth and realize, in many ways, it captures much of what I would want you to know of her character and spirit. Simply put, her death defined her life.

Momma was well into her 83rd year and had been plagued with ill health for years. Each time she had met her challenges with spunk and a gleam in her eyes, often the only weapons she had with which to fight. Daddy called it "intestinal fortitude". Guts. But that night in the ER she was sick and tired and broken. A fractured hip and pelvis were just the latest things to add to a long list of existing ailments, including kidney failure. She had been brought by ambulance and missed her dialysis treatment earlier in the day. After evaluations, the doctor left to make preparations to transfer her to Fort Worth so she could continue the dialysis and be treated for the fractures.

As she lay in the ER and we explained what was happening and why, she began to shake her head. "I want to go home". We repeated the importance and necessity of going..." you have to go to Fort Worth, Mom. You can't get dialysis here and you know you need the dialysis to live." She remained adamant, "I want to go home". She was of clear mind and had a complete understanding of the ramifications... going home meant she would die. If she was lucky, my mother would have one week in which she would be of sound mind and most comfortable. After that, the poisons not being filtered by her kidneys would take over. It would be a rapid and ugly decline from there over a few weeks, more or less. She understood. She smiled. She was at peace and never shed a tear. She never mentioned it again.

My sister, Robin, and I spent the next morning making preparations to bring her home. We rearranged the living room to accommodate a hospital bed. Mom had instructed from the hospital she wanted the bed set up in the middle of the living room; it would be more convenient for everyone and she would be most available to receive people that might stop by to visit. We made calls to family and friends to apprise them of the latest development. We met with the ladies from hospice and learned how to administer her medications. We made a schedule for the first week, providing 24-hour care with at least one of the family members there at all times. We were ready...or as ready as we could be. It was time to bring her home.

The ambulance brought Momma home and transferred her to her throne! Hail to the queen! She propped herself up in that bed and surveyed her kingdom. She approved. Thus began our last journey with her – a perfect journey marked by her laughter, warmth, and peace. I consider that week as her last gift to us.

The house was a hive of activity during the day as friends and family came to visit bearing food, cards, smiles, and memories to share. Each one got a big warm hug as they came and went, with plenty of laughter in between. Although they entered quietly and tearfully, knowing this was the end, they left feeling better...at peace... and smiling. She did that. That was my mother.

Nights were quieter. Blissful. We would gather around her bed after dinner – talking, laughing, sharing memories and stories. Eventually, one by one, we would go home and leave her in the hands of the caregiver(s) scheduled for the night. Mom had always been the last one in bed and the first to rise (always hit the floor on the run in the morning (*pitter patter*, *pitter patter *, humming or singing) There was so much to do! Even that last week, the party only got started the closer to midnight it got. That was my mother.

One night, a niece and family friend took a shift as her caregivers. After an exhausting day of meet-and-greet and long after the rest of us had left, mother was still sitting up in the bed and talking with the girls. She quietly surveyed the room from this new angle and declared she thought a certain group of pictures would look better if they were hung on a different wall. So, what did they do? They popped corn and had a picture-hanging party, Momma sitting there and dictating how and where. The girls laughed so much the next morning as they re-counted the evening's chain of events and their slumber party. They admitted they finally insisted Mom really needed to turn off the lights so **they** could get some rest! That was my mother.

The next evening, three of us (my daughter, niece, and I) gathered around the bed to do a crossword puzzle with her. Momma was an avid puzzler and word-seeker most of her life. And she was wicked good! It was what she and I often did together. I grabbed the Tribune, turned to the daily crossword, and began calling out clues and filling in blanks. Mom was hard of hearing and I almost always had to repeat the clues more than once; the girls would patiently wait to see if she heard the clue and give her a chance to respond.

We were about halfway through the puzzle when I came to a clue and hesitated. Call it stress or weariness or diminished mental capacity – but I sort of stifled a laugh as I verbalized the next clue, not daring to look up from the paper. "The clue is," (I hesitated) "the clue is 'dik-dik'. I could see the girls shuffling in their seats as Momma leaned forward in my direction. "What," she asked? What did you say". Again, stifling a laugh I repeated, "dik-dik, Mamma," and again the girls glanced at each other and fidgeted. We watched as she started her thought process... looking at the ceiling and biting her lower lip as she accessed the cache of words stored in her mind. The girls and I tried to not make eye-contact between ourselves and waited.

Finally, she did it... Mom repeated the clue aloud and in a strong voice, "dick dick" and the girls and I lost all control. We started laughing so hard, like junior high girls giggling at an inappropriate joke only we knew! Momma looked at us with fiery eyes, somewhat aggravated by our fit of laughter and left us with a gem to repeat for years to come... "What? Why are you laughing? I know what a 'dick' is! I just don't know what a 'dick dick' is!" It was a while before we could finish that puzzle. If we did. Knowing mother, I'm sure we did! But I remember little else. That was my mother.

Saturday. Mom had been in hospice a week. She was still going strong, her mind clear and sharp as ever; but we knew we were on borrowed time. Soon the dark days would set in; the kidney failure was pending doom and we would soon have to watch her deteriorate into someone we didn't know or care to remember. This day had been busier than usual. Many visits and words of encouragement and support filed in and out of the door, each greeted by Mom's wit and grace and gratitude. That was my mother.

Because I still worked full-time, I had been scheduled to be with her evenings (only a few hours after work and until bedtime) and weekends. It was quieter than usual this night, all having left after a hard day and busy week. Mom wanted to be moved to a chair for a while and a "change of scenery". After Dad and I settled her snuggly into a chair, he decided to go out for a brief stroll around the house and get some much needed air. I retrieved the little book we had made to keep track of those coming to visit and to record if they brought food or a card or a gift.

Sitting directly across the narrow room from her, I began to share the list of visitors for the entire week. I recounted all the visitors, the food and flowers and cards bestowed as love offerings. Only occasionally would she interrupt the reading as she had a thought or comment to share. I finished the list, closed the book, and looked across the room. She was smiling broadly, remembering the week and all that had made it special. Her eyes were clear blue and had that distinctive happy sparkle. And her last words on this earth... "You need to get some thank you cards. I want to send each one a special thank you..." That was my mother.

And she gasped. And she was gone. Just like that. Gone with her last breath.

She was special. She left us with an abundance of memories by which to remember her and a sparkling wealth of attributes we can only aspire to emulate. She was our gentle warrior and she died as she lived. Her last gift. Thank you, Momma.

Move Over, Elizabeth Browning

I've always enjoyed the art of language, joining thoughts and words into a string of sentences and finding the rhythm. I believe I may have been better suited in pursuit of the word than the numbers. I remember learning the vowels in first grade and pairing them with the pictures - a for apple, e for elephant, i for Indian, etc. It was fun and I felt I was on the edge of greatness! Learning to read the adventures of Dick and Jane and Spot was awesome. Learning to write with the huge pencils on Big Chief tablets, I was standing at the top of the world and would soon touch the stars.

I wrote my first poem in sixth grade, thirty minutes before Christmas break. Mr. Colwick told us we would be studying poetry when we returned in January so we should spend the final time writing a poem in preparation. A poem? The only thing I knew of poetry – it positively had to rhyme. Poems had to rhyme!

I grabbed my rarely-used ink pen with such anticipation! Ink pens were allowed only after permission was granted to use it instead of pencil on specific assignments. I scanned the room looking for inspiration. "Blue-Shoe ". "Shirt-Dirt". "Chalkboard, window, door, wall?" I could hear the clock ticking away the minutes. "Pencil. Book. Encyclopedia".

Oh, wow. I had nothing. I looked anxiously about the room. Most of my classmates were looking intently at the paper and seemed to be writing effortlessly. Billy, of course, was eating his eraser as Linda made her third trip to the water fountain. John had finished and was quietly basking in his victorious glory, the smirk telling me he had already mastered the next unit and was ready to proceed to something much harder. And there the rest of us sat, eyes darting about the room or staring at the blank sheet of ruled notebook paper.

I looked at the clock again and there was now ten minutes until the bell. On a day such as this there would be no staying after class.

Parents would be lined up around the school, impatiently waiting for us to come screaming out of the various doors. I could feel the breath leaving my lungs and sweat forming on my palms.

Mr. Colwick began gathering his papers and erasing the board, his bald head reflecting the light streaming in the window. My eyes followed the light to the window and there it was, the huge shade tree under which they (not me, but they) would be banished at recess for pushing in line or running when they should be walking or talking when they should be listening. "Tree," I thought, "that's perfect!"

My mind suddenly jolted with a kick start and flashed words rhyming with tree. "Bee. See. She. He. Knee. Free...". I grabbed my pen with new inspiration and confidence with three minutes until the bell. Uhmmmm... trees grow in a forest and a forest is magical and mysterious. I put my pen to paper and the words flowed effortlessly, smoothly, poetically. I know poetically because it all rhymed when I raised my pen triumphantly, as a rodeo calf roper raising his hands after "two wraps and a hooey"!

I will not divulge the unique creative thought processes of my brain but I will share my first poetic endeavor with you now:

As I was walking through the forest one day
I heard a little sound.
You won't believe me when I tell you
I saw an elf when I turned around.
He was so very tiny
But he sure gave me a scare.
He looked just like Mr. Colwick
Because he had no hair.

The End

....and the bell rang!

(my momma loved to tell this story)

134

My Selfish Agenda

Left Brain: analytical, logical, sequential, objective.

I've been thinking! I hear groans and I'm sorry; but sometimes Left Brain has a mind of its own and will not be denied! It likes to meander occasionally, noshing on various tidbits of information discovered decaying in the recesses of my mind. It chews and chomps and ruminates for a while before spewing them out in a indistinguishable tangled mass of sticky goo, leaving me to sort through the slimy chunks like a voodoo shaman sorting through pieces of bone and broken glass and chicken feet and trying to make sense of it all. Mostly, I rummage through the pieces and find I've been presented with just a puddle of worthless slime. Despite what some may presume, I generally keep those thoughts to myself. However, on rare occasions I discover Left Brain left me with a juicy morsel of value, something bright and sparkly hidden in the steaming pile to ponder. Please feel free to vacate and purge at this time. It won't hurt my feelings.

Left Brain dictates when I get an appliance or anything requiring operation/assembly I first step back and examine the schematics to familiarize myself with the product and read the instruction manual to familiarize myself with the operation. Doesn't everyone? I mean it's a logical and sequential process. I only proceed to actual usage when I feel properly informed and prepared. I suppose that's why I find most 'WARNING' tags and stamps and signs and yellow tape and graphics so infuriating! Dare I say stupid? For example, following is a short list of some of the WARNINGS included with a recently purchased chain saw:

WARNING: This chain saw can be dangerous! Careless or improper use can cause serious and even fatal injury.

WARNING: Do not cut near buildings or electrical wires if you do not know the direction of tree fall, nor cut at night since you won't be able to see well...

WARNING: Wear protective gloves when handling the chain. The chain is sharp and can cut you even when it is not moving.

WARNING: Muffler is very hot during and after use. Do not touch the muffler...

WARNING: Keep all parts of your body away from the chain when the engine is running.

WARNING: Do not operate when you are fatigued, ill, or upset, or if you have taken alcohol, drugs, or medication.

WARNING: Wear protective gear. Always use steel-toed safety footwear with non-slip soles; snug-fitting clothing; heavy-duty non-slip gloves, eye protection such as non-fogging, vented goggles or face screen; an approved safety hard hat; and sound barriers (ear plugs); safety chaps.

Left Brain began to munch about halfway through the list: *Is there really someone purchasing a chainsaw at this moment totally ignorant of its inherent dangers?* The manual is quite detailed (with all kinds of graphics and warning signs and symbols) but I'm thinking *there's no way this person would read the manual...the words are certainly too hard to understand and the pictures aren't in color!* Pity. How could someone this ignorant – nay, STUPID – even begin to know how to start the saw in the first place? I submit ...NOT.

Left Brain continued noshing. *Are there really those walking amongst us needing this additional guidance? They must be the ones giving plastic bags and scissors for toys to children and feeding them Styrofoam peanuts, desiccant packets, and glow sticks if it weren't for the WARNING. They would climb past the last rung on the ladder, stick metal forks and knives into toasters, and take the blender into the bathtub with them to mix margaritas without the WARNINGS. Obviously, they would consume mass quantities of household cleaning products, antifreeze, and paint if it weren't for the WARNINGS. They would stick body parts under the lawnmower, flick a Bic to check the level of gas in their tank, grab a filet knife to pick the rabbit out of their teeth (assuming they had teeth), and heat the can of sardines in the microwave but for the WARNING.* And thank goodness for the latest WARNING- I just saw on a 50 qt. plastic storage tub (complete with graphic), admonishing the user to not stuff their kid in the tub and seal with the lid! I'll be sure and add it to the long list of things I've already been told NOT to stuff a child into because it could cause bodily harm or suffocation. Thanks. I didn't know.

Who exactly are these people needing all this additional guidance for their own safety and that of their children? Do they truly exist? I do know if they 're out there...roaming the streets and/or woods some-where... they would NOT be reading the fine print on the labels and could not interpret the graphics. They are simply too stupid; I dub them Meatheads. It's for that reason Left Brain left me with the fol-lowing suggested agenda:

1. Remove all the unnecessary WARNINGS, those intended only for Meatheads.

2. If they really do exist, they won't for too long- so Win/Win for everybody.

3. Which will result in an immediate improvement in the collec-tive gene pool intellect.

4. Therefore, the labels on all products will then require only the most basic information regarding safety, operation, and usage

5. Thus, the important basic information we truly need will have much more space on the label...and finally... the "juicy morsel, something bright and sparkly hidden in the steaming pile..." referenced earlier...

6. **I WILL NOT HAVE TO USE MY MAGNIFYING GLASS TO SEE THIS IMPORTANT STUFF NOR WILL I HAVE TO FIND SAID INFO AMONG ALL THE USELESS, INANE, FINE-PRINTED GOBBELDY GOOK DIRECTED TO MEATHEADS!**

All I want to know are the dosage amount and times on this medicine bottle. Is that too much to ask? It's important information, don't you think? I will gladly sacrifice a few slabs of Meathead to the Goddess Clueless on the altar of DumbAss - if it means I don't have to constantly search for a magnifying glass.

Selfish, I know, and I only wish it was that easy. Unfortunately, we're treated as though we ALL eat paste and lick the windows. Shame. I haven't licked windows for quite a while.

Nice Balls, Betty

Dear Betty Crocker,

Re: Recipe for Holiday Sausage Balls

I'm not a great chef or culinary artist so when we were requested to bring a dish to the Christmas office party, I quickly turned to your cookbook for inspiration. I was scanning the pages for ideas and decided to try my hand at your Sausage Balls; they looked so appetizingly displayed on page 176 - round and firm and just the right size to pop in the mouth.

First of all, one does not "crumble" sausage from the tubular packaging. I think you meant to say "peel the disgustingly vile and slimy pork byproduct from the impenetrable protective plastic sleeve, squish the crap out it, then smear it evenly in the bottom of the skillet, stirring constantly over low heat until the grease absorbs, evaporates, or otherwise goes wherever the heck grease goes to disappear and the meat finally browns and cooks *into* crumbles."

Secondly, one does not merely 'roll' this mixture into balls. I think you meant to "put two tablespoons of the mixture in your dominant hand and squeeze like you are trying to milk gold from it. Don't give up and put some back into it. It's going to take some work. Schedule breaks."

Lastly, do you happen to use a special tool with your balls? Specifically, a tool to squeeze the slimy mixture into a sticky ball shape and guarantee all balls turn out the same size and shape? By late afternoon, the kitchen counter was overflowing with balls ranging in size from little marbles to balls that would choke a goat. These balls weren't pretty, either. Most weren't even balls, rather misshapen and taking more the form of a diseased peach pit. Perhaps a better name would be Pork Pits?

Be assured I'm not writing to complain. As stated, I'm not a chef of your status and take responsibility for my inability to whip the balls into shape. I simply wanted to share my experience. Also, I'm proud to tell you I was able to salvage the balls for the party. Some were marinated in my special hot wing sauce and served on toothpick skewers with a slice of jalapeno; I called them Buffalo Balls. Others were served in a split bun with ketchup, cabbage, and a generous garnish of Cheez Whiz from a can; I called them Ball Grinders. My personal favorites were balls marinated overnight and rolled in a mixture of coconut flakes and sea salt! Those were Salty Balls!

Thankfully, your recipe resulted in a generous amount; everyone ate all they wanted; I could hardly tell any were missing from the platters! I plan to freeze those balls and serve New Year's Eve with a nice Blueberry sauce. I think I'll call them ... uhmmm ... dessert.

Please feel free to share this information.

Sincerely,

No Time for DICs

I've always considered myself of relatively average intelligence. I'm in the populated area between that of an eccentric genius and one not walking into walls...at least not with the frequency and intensity requiring a helmet. Basically, that means I figure stuff out. When my intelligence reaches maximum capacity and begins to sputter under the payload, common sense engages. Tenacity and mule-headedness fire as after-burners and I blast through the wormhole into the light, floating as I bask in the quiet, self-righteous serenity of another mission accomplished. But I now find myself swirling helplessly in the dark abyss, unable to find my way to the other side. Confidence shattered. What brought me to this pitiful state and so torpedoed my frame of mind? I don't really know and therein lies my dilemma.

I stood on the deck of my home almost a month ago, sipping coffee to greet the day before going to work. That was when I first saw the hole dug under the edge of the house. I stood there staring at that hole and wondering what happened to my grand plan. I had problems repeatedly at that exact spot in the past, but that was before my intellect dictated I rebuild a section of fence I had removed and my common sense assured me that would keep pesky digging critters OUTSIDE that part of the yard. That project was completed months ago and had been successful...until now. "It's back," I thought. I wasn't too concerned, however. I had dealt with similar situations many times in the past and managed to complete damage control in a day...two at the most. I covered the hole and went to work with the self-assurance I would take care of that little problem in short order.

Yeah. Uh huh. Well, that was almost a month ago; what's ensued are a series of trials and frustrations as I've sought to outsmart the Mystery Meat. Yes, it's been almost a month and I can't even identify the thorn in my flesh. Armadillo? Raccoon? Skunk? After this long a time it doesn't really matter. I only know it to be a Destructive and Inconsiderate Critter, which I call DIC.

I've gone out night after night, stumbling around by flashlight to set the trap and perhaps catch a glimpse of the DIC. And every morning I open the back door hoping for the best and all I find is bait removed from the trap and a hole under the edge of my house. That DIC doesn't even trip the trap...just goes in and eats whatever it wants before retiring for the evening. If I forget to latch the gate, it comes in through there. If I lock the gate, it digs under. If I block where it digs under, it moves over and digs under the fence. If it happens to be under the house when I fill the hole, it digs out. If it's out when I fill the hole it will dig in. It doesn't matter what I use for bait or where in the trap I put it... the DIC empties the trap, then digs its hole.

I've dealt with his kind before, but this one has me baffled. It's like a ninja DIC! I feel its presence when I go outside. I think it is laughing at me, taunting me from the shadows. I think its evil intent is to run me insane and take over my house. It wouldn't be the first time a DIC tried it, but that's another story.

So, DICs BEWARE: I've worked hard over the years to maintain a DIC-free zone within the confines of this fence. You may feel smug now, laughing at me and sneaking around in the shadows. Mocking me to your DIC friends. Just know, I never give up and I always win in the end. Enjoy the shelter and free food while you can in your final days. And be afraid. I ain't got time for DICs! That's a fact!

One More for the Road

I've discovered getting older has its perks. You may call it rationalization; I call it enlightenment. Sometimes, it's hidden deep within the shadows and I must diligently search for something good in a situation.

I've known for many years three little words I hear in my head— ...just one more... is my worst enemy. Just one more... time or turn of the screw or minute or rung on the ladder or touch of salt, etc.... If I was a gambler, it would send me home desperately busted and dependent on the kindness of strangers. If I was a drinker, I would be the loud, obnoxious drunk thrown out into the gutter. This mentality catapults me into precarious situations, situations that if I had stopped short of that *just one more*... I would have been fine. It makes me push myself, at times, just a bit too far. And that is how I got the farm truck stuck last weekend. *Just one more foot and I'm sure I can back the truck where I need it.*

Stuck. But, it wasn't stuck badly; the old tires were simply spinning on wet, loose soil. It was practically sitting on top of the ground! I first tried to get it back on more solid footing by attaching a pulley to a tree and pulling with a rope. Stupid, I know, so blame that attempt on old age. (Another perk). It buried a little deeper.

Next, I took the shredder off the tractor and tried pulling it free with a chain. The tractor tires just spun, too, so at that point I just walked away - defeated and mad at myself and the predicament of my own making. I went by every afternoon after work to try again, *one more time*, thinking the warm sunshine would in some way work to my advantage. But each day the tires continued to spin. And bury a little deeper. I wasn't too concerned. Saturday was coming and that was the day I dedicated to freeing the truck, determined it should be out before the next rain.

Saturday morning, I could feel the rain coming...smell it...see it in the distance...as I gathered a shovel and jacks and haydite blocks and headed down to the truck. I knelt down to place the blocks and realized the true extent of my numerous *just one more*; I had managed to bury the truck (once pristinely perched on a nice bed of wet grass) up to the axle (in a mire of slippery, squishy clay mud). I was frustrated but not defeated and quickly set about lifting the truck and setting the blocks in the seeping, muddy ruts.

It started to sprinkle about the time I had everything situated like I envisioned for Project Extraction. Then, it started to rain. Hard. I grabbed the coffee thermos and ran for shelter, totally disgusted with myself. I sat under the awning, sipping coffee and thinking of anyone I would call to help me. Someone who wouldn't charge a lot. Someone with a bigger truck. Or a bigger tractor. And a bigger chain. Someone with knowledge and experience. Someone stronger. Someone who wouldn't laugh at my foible and could be sworn to silence. uh...NO. I knew I had to try again. *Just one more time...*

Thankfully spring showers can pass quickly, as was the case Saturday. (I'm certain I would have persuaded myself to give up the fight and leave it all if I had spent another minute glaring and cursing from beneath the awning). As it was, everything was already in place and ready to try. I couldn't walk away. I just had to try *one more time.*

I sighed as I put the truck in reverse, no longer full of optimism and expecting nothing. I hit the gas. The tires spun on the blocks as the truck jolted backward; I held steady as the smell of burning rubber filled the air, tires spinning and fighting to get the smallest bite of muddy clay. Then, I felt the truck relax against the strain. At the exact moment I backed that old truck onto solid ground the clouds parted, the sun shined down in all its glory and the birds began chirping a joyful song just for me. I did a dance as the agony of defeat immediately lifted from my old bones, replaced by the joy of victory!

It was then I had my epiphany...my moment of enlightenment. The mentality of "just one more" may be my worst enemy. However, I suddenly realized it is often my best ally and serves me well. It pushes and prods, challenges and coerces. Certainly, it gets me into trouble on occasion. However, there are many times I would give up if I didn't have that little voice inside my head daring, yet encouraging me..."just one more...". So, I'm thinking if I ever fall off the ladder and break my leg because the little voice told me, "just one more rung..." the same voice will be telling me "just one more hop to the truck" and then" just one more mile to the hospital."

Don't worry about me. I've got this! Well, me and the voice in my head that sounds an awful lot like Morgan Freeman! WE'VE got this!

Oyster Challenge

I've always been told I'm much like my father and living as closely as we do isn't helping the situation. Ask any of my family and I think they will agree. Is this a good thing? I suppose it depends on what aspect is being discussed, but I'll proudly carry the torch to my grave.

One thing both my parents taught us was to find humor in the smallest things. It's basically "don't sweat the small stuff and it's all small stuff" philosophy. Dad's catch-all phrase has always been "git yer priorities in order." I believe they developed this approach over time by facing one extreme adversity after another throughout their lives together, circumstances and events and weights under which most of us would either crumble or flee. They did neither. They (especially my dad) kept our family and home together by hard work, faith, and clawing nuggets of humor out of granite. This education has served me well in my life and I've tried to pass it on to my kids; it gets us through the hard times.

Dad had a bad appetite day yesterday. Last night he signaled he was finished with dinner by his customary draping of a napkin over the plate and pushing it aside. As I retrieved his plate to wash it I gently scolded, "I'm going to start restricting your dessert intake if you don't start eating better than this." We all (including him) know that to be an idle threat. We don't care if he uses Oreos to scoop hot fudge sundae if that's what he wants and he'll eat it. He flatly replied, "I hear ya." He sat there patiently with his back to the sink, waiting for his cookies or cake or ice cream.

It was then I noticed a can of oysters Robin (my sister) had dumped on us as a joke. I opened the oysters and dumped them in a bowl, grabbed a fork and sat it in front of him. He looked at it the longest time before asking, "what's this?" "Dessert," I answered, "go ahead...take a bite." He looked at it again. I'm certain by then the stench had wafted to his nostrils and he said, "yer not kiddin' anybody. That's oysters." I challenged him to take a bite, but instead he pushed the bowl toward me and returned the challenge. "Go ahead, Mikey, eat it. Mikey will eat anything." We shuffled the bowl back and forth a few times before it came to a halt, resting halfway between us.

We sat there... glaring at each other and then the bowl of slime and then each other again. (Cue the theme music befitting the situation from any number of old Spaghetti Westerns). I reached for the fork and looked Dad in the eyes, determined to take him up on his dare. I leaned over the bowl and started digging around for a "nice looking' oyster. He leaned toward me slightly, scrutinizing the process. I finally speared one and sniffed it, examining it closely for ...what?... I don't know! I sniffed it again, made a face telegraphing my disgust, and slowly took the fork to my mouth. I opened my mouth, totally focused on the ball of grossness riding on the fork and on deliberately forcing the grotesque critter between my teeth and on subsequently keeping it down. Just as it was within an inch of my lips Dad lunged toward me, slapped the table and yelled, "WATCH OUT!". I jumped and the oyster plopped to the table. "You're a jerk!" I said. He just smiled at his victory.

"You're a jerk," I repeated, as I stabbed another oyster and rushed it directly into my mouth. I started to chew. It was like the owl and the Tootsie Roll pop... "one, two, three..." before I spit it on a napkin, gagging and spewing, and trying hard to not say something nastier than the slime already on my tongue. GAG! "Gross! Nasty!", as I jumped up for some water. "That's disgusting! I'll never get this taste out of my mouth."

And he just smiled, gloating in yet another victory at my expense. After a time we took bets on whether Dory (his dog) would eat an oyster. She wouldn't. I lost again. *sigh* Next time, old man... next time!"

Pants on Fire

I know I'm not the only one whose mind meanders through a mine-field of random thoughts when performing thoughtless, possibly inane tasks.

I was working outside this morning, enjoying the gentle breeze teasing me with a hint of autumn. My mind eventually began to pick through a series of thoughts: prioritizing my to-do list, the weather, a cow, Trump vs. Clinton, FroYo Friday, the riots and race relations, another cow. Suddenly, my thoughts centered on methods of medieval torture – the Iron Maiden, thumbscrew, the rack, the breaking wheel, burning at the stake, etc. Terrible, I know. Horrid.

I wondered if they ever used anything, like... say... fire ants. The investment would have been minimal and the result would have been bone fide, verifiable torture. The Torturers would have dressed the prisoner in high top work boots, tight jeans, and leather gloves. The prisoner would then be led to a rather benign pile of rocks and ordered to move them from one place to another. As the first rock was overturned and the fire ants started moving and latching onto clothes, the prisoner would simply brush them away with a smirk. *Is that all you've got?* After a few more rocks were overturned, the first stings would be felt as the prisoner realized ants had gotten inside the gloves and attached to the hands. *Ok. That's not cool but nothing I can't handle.* The prisoner would smile slightly with jaws clenched, determined to keep pace with the raging ant horde by simply being more cautious.

However, while distracted, shaking gloves and peeling ants off the hands even more angry ants would have climbed inside the shoes and up the legs and inside the pants. *This is not good! Not good, at all!* The prisoner would quickly grab the pants legs, naively thinking the ants could be neutralized and dissuaded from additional advancement by such actions. *I should have insisted on The Rack!* The eyes would fill with tears at the realization foot stomping, slapping, and flailing would be to no avail; the prisoner would acknowledge utter defeat as the ants continued to advance and the bites began to throb. Hands. Ankles. legs. Waist. Still, the ant march continued undeterred. *Deliver me! I've got to have some relief! Please! God!* Finally, as a desperate attempt to halt the marauding horde's advancement... the prisoner would toss aside all dignity... along with the stripped gloves and boots and pants... much to the delight of the torturers and any passersby just happening by herding goats along the dirt path.

Yes, it would not have been a pretty sight - witnessing an innocent and unsuspecting victim of fire ant torture, stripped down and dancing the Clog and Boot Scootin Boogie simultaneously with uncharacteristic rhythm and without musical accompaniment- unless the screams, curses, and screeches count as music. You can ask anyone travelling the highway in front of my property this morning, and they'll agree. Not a pretty sight. Perhaps one of them noticed where my left boot landed. I never did find it! I'll buy another pair, though, because I'm not asking.

Peeing in the Gene Pool

Our survival depends on identifying certain elements of society that could lead to the total decline of civilization. They are elusive, able to blend into society unnoticed. If they remain in the shadows and are allowed to breed, we will devolve into a species of dysfunctional sub-humanoids void of critical thinking skills and incapable of utilizing the part of the cerebral we call common sense. They are peeing in our gene pool and must be stopped before it's too late.

Where are they? Maybe it's someone with whom you cross paths at Walmart? Perhaps one dined at the table next to you at Cotton Patch? I'm referring to specific idiots, not those of us incapable of assembling a credenza from Ikea without having two screws remaining. I'm speaking of the idiots among us who climb to the top rung of a ladder and keep climbing until they fall off the other side or operate appliances and tools in ways inconsistent with their intended use. They eat small bags of desiccant. They distribute plastic bags, pointed scissors, medications, and toys with small parts to children and have no concept of hazards related to suffocation, laceration, poisoning, or choking. They throw yard darts inside. They smoke as they fill their gas tank and hold firecrackers until they explode in their fingers. They drink cleaning products and put their heads into revolving ceiling fans. They grab hot light bulbs. They put all manner of substances obviously intended for external use in their mouth, eyes, nose, or ears. They don't realize edges may be sharp, surfaces hot, or substances poisonous. They need a message on every pack of cigarettes to remind them smoking will cause cancer and a disclaimer on a cup of hot coffee to remind them they're drinking hot coffee! This list is incomplete, but you now understand the magnitude of the problem.

The gene pool needs seining and these idiots would make for some big chunks! However, I've never actually seen one nor has anyone with whom I've spoken. How can they remain undetected? They must drool as they go up the down- escalator, wear underwear outside their pants, or repeatedly sing 'Itsy Bitsy Spider' under their breath (hand motions optional). How do they survive possessing no whit of common sense, ability to reason, or problem-solving skills? If left to their own devices, wouldn't they soon become extinct? They would cut, mangle, poison, choke, and suffocate themselves out of existence. Would that be a bad thing? Really?

Anyone making toast in their bubble bath or launching bottle rockets out their butt should suffer the consequences. It's the law- natural selection or God's will or survival of the fittest- call it what you will. I postulate continued governmental interference (FDA, OSHA, etc.) protecting these idiots from their own stupidity threatens the natural order of life (death). Common sense and logic regarding basic product safety issues should be cultivated in the home and reinforced by public education. Call me old-fashioned. "Don't be an idiot," our parents would warn when we started to do something stupid like eat kitty litter or swing the machete at our brother or drink motor oil. Occasionally, they would let us get a burn or scratch or break just to teach us cause and effect. We learned and evolved. Those who didn't, were maimed or killed. Either way, they didn't do it twice.

I'm not a conspiracy theorist but I have to wonder why the government interferes and protects them by requiring warning labels, disclaimers, and detailed instructions for proper use on even the simplest of products. Seriously Could it be the government protects the idiots among us to ensure they remain upright and breathing for voting purposes? It would explain a lot; don't you think? Someone must be voting for the idiots. I'm thinking it could only be other idiots. Just sayin'...

Pinball Wizard

I find it interesting how we think about things, the random thoughts occasionally bouncing around inside our brains like the metal balls in an old pinball machine – sometimes with the accompanying flashing lights and sound effects – 'DING! DING! DING!' -as the thought gets catapulted between the distractions set in its path and flippers frantically flailing to keep the thought in play and out of the drain. Pesky distractions like operating a moving vehicle.

I was driving to town recently for an appointment, cruise set on the 70 mph limit and enjoying the beautiful spring afternoon. Topping a hill, I was suddenly slowed by a big Buick creeper – the kind of car you just know is being driven by an old woman barely tall enough to see over the steering wheel, a matching set of white hair and knuckles, hands gripping the wheel at 10 and 2 and eyes squinting to keep the monolith between the lines. *Oh, great... (DING!) ... practically the only stretch of road in 10 miles where I can't pass."* My irritation was mounting exponentially to the distance travelled and opportunities missed for Grandma to scoot over on the shoulder for me to safely pass. Urghhh...

Then, I thought of my Dad. (DING!) One of his greatest fears as he grew older and more frail was loss of judgment and ability would rob him of his last morsel of independence – driving. He had always been a good driver, though a little too aggressive. We watched as his highway speed slowly dwindled with his health and confidence. As I followed that Buick I remembered the numerous times we had encouraged him, "it's alright to go slower Dad. You always told us to not drive any faster than we felt in control." But he harbored deep guilt for going slow, worried he was a nuisance to those following. Unfortunately, his compromise developed into a perceived need (more like obligation) to drive on the shoulder at the first sighting of a vehicle in his rearview mirror. He would drive for miles on the shoulder; I supposed it was his way of offering an advanced apology for going slower. I admonished him so many times, "Dad. PLEASE. Keep your car in the driving lane. DO NOT drive on the shoulder, especially over hills or around curves where you can't see what's ahead. It's a breakdown lane. People walk and bike over there. There are passing lanes. Impatient drivers can just wait to pass!" A melancholy suddenly invaded my space and I found myself (DING!) humming an old Joni Mitchell tune : 'I've looked at life from both sides now, from win and lose and still somehow it's life's illusions I recall... I really don't know life at all.' *I always liked that song.*

My own words to my Dad echoed in my mind as I choked down a heaping helping of self-served crow and relaxed, content to follow Grandma to the ends of the earth...or a place to safely pass...whichever came first! Fortunately, it was a passing lane. (DING!) *Go, Grandma! Keep it up! You're doing great!* I gave her an animated 'thumbs up' as I went by to indicate my support and encouragement; if she kept up her present pace she would absolutely be passing the courthouse square before dark. I smiled at the thought. A quick check of the rearview, however, caught a glimpse of the old woman's middle finger waving at me out the window! What? I didn't know how to feel about that as I continued to gain distance. Angry? Amused? Guilty? I already felt bad for losing patience. But now I had to wonder if she had mistaken my thumbs up as something more obscene. *Great... now there's some old woman going to tell everyone at Bingo how I flipped her off as I passed by!*

I stopped for that super long traffic light west of town, checking my mirrors and hoping it would change before Grandma caught up to me and looking to rumble. Fortunately, my attention soon switched from her to a group of girls walking the track at the park. (DING!) How cute they were - hair tied back in ponytails, bright colored tank tops and running shoes and length-challenged track shorts. I always admire the people out exercising on that track - walkers and runners of various ages, sizes, and shapes – sweating and working to better health. (DING!) *Note to self: I really need to do that, too...one of these days... maybe Monday!* But I noticed the girls weren't actually running OR walking; the gait was a slow, leisurely stroll. AND to add to the paradox... they each had a Big Gulp of soda in one hand and a burger in the other. (DING!) *I suppose it IS hard to run laden with quantities of fast food! You wouldn't want to suck cola up your nose or dribble mustard on the Adidas.* I watched them strolling and eating their burgers, talking and laughing among themselves. I couldn't help but ponder the obvious... (DING!) *So, did you pick up fast food as an afterthought on the way to the track? Or was dressing in athletic wear the afterthought, thinking you needed to dress appropriately for the park to eat your Jumbo Jack and cheesy curly fries? Have you calculated how many laps it will take to burn off that meal at your current rate of expended effort? I suspect you are more interested in making a fashion statement and to be seen, having no intention of allowing sweat to glisten upon your brow or stain that new sports bra. Sweat is yucky, I know.* They amused me.

I pondered the previous events as I made the last mile of my short trip... the paradoxes of being flipped the bird by a feisty little old lady and the junk food-laden workout of the young girls. Then, (DING!) *I will probably be an old white-haired woman by the time I decide to get to the track to walk and workout regularly. I hope I'm feisty, too. And I'll eat junk food as I walk if I want to...no guilt. Maybe I'll strap a pizza box and a chocolate shake to my walker. And I'll be stylin', too... I'll stuff my sagging girls into a hot pink sports bra and corral my lumpy, floppy behind into a pair of shimmering green shorty shorts. I'll walk slowly by then, in my lighted neon orthos, and probably irritate people having to change pace to go around a slow old woman on the track. I wonder if I'll flip them off as they pass by? TILT! TILT! TILT!*

Poop in a Box

How NOT to start a day: I was in transit and darted into a public restroom at 4:30 a.m., only to find myself in a holding pen for a one-stall facility. The stall was unfortunately occupied by a lady in the midst of completing her morning constitutional. It was extremely uncomfortable, standing on one side of a partition and listening to her moan and groan through the wall. She was obviously in distress and there was nothing I could do to help! I felt compelled to shout encouragement or try to talk her through it. Pass a note scribbled on toilet tissue? Perhaps she would appreciate the distraction of small talk? Or maybe I could sing a show tune? 'Luck Be a Lady Tonight' or 'Cell Block Tango' seemed appropriate...sort of. Poor lady was trying to stifle her business and I felt like I was cramping her style. I opted to take the cowardly way and quietly backed out the door to wait in the hall.

As I stood there passing the time (and her passing what must have been a Volkswagen) I quickly formed an image in my mind of the woman I could expect to come through that door. I considered the parameters of guttural volume, flatulent emissions ratio per square footage of available space in the small bathroom, degree of elimination difficulty, and extreme olfactory assault. I concluded the woman emerging would be very large and sweaty, her polyester pants stretched tightly over what they were trying to cover, and hair hanging in a stringy, unstylish mess. She would throw open that door, red-faced and out of breath, reeling from her rough physical workout coming entirely too early in the morning. I imagined what I had just stumbled upon in that urban version of a privy was the most physical activity she had experienced in a while...at least the most since consuming mass quantities of "fried chicken embryos and seared swine flesh" earlier in the morning...a snack to make it until breakfast.

I didn't have to wait long. I heard her stall door slam and immediately the outside door swung open; I struggled to not make eye contact. I thought SHE would be uncomfortable and wanted to spare HER additional embarrassment. That's how I roll...considerate that way. Imagine my surprise when this petite middle-aged woman waltzed by on a breeze, dressed in a tailored skirt and jacket...glasses...every hair in place pulled back in a tight bun. She shot past me in her shiny high heels...click, clack, click, clack...and pulling her small, wheeled attaché behind. She was obviously a professional woman on her way to catch a flight to an important business meeting. She presented herself as a woman in total control as she marched by, head tilted back and shoulders squared, jaw set, and ready to attack the day ahead!

I admit I was initially ashamed of my misguided assumptions and spatial profiling. Yet, she brushed past me as if I was nothing, a steaming pile of...well, something of which she had recent intimate knowledge. No greeting. No smile or nod of the head. What? How rude! I wanted to tap her on the shoulder and give an acknowledging nod as I pointed to the bathroom; "I know who you are and know what you did in there!" But, I didn't. She boarded her shuttle and I waited for mine.

However, on my brief shuttle ride I did find comfort imagining her stripped of her shoes and business prop attaché case going through Security. I imagined the alarms would keep beeping until TSA would tag her for the 'TSA SPECIAL', pulling her aside for the 'blower room' and 'magic wand' and cavity search. Each time the alarms would sound and the passengers observing this process would start stacking up behind her, all impatient and critical and looking like the Townspeople standing around the Frankenstein castle entrance demanding the culprit be presented for justice.

Finally, TSA would make a loud announcement through the speaker as they directed all attention to her (including her newly-acquired sweaty red face and stringy hair). "Nothing to be *alarmed* about, folks. Sorry-it's a little TSA joke. Anyway, don't forget to wash your hands after going to the bathroom. These newest devices will identify you as unfit for boarding until you complete the process. And *use* the soap." The crowd would collectively gasp as TSA slap an UNCLEAN sticker on her back and direct her to the facilities. I would walk by her at that time, smile, give a familiar nod and stroll away singing, 'They Call the Wind Mariah'.

It's all good in my world! But, Golly Gee, I sure need to find a bathroom!

Project Grandson

Project Jonah:

I want to thank all family and friends expressing love, concern, and support throughout this Project. From beautiful gifts to silent prayers and everything between, know you are appreciated. To our family holding vigil in the waiting room or from afar for his debut, I knew you wouldn't be anywhere else. It was comforting to know you were there; we felt your presence.

A special shout out to the other grandparents, Joe and Teri, for raising such a wonderful son. I know it wasn't easy and hasn't always been smooth sailing. He was a bit of a handful (I've been told that's a nice way to say it). However, you obviously planted him on a firm foundation as he stands tall and strong. You can take great pride in the man he has become. Thank you for sharing him with me.

Speaking of my son-in-law... YOWZA! What can I say about that boy who's become my son-by-another-mother by marriage to my daughter? His obvious contribution to Project Jonah has not gone unnoticed. I will save a lot of words by only saying: I could only hope any woman out there going through her own Project would have a man like him at her side. He has proven from the beginning he is vested in my daughter's comfort and welfare and in this little guy they brought home. I love and appreciate him for all he's done and continues to do. My daughter is blessed.

To my daughter... WOW! I knew she had it going on mentally and physically and intellectually. However, I was worried how she would handle the 'mystery' of labor. She likes things organized and clean and to be in control of her environment, which is NOT how one would describe the labor/delivery process. My girl proved she definitely has the right stuff and I'm so proud of her! Her husband and I stayed at her side and kept her focused, but she did the rest all by herself! I wish you all could have seen her in that delivery room! Well, maybe not... but it was a sight to behold... in a good way! Trust me.

In summary, I had a grandson Monday with the support of family and friends and a little help from his Mommy and Daddy. I'm sure some of you must be concerned, but I'm glad to report I'm recovering quite nicely. Well, I'm perhaps still a little tired and sore. My sleep pattern seems to be a bit askew but appetite is returning. All things considered, I was awesome! Actually, I've bounced back better than I anticipated so I should be able to have another one in about a year! Thank you!

Successful completion of PROJECT JONAH: PHASE 1! Now... It's all about the Grammie!

PSA

I apologize in advance if anyone finds the following recently published public service announcement offensive, but I feel compelled to share. If we don't protect our children, then who will?

This from a recently formed coalition of citizens following the USPS decision to destroy the entire collection of stamps in the 'Just Move' series "after concerns were raised the tiny pictures showed children doing dangerous things ... like performing a cannonball dive (without floaties), skateboarding without knee pads, and doing a headstand without a helmet":

The Announcement:

Dudes Offering Unsophisticated Citizens Help in Everything (DOUCHE) is intensifying its agenda to include non-contact sports and children's games and announced its intentions to have the following removed from store shelves by Christmas or restocked with modifications:

<u>Tiddlywinks and Pick-up Sticks:</u> All will be removed from store shelves immediately. It has been determined children may sustain eye damage if they do not exercise extreme caution and are not closely supervised. However, the manufacturer may agree to sell the items with two sets of safety glasses. Negotiations are ongoing.

<u>Play Dough:</u> It has been brought to DOUCHE's attention children occasionally mold anatomically correct human/animals/flowers and thus the clay obviously encourages promiscuity and sexual harassment. Additionally, some DOUCHE concluded the rainbow- colored doughs could send subliminal gay messages to children and lead to orientation confusion at an impressionable age. Finally, it is not considered an acceptable dietary supplement.

<u>Monopoly:</u> This game has been deemed irrelevant to the youth of today

having no understanding of discretionary and investment income and finding it increasingly difficult to count money and make change. Additionally, parents tend to give a spoiler and tell young players how the game ends – 'they all go to jail or bankrupt and the bank and tax man come and take it all'. Hasbro is addressing these issues with the addition of low-income housing, homeless shelters, soup kitchens, after-school daycare, and slum lords. Hasbro has also offered to include consoles with push-button pictures (based on McDonald's cash register design) and debit cards to make math accounting easier. However, DOUCHE suspects Monopoly is a cleverly disguised training tool for Republicans and Chase Bank CEOs, so it's doubtful the modifications will rise to the required standard.

Jenga: It has been determined this game makes young players extremely anxious and frustrated. Additionally, there is mounting concern of possible injury from falling Jenga pieces. A fully assembled Jenga tower will be on the shelves by the first of the year, no assembly required. Players will simply remove Jenga carefully from the box, look at it, and replace it in the box for next time.

Sidewalk Chalk: DOUCHE expressed concern that prolonged exposure to chalk dust will lead to unwarranted respiratory distress in children and possible death. They cited a recent study in Tanzania in which a lab rat was duct taped to a brick and fully submerged in chalk dust for two days. The rat showed definite signs of chalk dust poisoning and died two days later.

Yahtzee: DOUCHE cited multiple case studies identifying gambling addicts incarcerated for crimes related to their disease or currently in rehab. In all but two of the randomly examined cases Yahtzee had been played at least once in pre-pubescent or teen years.

Operation: It was suggested the humorous, yet incorrect naming of various body parts lead to medical misinformation and difficulty mastering biology and physiology studies later. It was further suggested that could explain our inability to keep pace with other countries in science-related disciplines. The big red nose and buzzer are especially offensive, constantly reminding children of their lack of skill and coordination and often result-ing in arguments and tears of frustration and embarrassment.

Board Games in general: DOUCHE re-stated its mission and assured the public this list is not complete. They vow to continue their vigi-lance and plan to have all games with spinners banned by summer. These games promote unnecessary competition between friends and a destructive hierarchical ranking when one player is allowed to go first (or take a turn) and the others are required to sit and watch. Board games remaining on the shelves will be those providing a spin-ner for each player. All players will spin at the same time and move together directly to the Winner's Circle of Love where they will find a medallion declaring "We Are All Winners". Certainly, the new versions will require little or no time to complete but DOUCHE assures parents there will be much less arguing, no hurt feelings, and all the little chil-dren will have a heightened sense of self-worth and personal triumph.

Although DOUCHE admitted its resources are currently directed at childhood pastimes, it assured the public it remains dedicated to the eventual eradication of anything anyone anywhere may find offensive. They have formed a special committee, Banning All Gaffes in Speech, to examine phrases and vernacular currently used in conversational speech and will be publishing their recommendations shortly. The spokesperson for BAGS was recently quoted as saying, "DOUCHE and BAGS, working hand-in-hand in a concentrated effort, vow to provide a cleansing of corruption and impurities in all areas assaulting our sensibilities. We will scour every nook and cranny and dark space in search of offensive matter. We WILL cleanse and purge. Soon every man, woman, and child will be able to take a deep breath, free from the dark offensive cloud surrounding us all. We vow to crawl so far up into your business it will be impossible to determine where you end and we begin! This is our promise." When asked how they respond to those who may be offended by the extent of their extreme intrusion, the DOUCHE-BAGS shrugged their shoulders, made the universal ob-scene sign, and quickly exited the building.

Respect the Weathered Men

Sitting here on Day 4 of a self-imposed quasi quarantine due to coronavirus (or in my hermit-life is commonly referred to as Wednesday), I'm still at that awkward stage between thinking about the myriad of things I could be doing around the house or actually getting up and doing them. I've been feeling a real need to pace myself for what may be the long haul and don't want to burn out too soon. It makes sense to me. Anyways, as I sat around thinking about my relatively new slacker existence in this relatively uncharted state of the world, I received notification that church services must be suspended until further notice. What? I immediately thought of my dear departed parents having to exist in this new world order. How would they have reacted under these circumstances? I think I know.

**

When my Dad was a kid (which would have made the time in the 1930's) he and his family headed out for a rare overnight outing away from the stresses of Depression poverty and working this old sandy peanut farm. His father was a no-nonsense old man; if he (or his boys) weren't plowing behind a team of mules or working the fields with a gooseneck they were lollygagging and he didn't approve of lollygagging. The only exception was going to school; he approved of books. Books, but not basketball. That fishing trip was actually the only time Dad talked about his father participating in a leisure activity. Rare, indeed. I suppose a nice spring day following a rather harsh winter gave him the push he needed. The hard work of plowing and planting would come soon enough for all of them.

Grandparents, aunts, uncles, and cousins loaded a couple of wagons with cane poles, quilts for bedding, lanterns, a bit of food, and the oldest folks to make the short pilgrimage to the choice fishing spot - a creek just over the hill and down the road and across a few pastures.

The kids scampered ahead with their poles slung over their shoulders, laughing and chatting as they excitedly anticipated the slower wagons and mules making their way across the rough terrain to join them. Upon arrival, the wagons were quickly unloaded and camp set up under an old oak tree a short distance from the creek bank.

This spot was a prime fishing hole for perch and crappies, often trapped in small pools along the otherwise dry creek bed. Most of the kids knew it well, a favorite spot for sneaking off on a Sunday afternoon to explore the meandering trail of dry creek bed. The women busied themselves with nesting the camp as most of the men sat around talking crops and rain; the kids ran the creek bottom, occasionally returning to drop an impatient line in a pool of water. One older aunt, though, had found just the spot. She managed to climb out on a limb that had fallen across the creek and suspended just over a deeper pool. She was soon tight lining little perch and crappie, tossing them over at the gaggle of screeching kids fighting over whose turn it was to grab a fish to run up the bank to the camp to be be cleaned and thrown whole into a cast iron skillet full of hot boiling lard. As the sun set they were already feasting on fried fish and corn pones, followed by dried peaches by the handfuls for dessert.

It had been a good day. The adults sat around the fire a while- men chatting about the work ahead and the women about the gardens to soon be planted. The kids darted about and poked at the fire but it wasn't long until it was time to get the beds ready for sleeping - "early to bed and early to rise", which was their way. Some beds were made in the wagons, quilts spread and inviting. Others were laid out on the ground under the wagons. Most of the older kids (including Dad) preferred the creek bottom; with a little work to move a few rocks and sticks, there was a nice bed of soft sand on which to spread a quilt. They were strongly discouraged from sleeping there, but the less cautious among the adults finally agreed to grant them their wishes for privacy and independence.

As the fire burned low, excited chatter about the trip and fishing and night sky gradually turned to hushed whispers. My dad could hear his father and uncle talking quietly. He looked and could see them silhouetted in the moonlight against the darkness. They would look to the north and point, scratched and spit. They would stroll around for a bit, then point and scratch and spit. He strained to hear the conversation, but their voices soon blended with the sounds of frogs, cicadas and crickets as he slowly faded into a restful sleep on his bed of sand.

At some point in the early morning hours before dawn he was startled awake by loud shouts and frantic yells. His father and uncle were rousing everyone from the creek bed with shouts of, "head to high ground now" and "grab your beds and get up on the bank". Sleepy kids grabbed quilts and shoes and stumbled out of the creek bottom, pulled up the bank by frantic adults or pushed from behind. Younger kids were crying, older kids were perplexed. "Why? What's happening?" There were no obvious signs indicating they should have had a blissful sleep interrupted. No snakes. No coyotes. No wild hogs. Nothing.

The wagons emptied as everyone gathered to the chaos to find out the reason for such a commotion and seemingly unwarranted interruption to their peaceful night. My Dad's father and uncle were joined by a couple of other men, as they pointed to the northwest. They had taken shifts through the night keeping a watchful eye on the sky to the north and west, the lightning illuminating an ever increasing expanse of dark sky in the distance. "But it's not rainin' here!", some of the kids protested. "Not even a sprinkle! Look? We can still see the stars above!" "Doesn't matter," was the answer. "All that rain up north has gotta go somewhere. Better safe than sorry. You kids make your beds up here to finish out the night." Amidst a few mumbles, everyone settled back down on higher ground and waited for first light.

The sun rose to bright blue skies; it was just another beautiful spring day as the group slowly started stirring. "See? All that fuss was for nothing," the kids grumbled as they gathered firewood for a quick breakfast before breaking camp and heading home. It was as they sat around chatting and making plans for loading the wagons they heard a low rumble in the distance. "What's that?" Everyone sat quietly, straining to get a direction and source of the odd noise. It was then a wall of water tore down the empty creek bed, pushing branches and debris aside as it continued on a path downstream. "Whoa!", the kids gasped, crowding the creek bank for a closer look. "What was that?" "That, boys, is why you never make your bed in a low spot and close your eyes, thinkin' all is well. Just because it's not raining on you doesn't mean you're not gonna git caught up in the wash. You gotta look around, look at the signs in the distance. It's rainin' somewhere."

My parents were people of optimism and faith. This is not interpreted as blind faith- a belief it's all in God's hands and there is nothing to be done- God will provide and care for the faithful. Mom's faith was translated "God helps those who help themselves," which I heard her repeat many times. Although not Biblical in origin, it is in philosophical terms. Dad's daily walk was translated, "faith is the substance of things hoped for, evidence of things not seen" and "faith by itself, if it does not have works, is dead." They were both believers, yet their faith required effort and actions for any hope of blessings from that faith. Although Dad often toed the boundary dictated by Common Sense (especially in his later years) he rarely overstepped. How would they have reacted to these circumstances, a coronavirus world making unprecedented demands on their faith, patience, and endurance? I think I know.

Dad learned a lot about 'living a good life' from the words and examples of the Bible. He also learned a lot from just 'living life good' and its experiences- like that fishing trip to the creek. That old creek taught him to listen to old men walking in circles, spitting and scratching- men who had spent many years studying the sky and reading the signs. It also taught him to "never make your bed in a low spot and close your eyes, thinkin' all is well. Just because it's not raining on you doesn't mean you're not gonna git caught up in the wash. You gotta

look around, look at the signs in the distance. It's rainin' somewhere."
He would have followed protocol.

Rise of a Megadong

They said I'm tenacious and too particular. Well, actually, they said
I'm entirely too dang hard-headed and anal retentive. *Whatever.*
Considering these are relative terms subject to interpretation and
impossible to quantify, I simply smiled and thanked them for the com-
pliment. They weren't amused.

I never had more than a passing fancy of wind chimes, occasionally
purchasing a cheap one at Walmart and repairing it over the seasons
until nothing was left to tie to a string. One day not long before retirement, I was at Ace Hardware and hesitated in front of their large,
more expensive chimes. *Nice! But expensive. Too nice and expensive
to hang out in the Texas weather.* I lingered before the display, making
notes of what a Texas-sized wind chime would look like, how it would
be constructed to withstand our inclement weather and the ravages of
time. I was inspired and tucked that into my mental file labeled, 'POST
RETIREMENT PROJECTS'.

That day of liberation finally arrived; the day of gold watches and cake!
After thirty years of crunching numbers sequestered in offices and
shackled to desks, I was free to get out in the sun and do whatever
old retired women do! *Where do I start? There's so much work to do
around the house and farm! Work?* I had a fleeting moment of guilt.
But I don't want to work today. I WANT TO PLAY! At that moment I
heard the sickly, faint tinkle of an old wind chime held together now
by bailing twine and Elmer's glue. The sound started the rolodex in my
brain spinning, choking and sputtering like an old washing machine
before grinding to a jerky halt. *Ahhh, yes! I remember! Project Wind
Chime!* Retirement had officially started!

I began a chime crash course on Google - basic construction and relative dimensions, the science of tones, and studies of oxidation rates of various metals. The kids would ask occasionally, "what are you doing these days, Ma?" to which I'd answer, "building a wind chime." They'd smile politely and nod, "Sweet, have fun with that." After days of research and numerous schematics, I jumped in the old farm truck and headed to town with its lumber yards and hardware stores. I loaded the truck — four 10' sections of 2" steel conduit, 3/16" inch cable, a stock sheet of ¾" plywood, and a various assortment of chain, rope, tools and hardware! It was a busy week of drilling, measuring, sawing, and modifying before I finally stepped back to survey my handiwork. Assembled, it measured 15 feet tall, 4 feet wide at the halo, and I have no clue how much it weighed. *Wowser*! It was truly a monolith worthy of the moniker, Texas-Sized! *This is epic!* Absolutely puffy with pride, I slowly deflated with the realization I hadn't given much thought of WHERE to hang it. And most importantly, HOW? *Texas-sized, indeed*! I trudged toward the house down but not defeated, determined I would hang that testament to retirement in a tree — if it killed me!

The next few days were spent figuring out the best way to finish Project Wind Chime, lying still and silent in a heap on the ground. *I wonder how she* (now dubbed Texie) *will sound?* Perhaps the magnitude of finishing the project gave me pause to consider quitting. *What if the tones are unpleasant? Or loud? Or unrelentingly irritating?* If so, the project would end with nothing to show but a swaying pile of clanging scrap metal, chained high in a tree! *That would be a major fail!* Fortunately, (sometimes unfortunately) I can talk myself into anything given enough time and decided to plod onward with a renewed store of tenacity. After much deliberation, I decided on THE branch. Strong oak branch. Twenty feet high. In a tree appropriately distanced from the house — just in case.

The HOW was more of a dilemma. There was an abundance of willing hands on standby to help; the same hands that would want to choke me for not asking. But this was a solo mission, and I was determined to figure out how to safely get Texie home. I walked around that old tree, considering the angles, logistics, available maneuvering space, and equipment needed to safely hoist and secure her twenty feet in the air. *Phase 1: Tie the pipes together and drag them behind the ATV to the tree; wrestle them to an upright position leaned against the tree. Phase 2: Back the farm truck into the correct angle to safely support the ten-foot ladder, fully extended to twenty. Phase 3: Climb the ladder to prepare the branch, hang support chain, and drape hoisting rope. Phase 4: Climb down the ladder; attach the rope to the ATV hitch and drive forward to hoist the chime into position. Phase 5: Climb the ladder; attach chime to support chain and detach hoisting rope. Phase 6: Climb down the ladder; attach wind sail to its cable. Phase 7: Step back and bask in the Glory that is Texie, The Texas-sized Wind Chime!*

In my ideal world, this plan took an hour to accomplish; in the real world, it took all day. (I may have failed to include time for SNAFUs, redoes, and coffee breaks). The sun was setting as I added the final touch – the piece de resistance homage to my Dad – an old International truck hub cap to serve as the wind sail. I proudly stood back and gave the sail a big push to sway Texie into action. *Nice! She sounds good! The tones are deep and rich, somewhat melodious. And not so loud as to be annoying! Epic!* I continued banging the hammer into the pipes; it was music to my ears.

The kids arrived home and followed the odd banging sounds. They saw the ATV and tools still scattered about the scene. They saw the truck, the ladder still extended into the tree. Their eyes slowly trailed from the truck and ladder, up the tree, following the full length of Texie to her halo. They were impressed, I'm sure, as I regaled them with the construction details. They seemed more interested, however, in how it came to be twenty feet in the tree. "It's awesome. Truly. But, you should've asked us for help," they finally said. After a proper scolding (some stuff about broken hips and nursing homes and other stuff about knitting and watercolor and reading clubs) they turned to walk to the house. I heard one them mutter, "you're entirely too dang hard-headed and anal retentive for your own good!" *Maybe but I don't think so. Whatever.* I gave the wind sail another big swing. *Sweet!* The tones were faint, but deep and rich and melodic! I gave the sail a few more shoves before following behind. *You'll see! This will be awesome. All we need now is a nice breeze! Just wait!*

So, I waited. And waited some more. A month passed, during which time I often visited Texie. I set a lawn chair beside her, sipping coffee and coaxing her to let her freak flag fly. On breezeless days she'd silently stand there mocking me and I'd swing the sail, forcing her into action. Occasionally, the breeze was enough to breathe life into the cheap chimes scattered about the farm and they'd dance and sing. Texie simply swayed and whispered quietly. I discovered some unfortunate miscalculations regarding her size. 1)it required a significantly greater force to make her budge. 2) only a strong, solid strike from her hammer would evoke a tone to be heard at any distance. *That presents a conundrum!*

I was disappointed but not totally whupped and began to consider my options. *Even I can't control the wind; it is what it is. But there will be plenty of days with enough wind to make it work; this is Texas.* Accepting that meteorological fact made me feel more optimistic, but how to make her heard at the house eluded me. This project was not turning out as I originally envisioned. In my dreams, I would relax on the deck and listen to her deep, rich tones serenading me. Or I would be lulled to sleep by her sweet rhythmic sounds assuring me she's on duty and all is well. *Epiphany! She's too far away! I control the distance; I simply need to move her closer to the deck! I'll be able to see and hear her!* Problem solved.

And that's what I did, following the same procedures and equipment-use as outlined above. I moved Texie, taking her down from one tree, dragging her around to the other side of the house, and hanging her in another tree. It took all day and required some sweat and sore muscles but the results were awesome (yet worthy of another scolding from the kids). *Whatever.* Project Wind Chime successfully accomplished, I could finally bask in the glory. On the nice breezier days, I will enjoy her melody as I relax on the deck or putter in the yard; on breezier nights, I will drift off to sleep to the sounds of her rich, smooth tones. Texie was home and as majestically wonderful as I imagined. *I love it when a plan comes together!*

FOOTNOTE: Life with Texie has been great and I've enjoyed her as I had envisioned. HOWEVER, I was startled awake at 5:00 this morning from a sound sleep by an incessantly loud clanging and banging noise, heard clearly between piercing claps of thunder. It was unfamiliar and relenting, somewhat like sheet metal being angrily ripped off a roof by high wind and slammed mercilessly into a tree. I stepped onto the deck to determine the source. Who was outside at five o'clock this morning in the rain removing the hammer and sail from a mega chime, dodging four wildly swaying 2" pipes as she cinched them together with the belt from her robe because the wind was blowing a gale determined on beating a certain Texas-Sized wind chime to death? Yes. It was me. And as I changed into dry clothes I'll admit there was a fleeting thought to move Texie again. Don't worry, family. THAT would truly be the definition of too dang hard-headed and anal retentive for my own good. I'm not.

Rhythm of the Falling Rain

Listening to the drought-busting rain continue to cascade across my roof and reminiscing of childhood days – days before computers, iphones, ipads, and TV; days back when our hopes and dreams were free and not tethered to a functioning internet.

My youth did NOT predate the television era despite what you may think, only a television that would actually work and get a signal during rain. We did have an old black and white that would receive 4 channels out of DFW and it worked pretty well – on sunny days...with no wind...if we hadn't misplaced the channel-changing pair of pliers... AND if we could position the foil just right on the antennas. But, on a day like today my sister and I would think, "we know it is wet and the sun is not sunny, but we can have lots of good fun that is funny!"

Some of our activities on rainy days included the following:

- EMPTYING THE TOYBOX: We would empty the little red box with no lid of its limited treasures, being entertained to various degrees by the mere chaotic act of digging and tossing. There were always things we forgot which had settled to the bottom. *I wondered where that was*! It was fun to sit in our room and pick through the mess, sharing the treasure trove and stopping to play together with some random object or game we found.

- ROLLING AND BOUNCING BALLS: When we were extremely young, I remember sitting on the floor and rolling a big ball between us. We weren't allowed to throw the ball in the house but rolling and bouncing was acceptable. Unfortunately, we would get too adventurous and knock something over...usually because we HAD to throw it or try for that ONE BIG BOUNCE. Living on the edge; that's how WE rolled!

- SHOOTING SMALLER BALLS: As we got a little older, we created games using smaller balls (usually the ball from our Jacks or the ball at the receiving end of a broken Paddleball). Several variations using these balls developed over time included shooting/ bouncing the balls into an upright bucket or tin can or rolling the ball across the floor into a can lying on its side. I thought it was fun but SHE tired of these games quickly and moved on to develop her talents elsewhere, leaving me to my own creativity. I was easily self-contained in my own head and enjoyed developing these useful skills. I learned our linoleum-covered living room floor was uneven and tennis balls and (especially) golf balls were the BOMB for such games. My mother, however, couldn't tolerate the golf balls bouncing across the floor, hitting walls and tin cans for an extended time. In retrospect, she actually had the patience of a saint!

- PLAYING SCHOOL OR CHURCH: These are self-explanatory. We took turns being a teacher or student. For school, we would read and do worksheets we had around or mom would make us some. We graded papers and colored and cut paper and raised our hand to ask a question or get permission to go to the bathroom. We had recess and snack breaks. Playing church consisted mostly of singing hymns, reading some random verses, and eating crackers and juice. We played nice because we always wanted to be good in school and never wanted to be a sinner.

- BUILDING A TENT: This activity was almost exclusively something we did at Granny's house when we stayed with her. But occasionally, on a rainy day, we would pull out the blankets at home and build our tent house in the living room. We would sit under there and whisper and talk and tell secrets, sing, play games, etc.... until SHE would knock it over and we would get mad because you can NEVER get a tent to go back right once it's been knocked down. It just doesn't work as well.

- TREASURE HUNT: This game consisted of hiding random objects (marbles, fake jewelry, small toys) in the house and making a map for the other to follow to the treasure. I loved doing this and we even played this outside occasionally. We had fun ...until we couldn't follow our own map or remember where we had hidden the treasure. I think we would eventually find it at the bottom of our toy box on the next rainy day.

- PIRATES: This was like a treasure hunt, except mom would hide an unknown treasure (we didn't know what it would be) and make the map. Then, we could look for the treasure together.

It was fun and the treasure was always a surprise – usually a treat to eat.

- HIDE AND GO SEEK/TAG: These were our favorite games outside. However, it is not as easy in a small house with nowhere to hide. It was more of a quiet -game -with –evasive- maneuvers -game. The options were limited but we would try. Mostly, we would try to stay out of sight around a corner until we had a chance to make a mad dash to base or tag. We had fun ... until Mom got involved and reminded us to stop running in the house. Busted!

- PLAY IN THE RAIN: On a warm summer day and a gentle rain, like today, we loved to go outside. It was awesome to feel the cool drops against our skin. We would run in circles and giggle. We would catch the drops, splash in puddles, and play in the mud. We would wade in the bar ditches and float random leaves or paper as tiny boats. We would toss rocks to make a splash. It was fun and we never melted, drowned, or got sick.

- SIT AND WATCH IT RAIN: Sometimes, it was nice to just sit quietly and watch the rain. We would watch the drops splash in the developing puddles. We would watch the birds land and shake off the wet, then take off again. We would watch the cars go slowly by on the street, feeling hidden and snuggly in the dry confines behind our window. We would point out things and talk in hushed tones, as if the magic of the veil would be broken if we talked too loudly. And we would plot our next move... selecting from the list above... or to just sit a little longer and enjoy the wonder of it all.

Those were peaceful days, days when a nice rain gave you permission to slow down for a while. Days before everyone sat in their respective corners entertained by their respective electronic devices connected to their respective contacts. Days filled with adventures and challenges of our own making. Days of introspection and communication on a most personal level. Days to share and learn. Good days.

But, enough introspection for now! Dang this rain! Wonder if my internet is back up and running yet? I have Googling to do! Reminds me of that old television...

Second Verse, Same as the First

Annual Reflections Upon Standing in Front of a Mirror in My Birthday Suit

Sags and bags where once was tight,
Creaks and leaks and hazy sight.
Spots, dots, and peachy fuzz;
Clots, shots, and ears that buzz.
Wrinkles, crinkles and big blue veins;
Meds, dreads, and dribble stains.
Squishy and jiggly, floppy and droopy
Document the BP, heart rate, and poopy.*
Thoughts derail and leave the track
Or go in a tunnel and never come back.
Head too hard and skin too thin,
But no desire to begin again.
Golden Years have officially begun,
I can't wait until I'm sixty-one.

(*I was kidding about poopy... it rhymed with droopy. I dropped the line about 'having fits'... rhyming proved problematic.)

***

Sags and bags where once was tight,
Creaks and leaks and hazy sight.
Spots, dots, and peachy fuzz;
Clots, shots, and ears that buzz.

Wrinkles, crinkles and big blue veins;
Meds, dreads, and dribble stains.
Squishy and jiggly, floppy and droopy
Document the BP, heart rate, and poopy.
Thoughts derail and leave the track
Or go in a tunnel and never come back.
Head too hard and skin too thin,
But no desire to begin again.
Still tripping the light in ortho shoes
Dancing my way to sixty-two!

***

Blah Blah Blah...
Pain and swelling in my knees...
Think I'll just stroll to sixty-three.

***

Blah Blah Blah...
Let me sit a minute, maybe more
Then maybe I can crawl to sixty-four!

***

Blah Blah Blah...ad nauseum...
Barely hanging on, but thankful I still drive
I'll just take my truck to sixty-five.

***

O.K. Blah Blah Blah...One more time...
I'll grab my meds and mix my fix;
Primed, posed, and propped
to greet sixty-six.

THE END?? ('m hoping not.)

Seeing in the New Year

How did I "see" in the New Year? ... with one blackened eye and the other harboring foreign debris requiring professional extraction. Do you think it's an omen of things to come? Neither was of any consequence; however, if any inquiring minds want to know...

The blackened eye was the result of a common household injury; I hit my head on the towel rack going to the bathroom. Despite my daughter's argument to the contrary, I'm certain that happens to others all the time and all over the world. Well, maybe not Ethiopia or Bangladesh or Alabama. But a lot of other places. Like most people of a certain maturity, I make frequent trips to the facilities and usually more than once nightly. Do I ever turn on a light? No, I do not. I've never found it necessary to 1) subject myself to the inevitable retina burn or 2) be brought down the runway like a jumbo jet coming in for a landing. I'm usually persuaded to action by the gentle beaconing of nature's call - a slight nudge in the bladder and whisper in my ear, "OK, Hon...it's time." I get up in due time and make the trip to and fro in the dark without being fully wide-eyed. These are nothing more than an inconvenience and do little to interrupt my sleep. It works for me. At least it did...until that one time...

My dog had a call of nature of his own, whining and barking at the door. He never needs to be put out at night, so this abrupt interruption to my routine was a bit disorienting. I stumbled out of bed and trudged along sleepily to let him out, deciding I would take advantage of the situation and go myself -just in case I needed to go later. I call this activity "Bladder Banking"- to put some time on the old meter, so to speak and add some length to the fuse. I must have been more discombobulated than I thought; latitude was on target but I missed my longitude by approximately 2 degrees, hitting my eyebrow ridge full-force just above the outside corner of my right eye. I didn't turn on a light at that time either because I was distracted by the 'stars' – they were so pretty. Anyway, I continued to feel for blood, certain it must be gushing from an open skull wound. Satisfied it was not bleeding and simply a solid hit, I let the dog inside and went back to bed. The next morning, I had a shiner resembling a smeared, shaky application of blue eyeshadow and black liner...sort of the 'morning after' look. The fiasco was not without merit, though, providing additional fodder for my immediate monkey gallery. "How was that even physically possible?" "Did you turn on a light? No? Well, duhhhhh...". "Gee, Mom, your eye looks like a hooker's makeup on Sunday morning." I'm grateful for another opportunity to bring amusement to their otherwise mundane lives. They seem appreciative.

The debris in the left eye started less dramatically, a small speck of something carried on the ample breeze as I worked outside. Figuring it would eventually dislodge itself by the application of eye drops and the incessant blinking, I passed a few days looking like a battered boxer with Tourette's - one blackened eye and the other teary, twitching, and blinking involuntarily. I decided as the weekend approached and holiday Monday to follow, I would go to the optometrist so they could determine if there was actually something in my eye or merely a scratch. Either way, I was looking for some relief – the kids were starting to repeat their "poor old Mom" jokes.

I stopped by the optometrist's office without an appointment and they graciously worked me into their loaded queue. I was taken back immediately for an exam and the doctor arrived shortly. After pressing my face into the Dial-a-Goggle for a view it was determined I did, indeed, have something embedded requiring removal. She glided across the floor on her rolling stool (I felt a bit too gleefully and enthusiastically), waving a small sealed package in the air. "Don't worry! I have an extraction instrument in this little package that will get that out in no time. I'll deaden your eye first with some drops, then extraction. You shouldn't feel a thing. But...be very...very... VERY still. Don't move." After the drops were applied, I sat with my eyes closed in the dark and heard her ripping into the package. She rolled her stool even closer. "That should be long enough for the drops. Now...remember...don't move." I didn't and it was over in a matter of seconds.

"There! I got it!", and I felt immediate relief. As I sat there and blinked a few times, she rolled the stool back and away. "Hummmm," she said, closely examining the tiny source of all my recent discomfort. "I'm not sure what it is...maybe a seed hull of some kind? Want to take a look?" I focused in her direction to see what she had extracted from my eyeball and she was not waving some sophisticated, calibrated, and celebrated surgical extraction instrument. She was waving a big needle...like a big sewing needle...A NEEDLE! She must have seen the horrified look on my face; she shrugged and laughed, "yeah...it's like a big needle. I don't like to tell the patient that until AFTER..." And as I was processing that thought and leaning forward to see whatever she had removed from my eye...SHE DROPPED IT! Needle and all! "Ooops! Well, maybe it's still stuck on the end". She bent over, picked it up... then...DROPPED IT AGAIN! *What tha...?* She retrieved it a second time but, obviously, the speck was lost forever by that time. After her last instructions, I thanked her for her time and the immediate relief, paid for the service...and made a hasty retreat to the truck to check my eyeball in the rearview mirror. Yep. It's still there. Still numb. Still inflated and no blood. I was satisfied and drove away, feeling like my 'normal' self in just a few days.

So, I 'saw' in the New Year a bit battered. But also very grateful for my health (even an old weak bladder), my vision (old eyes, but I can still see the stars), my dog (UNLESS he makes a habit of waking me at night), a fumble-fingered doctor (she was steady when it counted most), and my family (who promise to provide the best care in my golden years, best care MY money can buy). It's all good! May you all be as blessed in the new year!

Shut Up and Eat Your Freakin' Happy Meal

I took my grandson (The Jonah) for a Happy Meal today, weather being as it was. Sitting in the play area, I soon discovered one thing that irks me more than kids and teenagers whiling away time on their electronic diversions; it's PARENTS WITH CHILDREN whiling away time on their electronic devices. Parents with small children who want nothing more than a few moments of focused attention directed toward them. Those parents and one parent particularly.

This gal's two kids (maybe ages five and three) made numerous trips from the playground equipment to her table, begging her to watch them play and climb. She never looked up from her phone or responded to them in any way, even as they stood hovering and chatting at her. Nothing. No, I'll amend that statement. The only time she made eye contact was when she shouted loudly (screeched) at the younger child for sipping from her drink! The mother grabbed the soda cup- "That's MY drink. You have your own coke. Go find it! It's wherever you left it!" After yelling rudely and waving them off, her attention went immediately back to the phone. They ran back to the equipment and climbed to the top - stopping at every level to look through the webbed enclosure and shout, "Momma! Momma! Watch! Look at me!" After one last poignant attempt to capture her attention, I could actually see the frustration in their faces as they climbed on - deflated, defeated, and disappointed. Sad.

How many precious moments with her kids will be wasted and lost? I wondered how long it will be before they stop asking her to watch? How long will they try to compete with the electronic devices for her attention before giving up completely? How long before negative and destructive behaviors result from her neglect and indifference? I'm thinking only as long as it is before they have a device of their own in which they, too, can lose themselves and not have to care.

No restarts or resets in real life. Sorry.

Snow Days in Texas

Weather is a topic of conversation much of the time in Texas. Most of you can relate to what I'm saying, but others may need a bit of guidance to relate. Much of the time conversations are centered around the heat - a short exchange at a checkout register, "Whew-Weeeeee, it's hot today." (Translated: Day 22 of 100 degrees or greater, I may have to turn on the AC and dig out my t-shirts). "Yep". (Translated: "I totally agree with your assessment). And many times the conversation is, "Shore could use some rain". (Translated: Day 97 with no precipitation, the coastal field is burning, won't get another cutting, will have to sell my cows, bankruptcy imminent). "Yep". (Translated: "Indubitably).

On rare occasions we go to sleep with our fans blowing cool air and awaken to rain and sleet blowing in sideways on a strong north wind, dropping temperatures, and developing frozen ice on windshields and sidewalks by noon. Days like this cause a real stir, especially in a school. The halls are buzzing with excited chatter, phones are ringing as concerned parents wonder if school will dismiss early, if the buses will run, if they need to come get their kids. Coaches call to discuss cancellation of pending travel and activities and other schools call to inquire what our plans for the day are looking like. The kids' first question, "is it going to snow?" followed by "can we make snow angels in this stuff?" They gaze in wonder out the doors and windows, amazed at the slightest accumulation of anything white on the ground or rooftops; the tiniest icicles are cause for celebration. The kids on my bus route were absolutely giddy on their short ride home this afternoon, animated and giggling and pointing out the smallest details indicating their little world had been touched and altered from the previous day by Mother Nature's hand. As I dropped them at home they each would try to make a snowball, only to watch the small granules of sleet fall through their fingers and blow away in the wind. They would try to slip and slide on the frozen ground, unsuccessfully, before skipping joyfully into their warm house.

Watching them, I couldn't help but be transported to another time and place and remembered how my sister and I felt on mornings like today when we were kids. Dad was Superintendent of Transportation for the school district. He and the District Superintendent made the decision on snow days as to whether it was safe for the buses to make their routes both to and from school. The phone would ring early in morning, waking us from a sound sleep. We knew it would be the Superintendent asking Dad's opinion. Robin and I would huddle together under the warm covers, whispering excitedly and wondering what the answer would be. Most times, Dad would talk to him briefly before getting dressed and leaving. We knew this meant he was going out in the pickup to drive on the streets and some of the worst county roads, checking for ice and accumulation before offering an opinion.

We would listen to the truck drive away, giggling and snuggling and whispering. We would venture a quick peek out a window and discuss our plans for the day. Morning cartoons and Slam Bang Theater. Hot chocolate and cinnamon toast. A snowman. Maybe we could make a sled and pull each other for a ride. Sometimes we would fall back to sleep but we always knew when Dad's truck came home. Then... those long, tense moments to follow. We would hear him stomp the snow from his shoes and his footsteps as he entered the house. We snuggled closer and got very, very quiet- covers pulled far over our heads. We listened to his steps as he walked to the phone in the hall. Dialing. Dialing. We clasped each other's hands and held our breaths. Waiting. Waiting. Daddy would hang up the phone, but we knew the routine. If he walked away from the phone it meant they had decided it was safe, school would start as usual, and we had just wasted two hours of good sleeping time for nothing. However, if he started dialing the phone it meant all our dreams for the day would come true.

We were quiet and still, our breaths slow but hearts racing. Anticipating. The first "*click*" of that old rotary and we would look at each other and hug, doing a happy snow day dance under the covers. I know now Daddy always knew we were awake, but he never scolded; he let us have our snow day adventure. And at that time, we felt special and invincible, privileged to be the FIRST KIDS to know there would be no school that day! Knowledge is power and for that brief moment in time we were queens of the kingdom. Even if we were the only two citizens of the kingdom and the only ones to know.

I appreciate the excitement a day like today brings. I enjoy the change in mood and conversation. I relate to the anticipation and the wonder of it all. I understand the kids wanting so badly to fashion a snowball from sleet and make ice angels and break a tiny icicle off the rearview mirror to watch with wonder as it melts in their hands. It's a rare thing and rare things are precious. Soon enough our conversations will return to the customary heat and drought and unrelenting sun.

And that day can NOT come soon enough for me! I hate winter, especially days like today. I said I appreciate and understand them... I never said I liked them.

Socks, a Simple Luxury

"There's my person without feet today". I half-mumbled this to myself years ago as my son and daughter and I got out of the car on the downtown square. She asked what I meant by saying that, as the lady obviously had feet. I explained the story of a man who once complained he had no socks until he met a man who had no feet. "When you're feeling sorry for yourself about anything, you can always find someone who has it much worse than you; it puts things in perspective and makes you feel better. You just have to keep your heart open to others around you." I don't recall after all these years why I selected that particular person to be 'my person without feet' that day. I only know they were struggling – physically, emotionally, or financially – to an extent the kids, upon further evaluation, understood exactly what I meant. My daughter would prove this to me years later as my mother had been admitted to the hospital- again. Although Mom fought another five years, I felt at that time she wasn't going to win the battle. My daughter came rushing up to me as I stood in the hall, not crying so much as tears rolling uncontrollably down my cheeks and not having had time to compose myself. She hugged me and whispered, "I'm sorry, Mom, you couldn't find someone without feet today." I smiled...

I've lived long enough I don't sweat the small stuff and consider most of it small. Last Monday I was in Logan airport for my 1,800-mile flight home from vacation. I live by a few simple rules when flying. First, I acknowledge all control of my immediate future was relinquished to the abilities and sensibilities of total strangers the moment I entered the security line. I accept if they (TSA) come toward me with a probe all I can do is ask, "is a 45 angle sufficient or should I grab my ankles?" Second, I must sit back and relax and have faith all will go according to plan...that Mike tightened the bolts and kicked the tires, Bubba threw my luggage in the underbelly, Chet and Biff in the cockpit are rested and sober and capable, and no one gave the controller a wedgie in the bathroom. Third, my ability to thwart a terrorist attack with a copy of Air Mall and a Styrofoam coffee cup before successfully landing the 747 is against all odds. Last, I accept the fact that the Indian/Iranian/Lebanese/Nigerian behind the counter (any counter) is void of both English-speaking skills and empathy. Acceptance of these conditions generally allows me to 'go with the flow' and enjoy the ride.

However, last Monday pushed my buttons in an unexpected way, testing my metaphysical timbre. As I checked in for my flight the lady-behind-the-counter informed me it was delayed an hour and we wouldn't depart until 12:45. I shrugged – an hour is nothing in 'travelese'. I found the gate with the other Texas-bound travelers and settled in. *Little did we know that one hour would eventually devolve into a five-hour delay before total cancellation, followed by an hour in baggage claim to retrieve my bag, four hours standing in ticketing to reschedule for the next flight...which would not be until the following afternoon with a 3 ½ hour layover in Charlotte, arrival at DFW at*

11:00 pm and Erath County at 2:00 a.m. NOT HAPPY! Additionally, as I had been texting with my sister all afternoon because my father was ill and at the doctor's office I was down to little/no power on the cell phone and no way to recharge it. I listened to the flight cancellation announcement as I read a text Dad had been admitted to the hospital with pneumonia and heart failure. What? This was not good! NOT GOOD! I frantically searched for someone...ANYONE... with no feet! ANYONE?

Five hours waiting for the flight had been ample time to familiarize myself with those around me. Four hours inching forward in the ticket line helped reinforce the assessment I shouldn't complain. I was calm and centered. I could look around me and see several families now stranded with exhausted, hungry children. I could see the elderly, tired and apprehensive. There were businessmen, nervous their life and livelihood would implode in their absence. First class and coach, young and old, fit and infirm – we had been equalized in the oddest, most unexpected way.

I had found my people with no feet when I needed them most, and I thank you. Thank you, Young Mother traveling alone with three small children, the youngest of which has medical problems. I wish you well and hope you made it home safely. Thank you, older woman who had a knee replacement two months previously and is scheduled for another soon. You bitched and whined and griped enough for the both of us. You got on my last nerve, but I hope you are back on your feet soon. And thank you to the Asian couple traveling with a bratty, obstinate teenage girl- and thirty pounds of frozen live lobster purchased at Logan Airport's Legal Seafood! I owe you a huge debt for helping me keep my chin up through the ordeal, knowing things could be much worse. I could have been sitting on $350.00 of thawing and soon-to-be-rotting crustaceans! So, thanks to you all for helping me through this most trying ordeal and helping me keep perspective. Thank you for being my 'no feet' people.

I wonder, though... Sometimes I get a creepy feeling that someone is watching me. And when I get that feeling I have to wonder if it's possible someone could be looking at me and thinking *'Awww....you poor dear. You're my inspiration for the day. I could be YOU!"* Is that possible? Do you think? Nahhhhhh!

Sorry, Not Sorry

In November I took a temporary position as a school custodian, working at night. After a few months it had become routine and I'll admit, somewhat of a drudgery, which I hope excuses the following account of my unprofessional lapse in ethical behavior.

Recently, I was trudging along and vacuuming a classroom for the umpteenth time that night and contemplating self-actualization - how exactly does one recognize that point in time when it is attained and if so, once realized, can it slip from one's grasp? Or I may have been thinking about how much it sucks to be me? I'm not sure... my thoughts jump around. Anyway, I was vacuuming and noticed a jigsaw puzzle on a table from the corner of my eye. *Hummmm...* I continued my vacuuming, but my eyes were repeatedly drawn back to that puzzle. It had two straight-edged pieces missing from the border. TWO, one on the left and one on the right. *Hummm... I wonder...should I? No! I shouldn't!* I abruptly turned my back on the puzzle and vacuumed to the door, the ethical argument still echoing in my head.

Finishing the task, I unplugged to venture forth down the hall on my path to self-actualization. However, like a moth to the flame, I was soon standing over that demon puzzle and ...BOOM! POW!... had those two pieces found among the chaos and placed in less than a minute! I felt like a genius! *Oh, yeah!* After basking in my victorious moment of glory, I turned and exited quickly, as if someone would see and report my breach of conduct.

I laughed to myself, however, because it reminded me of that pivotal scene from 'Goodwill Hunting' when the genius night janitor solved the math challenge on the chalkboard. I danced along on air the rest of the night, feeling much better about life in general...maybe even a bit superior! Those sixth graders never knew what hit 'em! **BOOM!**

Special Delivery

This is the first Christmas I have done most of my shopping online. It has been interesting to be on the receiving end of the various delivery services' deteriorating holiday spirit and waning enthusiasm. The first deliveries were brought up the drive to the sunporch, inside, sheltered from the weather and gingerly placed on a chair. *Merry, MERRY Christmas!* Then, they were brought up the drive but laid outside on the front steps or under the carport on the ground. *Have a nice Christmas!* Next, they could be found at the fence gate (but nicely wrapped in a plastic bag for protection). *Happy Freakin' Christmas!* Most recently, they seem to be tossed out of the moving vehicles at the gate and often in the middle of the driveway or in the grass (no plastic wrap, no nothin'). *Hey, Lady! I've got your Christmas right here!*

Bless the U.S. Postal Service! Perhaps it's their credo of "neither snow nor rain nor heat...", but I so appreciate their dedication to duty! Living on a rural route, we often have deliveries not fitting the smaller mail receptacle on the highway. We have several mailmen and each is so kind to bring such deliveries up the county road, down the driveway, and deposit the mail and package on a bench inside the sunroom porch. Every time. All year.

Amidst the throes of the recent ice storm there was an unexpected knock at the door; I opened the door to a postal employee, mail and package in hand. He had braved the slippery slope in true postman style -a cute, young man I had never seen before. I invited him inside to get warm, but he politely declined and kept his distance - a testament to his professionalism, I assumed. However, he acted very oddly. (Sort of like a guy going on a blind with a vision of the girl in his mind but when she opens the door and is nothing like he imagined and he can't hide his disappointment and awkward reaction or make his escape soon enough...sort of like that. I think. I don't know personally. It never happened).

Anyway, he continued to be extremely fidgety and nervous as he verified my address and identity, practically backing toward the exit as we spoke. I understand him being in a hurry to get away to his rounds, yet he seldom made eye contact. And, I noticed his weird, embarrassed side glances in my direction. Did he doubt I was being truthful? Was he that shy or socially inept? *Poor, dear.* I expressed my extreme appreciation to him for delivering my package so promptly. I excitedly gushed on and on about how I had been anxiously awaiting its arrival for weeks and was relieved to finally have it in my hands! Upon this declaration, he suddenly looked up and smiled at me slyly on his way out the door...an uncharacteristically confident nod of the head with an almost inappropriate smirk...two thumbs up! Weird! Right? Like we were in on the same joke. Strange fellow, indeed.

I looked through the mail on my way to the kitchen looking for any clue to his odd behavior. There was nothing, just a collection of junk mail and a few bills. Oh...and the package wrapped in plain brown paper, **SPECIAL DELIVERY from JoyToys** I had been expecting. The encounter was perplexing, though. I don't get it. Oh well, I suppose it will just have to remain a mystery. An enigma, for sure.

Stay on the Trail

I know my family (and others) wonder at times if my elevator goes all the way to the top floor. It's alright as I do little to dissuade their assessments, certain one day they will recognize my eccentric genius for what was and write a ballad about me. Meanwhile, however, they continue to scratch their heads and talk amongst themselves – no doubt discussing whose week it is to "keep an eye" on me.

One thing they question is my desire to work outside. I don't putter around in matching shorts and tank top, flip flops, and styling hat - sweet tea in one hand and phone in the other. Indeed, I don my torn and stained jeans, work boots, and leather gloves to hit the trail in search of sweat, scratches, and dirt. I have various motivations to spend my down time in such a way, but the one relevant to this discussion is the liberation of my mind from my body. Again, my family will laugh at this notion and snip, "What's the deal? You walk around all the time with your mind and body in different places!" To which I will reply, "Oh, yeah? Whatever!" – because I'm full of quick retorts like that.

For a more profound explanation, working physically in such a way allows my mind to go everyplace and/or nowhere. I can contemplate my navel or the circle of life, consider the validity of the theories regarding our search for self-actualization or wonder at the processes necessarily present leading to the discovery of fire. Conversely, my mind may pose questions as to who named the doodle-bug, why can't those adventurers on NAKED AND AFRAID have clothes and shoes when even Bear Gryllis is allowed clothes and shoes, or how big will my ears be when I die? Sometimes the thoughts bounce from one thing to another like a game of Plinko; other times, they get stuck on a theme like they're playing on an old scratched LP. Either way, my mind is occasionally not in the moment; instead, it's wandering and sniffing a trail much like one of Dad's old coon hounds, nose to the ground and oblivious to the surroundings and pesky interferences. Well, sort of like that; his hounds never left the trail to chase a squirrel.

I jumped on the tractor to finish a little shredding job. After completing that phase, I returned on the four-wheeler to continue the task of taking down an old barbed wire fence. I soon became agitated, however, dodging the same low limbs I had dragged myself under repeatedly on the tractor; I grabbed the loppers for a quick *snip snip* to rid myself of the inconvenience and nuisance they caused. It was only much later, as I sat down to cool and get a drink, that I noticed the yellow jacket's nest – just above where I was now sitting on the parked four-wheeler.

I marveled at my good fortune; I should have been stung repeatedly by angered, displaced yellow jackets as I had driven the tractor under that limb repeatedly and walked all around it snipping. *Wow, that's a huge nest! How could I have missed it? Oh, I must have been thinking about something else.* Sometimes it's good to evaluate a sequence of events and consider possible improvements should the situation arise in the future.

As I returned to the fence, cutting and rolling the old barbed wire and grubbing the decayed cedar posts, my mind sniffed out and returned to its meandering trail. I thought of others doing this kind of work on a hot afternoon. I wondered if their minds tended to wander hither and fro and if that's why they do what they do. Is that why my Dad could always be found out here until his body, worn and frail, trudged to the house to sit out his last days in a chair? And what did he think about as built these very fences I now so unceremoniously must take down, cutting the baling wire he strategically tied and ripping out the posts he planted? And what did he think about as he sat in his chair those last years- building these fences? I wished I had asked him these questions when he was around to provide an answer.

My mind continued further down the trail. How many more years before I have to sit and stare out the window and what will I think about then? And does this mind travel phenomenon explain how people run over themselves with their own tractor/shredder after years of operation? Or overturn their four-wheeler on the same property upon which they've run it for years? Or cut off their leg with a chainsaw?

Or perhaps even absent-mindedly thrust their face repeatedly into a yellow jacket's nest? I don't know but it's something to think about, right? And I will the next time I work outside.

But first, I have to make a trip to TSC for a new pair of work gloves. It seems I misplaced the left one. I remember removing it, thinking I didn't really need it at that particular moment and could do what I was doing just fine with only the right glove. Unfortunately, I removed it and can't remember where I took it off or where I put it. I must consider the possibility my mind was elsewhere and thinking about other 'stuff'. What? I just don't know at the moment. Maybe if I keep thinking about it... **SQUIRREL!**

Super Mom, Not

I did my Christmas shopping this morning...gifts and food items to prepare for festivities tonight and tomorrow. My family will tell you I don't usually procrastinate on the whole Christmas thing. Historically, I do all the shopping on the night BEFORE Christmas Eve. That's timely, right? Alas, I wasn't motivated last night so I waited until today. Christmas Eve! *sigh*

As I strolled the aisles with my detailed listing of items my mind drifted to memories of Christmases past, back in the days when I used to beat myself up for not being Super MOM! I have spent my time in the dark abyss cursing myself for not being more like *THEM*...the working June Cleaver types "bringing home the bacon and frying it up in the pan" moms, all with every hair in place and in a tailored business suit. Those moms having their trees up at Thanksgiving complete with handmade ceramic ornaments and knitted tinsel, a star they fashioned out of recycled aluminum cans in their spare time. Those moms with the gifts overflowing and spilling from beneath the heavily decorated limbs well before December, gifts gathered and wrapped throughout the year and successfully concealed in closets and attics and under beds. Those moms with the goodies wrapped in tight little parcels and jars for timely distribution to everyone from the CEO to the mailman. Those moms with the perpetual giggle in their voice and smell of vanilla. Those moms!

Yes, there was a time I felt inadequate and out-of-sync. Time and experience led me by the hand into a sense of peace and well-being with the realization of the following: 1) SUPER MOMS must be a myth. No one can be that efficient AND happy all the freakin' time. 2) I'm actually efficient as I am. I'd like to see a Super Mom get it all done in just half a day! On Christmas Eve, no less! 3) I never have the money to pretend like I have the money to spend on frivolities. 4) I spend quality time with my family throughout the year and buy 'things' for them as I want or they need. We are basically satisfied. 5) I did not raise petty children, jealous or envious of the possessions of others. I'm proud my kids would rather hang out with me than hand over a list of 'wants'.

So, yeah... maybe this is rationalization on my part. I know I will always wish I knew then what I know now; I honestly would have done some things differently. Some things better. I regret I wasn't perfect and made mistakes; I would do better if I had the opportunity for a do-over. However, I can only keep learning and do the best I can, be the best I can be. I'm hoping that redeems me for past lapses and inexperience. I hope, in some odd way, that comes closer to making me a Super Mom than imaginative wrapping and smelling of vanilla.

Sweet Rejection

I'm not an outstanding personality. I'm old, tired, and grumpy. I have no fashion sense and am only moderately attractive, meaning I have most of my teeth and hair. These characteristics precede me and I'm usually discounted, rejected, and invalidated immediately at (1) first sight or (2) the moment I speak. I accept this.

However, I spent 7 hours yesterday being observed and evaluated. I was paraded back and forth before well-dressed professionals numerous times, asked my opinions on serious issues, and discussed behind closed doors. I thought I truly had a chance. I was, after all, a finalist! Only after an entire day was I rejected and deemed unworthy! Imagine that! It took them all day to decide! I wasn't immediately turned back at the door or told the position was filled. It took them ALL day to decide I wasn't what they wanted or needed.

I can't speak for the other 78 people rejected in the jury pool, but I thought it was a very good day indeed! Thank you, Criminal Justice System, for the validation. I needed that! Maybe next time!

Surviving the Daily Grind

Perhaps my kids are right; they've been telling me I have a drinking problem. A little sip to get me going in the morning. Drinks throughout the day to keep me on track and moving. A full thermos or travel cup every time I leave the house. A tad nip in the evening to relax me for sleep. Some consider this excessive; I believe it to be basic maintenance and motivation to remain in forward motion.

Oddly, the kids don't perceive the quantity I drink to be problematic. They do, however, criticize the quality of what I drink and the modus operandi for procuring it. After the events of this morning, I've had to admit they may be correct in their assessment. Perhaps I do have a drinking problem.

***

I've been drinking coffee for as long as I can remember. It's what I do. But I've never been mistaken as a connoisseur of fine caffeines, a coffee bean aficionado, or a Starbuck's Diva. I've always bought store brand grounds in big gallon buckets - the cheap stuff. When the kids moved in (to take care of me), I was informed my coffee was swill and not suitable for human consumption. Alright. So we installed a coffee bar- a small bureau in the kitchen for the Bunn and a coffee bean grinder, shelves for 'fancy' coffee beans in bags and air tight canisters, a cabinet for travel mugs and thermoses, and hooks to hold our combined collection of prized coffee mugs. This is my new normal. I've accepted the changes without complaint, believing compromise to be the foundation for a successful venture into cohabitation. It was a generous gesture of good faith on my part, a sacrifice for the greater good. (Well, that, and because their coffee is actually so MUCH, MUCH better!)

The greatest adjustment, however, has been living in the same house with the grinder. I now must select the beans, open the grinder, pour the beans, grind the beans, transfer these fresh grounds into the Bunn...only then can I finally brew some coffee. I find this process to be extremely labor intensive and slow when all I want is a dang cup of coffee!

This is especially true in the mornings. Momma was the first to rise and shine; she hit the floor running and humming or singing a hymn or Frank Sinatra or some silly song of her youth; she never slowed down until she was the last in bed at night. Dad started on a slow roll and managed to maintain it all day. His mantra was, "if God intended for me to see the sunrise he would have scheduled it later in the morning". I'm not grumpy, exactly, but simply disheveled and disoriented. I don't care to be jolted awake, jump starting my passage from a blessed slumber into consciousness by something loud and irritating. (I've been single by choice for many years for a reason!) Also, cursing or stomping a kitchen appliance won't set my path toward a happy day! Finally, it's never a good idea for me to operate heavy machinery BEFORE I've had a few cups of coffee; I could lose a finger, maybe a hand. The grinder does sound suspiciously like that wood chipper from "Fargo". I dubbed the grinder FARGO - Ferocious Auger

Ripping Gnawing Obliterating. That image from the movie can almost put me off my morning coffee. Almost.

The kids have mercy and sympathy, leaving at least one cup of coffee in the carafe when they leave for work; that's just enough to get my eyes open but not quite focusing. To make additional coffee to get me started sans the wood chipper, I add a big scoop of my cheap stuff on top of their used coffee grounds in the Bunn's basket and pour some water through - a fast, economical, and safe way to get some more coffee flowing in my veins. They consider this plebe's brew to be disgusting and cheap, as they do my alternate morning method of scavenging leftover coffee from whatever source and heating it in the microwave. All to avoid the morning grind. Whatever.

This morning, after I drank the 'mercy' cup they had provided, I discovered my stash of 'Boone's Farm' coffee grounds was depleted. The canister was empty but certainly the gallon bucket was stored away. I searched and rummaged through the pantry, coming to the bleak realization there was nothing. Nothing. I glared toward the grinder with dread and loathing and thought, "It looks like you may get a finger this morning, FARGO! I've got nothing."

Then, suddenly inspired, I remembered the jar of instant coffee reserved for EMERGENCY ONLY situations stashed behind the canisters of beans. (Considering instant coffee my only choice for a morning beverage addresses my level of desperation.) I reached behind the coffee bean bags and canisters and filters, feeling around blindly for the distasteful jar of java. My heart filled with joy as my fingers grasped something unexpected. A sampler of coffee perhaps? I then remembered my son had sent some Kona coffee samplers home with me when I visited him in Hawaii. "I thought we had tried them all but must have missed one! "YES!" It wasn't precisely the shape and size of most coffee samplers and the contents were a finer texture. However, being from Hawaii I accepted it would be packaged differently. I squinted my eyes tightly and the graphic of a Hula dancer came into focus...and eventually the word, 'COFFEE'! That's all I needed to know. I was ecstatic, a morning catastrophe narrowly avoided.

I pulled the basket and added some of the Hawaiian blend to the older used grounds, poured some water into the machine, and anticipated enjoying a unique gourmet coffee! "And there's enough left to share with the kids later! They'll be so surprised!"

The aroma of brewing coffee filled the air. I sniffed deeply. "Odd, yet familiar aroma. What is it? Cinnamon? Chai? Hazelnut, perhaps." It didn't have a bad aroma, just not quite the coffee I'm used to drinking. I was puzzled but undeterred, anxious to have another cup of hot coffee and get my day started.

I poured a steaming cup, still intent on identifying its unique bouquet. I lifted the cup to my lips and took my first sip. "Hummmm..." I hesitated before taking another sip. "Maybe the taste will improve as I drink more and get used to it? What IS that smell? Is my tongue starting to tingle?" I continued drinking, although I can't say I was enjoying it. Actually, it was a struggle to continue but I was determined to drink it...and like it.

Eventually, as I neared the bottom of the cup I started to feel a burning sensation in my mouth. "O.K. The coffee has some spice or pepper added, perhaps something exotically Hawaiian! How exciting!" I finished the cup thinking, "But, it really doesn't taste very good. And my mouth is on fire! It's alright, though."

I poured another cup, still uncertain I could drink it. "Maybe if I knew what this mystery smell is and what's adding spicy heat I could enjoy it more?" I grabbed my reading glasses and began exploring the label. I read it twice. Twice, to be sure there wasn't a mistake. It seems I had infused my morning brew with some Hawaiian coffee and spices, for sure. However, it was coffee and spices meant as a rub for grilling chicken or pork. UNCLE'S LU'AU COFFEE RUB! It did have a hula dancer pictured on the label. It did have 100% Kaua'i grown coffee. Also, paprika, sea salt, sesame seeds, garlic, onion, and a variety of other things...but, all organic!

So, yeah, I had been drinking stuff meant to be rubbed on a pork's butt. "Well, that's interesting,' I thought. "I KNEW it had coffee in it!" No, I didn't drink any more of my special Hawaiian brew. I was oddly wide awake and up to the task of facing off with FARGO...first thing after I brushed my teeth and drank a lot of water.

I'm sharing this SNAFU with you, but please don't tell my kids. This will only serve as more ammunition, another reason for them to insist "See? This is why you need a keeper!" I, however, insist I'm fine. It was coffee...sort of...so, I was right. And all organic ingredients, so that's good. Also, I don't have a drinking problem; I do have a slight eye issue, but nothing drug store readers hanging on a string around my neck won't fix. And as a super bonus, I have some nice Hawaiian rub to try on our next pork loin. I'd say it was a productive, yet fairly uneventful start to the day. It's all good!

Texas Sized Blessing

May there be no surprises when tha morning sun rises
And it finds ya fit as a fiddle...
Yer barbed wire stretched tight, yer buckle bright,
And yer table piled high with good vittles.
May yer chickens be layin' and yer mule be brayin'
And yer outhouse stay upright in tha wind...
May tha crick never rise, possums leave fruit for your pies,
And tha hawgs stay put in their pen.
Corn with no crows, no weevils in the boles,
The skunks always spray downwind,
Yer hoss never buck, or yer pickup git stuck,
And yer Skoal stays fresh in the tin.

May your boots always shine as they scoot with the line,
Yer churn overflow with cream,
Tha catfish be bitin', the flies never lightin',
Yer Wranglers stay strong in tha seam.
May yer gravy be lumpless, the back forty bumpless,
An' ya never see yer cuzzin on 'Cops'...
Ya know when to hold 'em, never have to fold 'em,
And yer ol' barn be bustin' with crops.
May the herd keep growin' and blue ribbons when showin',
May tha kids remember to close the gate,
Yer hounds stay sound, nose to the ground,
And your twenty-two always shoot straight.
May yer life never be lackin', yer latigo slackin'
Yer John Deere never fail to start;
Yer pumpjack keep drillin', the banjo keep thrillin'
And love stay hunkered down in yer heart.
As day turns to night and tha cold wind bites
May yer woodpile be always stacked high;
Good health, good kin, good wealth, good friends
And may ya always keep your powder dry.

Thank You, Antique Roadshow

DURING THE SPAN OF TIME THAT IS MY LIFE THUS FAR, I HAVE:

- Pulled my hair out and split a few; won (or lost) by a hair; let it down and blew in the wind.

- Had my nose out of joint or to the grindstone or in somebody's business;

- Kept my ears to the ground or peeled; been up to them with work or crap or whatever.

194

- Had my mind frazzled, boggled, and blown; been out of my mind, at wit's end or mentally drained.

- Seen things I would rather forget & hard times; looked until my eyes crossed and before I leaped;

- Seen the light but not the forest for the trees and didn't see it coming.

- Watched the world go by, my Ps and Qs, my mouth, my step, and my manners;

- Screamed my head off and talked until I was blue in the face.

- Muttered under my breath & whispered sweet nothings; voiced opinions; kissed off a few.

- Held my tongue, bit my tongue...even swallowed my tongue;

- Bit my lip, sealed or smacked them; kept a stiff upper one and dragged the lower one;

- Bit off more than I could chew; or the bullet or nails; chewed some fat.

- Made it by the skin of my teeth; kicked in the teeth; teeth gritted or gnashed.

- Swallowed my pride; ate crow or my feelings; chomped at the bits; spit into the wind;

- Whistled Dixie in the dark or through my hat; spoken out of turn; sometimes put my foot in my mouth.

- Took it on the chin; held my chin up; made it by the skin of my chinny- chin- chin.

- Turned the other cheek or spoke with my tongue in my cheek; danced cheek to cheek.

- Been slapped in the face; had stuff thrown in my face; dealt with two-faced; faced the music.

- Necked and stuck my neck out while avoiding the appearance of it being too stiff;

- Kept my shoulder to the wheel; carried the weight of the world, sometimes a chip; invited others to cry on them.

- Had my arms twisted and been up in arms; pulled myself up by my bootstraps; patted my own back.

- Rubbed elbows and bent a few, been up to my elbows and used a lot of grease;

- Been handy; hands up, hands down, and hands out; busy hands, idle hands; hands tied, hands slapped.

- Worked my fingers to the bone and stuck them in many pies; twiddled them and sat on them; shot a few.

- Had my back up or against the wall; backed into a corner and had to back up or down or out;

- Had my heart broken and the heart to do it again; it has stopped, raced, skipped a beat;

- Been punched in the gut, sick to my stomach or had it tied in knots; butterflies;

- Shook my bootie; dragged my butt and had it kicked, sat down, chewed, and a fire lit under it; took it up the WaZOO; had a cob up it; unsure whether to wind my butt or scratch my watch; kicked some and took names.

- Been brought to my knees, knock-kneed, weak kneed, and knee-jerked.

- Had my leg pulled; been on my last one before, given a leg up.

- Kicked up my heels or had something nipping at them or dug them in.

- Hot-footed it, pussy-footed it, walked in others' footsteps.

- Tippy-toed, twinkle toed; had mine stepped on and stepped on a few.

- Stepped forward, one step at a time; backtracked; stepped out in good faith;

- Stood... up, back, down, over, side by side, on my own; walked on pins and needles.

- Ran the extra mile; wore others' shoes; stayed the course; leaped to wrong conclusions.

- Tested the waters and jumped off the deep end.

- Stayed in line or stepped over it, maybe toed; marked my time; hopped to it; kicked against the goads;

- Ran in circles and out of gas or on empty; jumped through hoops; reached for the stars;

- Danced a few jigs and to a different drummer.

- Knocked down, knocked over with a feather; knocked up; run over; pulled in all directions.

- Rolled over by a steam engine; thrown to the wolves; tossed aside; exhausted my options.

- Made mountains out of molehills and climbed out of holes I dug.

- Tossed cookies and thrown fits; caught hell, raised a little, gave a little.

- Green with envy; red-eyed, red-faced; brown-nosed; yellow-bellied; blue.

- Weighed options and measured my words; counted the costs and counted my blessings;

- Backed up to punt; struck out and hit a few out of the park; took hard hits and scored a few touchdowns; been beaten to the punch, against the ropes; won some hands; slam dunked.

- Chewed, screwed, and tattooed; rode hard and put up wet; pulled through the keyhole backwards.

- Side swiped, rear ended, broadsided; hit head on and from behind.

- Left once, right often, forward seldom, and backwards occasionally; mostly centered.

- Lit a shuck; burned the midnight oil and the candle at both ends; tried to let my light shine.

- Worn; worn down, worn out; beat up; beat down; put through the wringer.

Excuse me if my patina is showing and offends you. But I've earned it - every wrinkle, crinkle, crease, and scar; every gray hair, age spot, creaking bone, and medical bracelet. Besides, it adds greatly to my value. I learned that on the Antique Roadshow!

The Apprentice Goes on Tour

Clearing the briars, brambles, and barbed wire on the farm...also known as my escape and reflective time. It seems I've spent a lot of time out there this year, escaping and attempting to make sense of this cluster commonly known as 2020. I consider myself 'essential personnel' reigning over this Empire of Dirt, so social distancing and staying home has not been a huge sacrifice; I've tried to do my part as requested. Scratches, sweat, thorns, and poison ivy seem the better choice if the only alternative is to go 'out there' into the ether. Also, it keeps me out of trouble and gives me something constructive to do outside. And time to think.

The past two weeks since the 2020 election and ensuing drama have given me much to consider as I've snipped, hacked, and shredded. As I attempted to think through the events and make sense of the current state of affairs, one thing became evident to me: Donald Trump spent 15 years hosting *The Apprentice* and it was a grand stage show of things to come, a glorified and extended dress rehearsal for when he took his show on tour to Washington, D.C. It's even had commercial breaks and scripted dialogue. Wow. Think about THAT... the past four years have actually been a filmed reality show, 24 hours a day, 7 days a week, not including Trump Twitter time! And we all had front row seats!

For the conspiracy theorists out there, look no further than the similarities. *The Apprentice* and the Trump Presidency were both 'reality' shows, though that basic premise continues to be denied by those behind the scenes and closest to the action. Both were televised to the masses, designed to entertain the demographics and desires of the perceived fan base. Both were presented by Donald Trump, produced by Donald Trump Productions, and hosted by Donald Trump. *The Apprentice* was based in Trump Tower and the Presidency was based in The White House, another similarity too obvious to reject or ignore. Donald Trump commanded the Board Room, President Trump commanded the Oval Office. He was flanked (*The Apprentice*) at crucial decision moments by his advisors, consisting of familiar loyal family members (Ivanka, Eric, or Don, Jr.) or an occasional outsider considered worthy. Oddly, he often ignored the advice of his own panel and proceeded as he wanted regardless. Seems familiar?

A true conspiracy theorist could not discount these additional similarities between the two Trump productions. During his tenure in both shows, Trump featured and promoted his properties, products, and brand and those of his 'advisors'; drama was encouraged, controversy applauded, and ratings(popularity) continuously scrutinized. Disloyalty, confrontation, and aggression among the ranks was a necessary part of the contest as a sacrificial offering(s) would be required. The various tasks *The Apprentice* contestants undertook had actual measurements and statistics to objectively evaluate success or failure, interspersed and often supported by the opinions of experts in the field. In the end, however, all eyes turned to the CEO sitting in the big chair behind the big desk; he had the final word and total discretion in all decisions. Yep. I see the pattern.

Additionally, the premise of both shows centered around controversy, competition, confrontation, backstabbing, backbiting, and undermining. Each episode ended on a negative note as a lone weary combatant entered the Board Room to be interrogated, intimidated, humiliated, and berated by the CEO. Then, with the point of a finger and a smile, the CEO would wave the contestant away from his presence in a dismissive gesture and the words, "You know what? I don't like you. You're fired!"

So, yeah... I really believe I'm onto something. The past four years have been a staged production. Will there be spinoffs? Sequels? Will there be reruns in syndication? *The Apprentice* had a long run and spinoffs and reruns are streamed in syndication. So, maybe? Probably. It's impossible to predict because the final episode in the White House production has yet to be written. The previous episodes were real cliffhangers - considerably more substantial and consequential in scope than the popular, "Who shot J.R.?" We remain tuned in, hoping for a nice ending and final credits to run.

It would have been helpful if the last minute of the last episode of *The Apprentice* presented in the following way: The contestants were all lined up before the big man in the big chair behind the big desk, flanked by his 'advisors' and yes men. He is looking down from his perch, loudly berating them all - exposing their weaknesses and insulting their intelligence. He intimidates, threatens, belittles. Finally, one single person steps forward. She points her finger at him and looks him in the eye. With a strong, courageous voice she yells, "You know what? We don't like YOU and we took a vote. YOU'RE FIRED! Leave the Board Room." Reality imitating fiction?

Unfortunately, that scenario never happened and it's a pity. It would be informative to have seen and documented his reaction and how he made his final exit. If so, maybe we would now know how this White House Trump production is going to end. I do know, however, it will not have a happy ending. It can't. It's not an option. It's not in the script. This will remain a sad, embarrassing time in the annals of American history. There is no pride to be had. No one will walk away from this show unscathed. There will be no happy dance, no cause for celebration. We can only continue to tune in, sitting idly as we anticipate a slow fade to black.

I'm tired and ready for the final curtain. CUT! AND THAT'S A WRAP! Bring on 2021!

The Gambler

Our eyes locked briefly over the gaming table. He had insisted on dealing, but I was fairly certain he had just switched the top two cards in the deck to his advantage. *Should I accuse him of cheating? What if I'm wrong?* Rather than make a hasty accusation, I decided to ignore it and play on. He dealt a few more hands and I was slowly making progress. Then- it happened again! I saw him stealthily switch the top cards. Oh, it was slick! Very slick, indeed! But I saw it and couldn't let it go. I didn't want him to think I'm a mark for his con; I'm not some naïve and inexperienced patsy. We exchanged a few words. Although he never admitted to any sleight of hand, he assured me it would not happen again. We proceeded.

Soon, however, he dealt himself a card he didn't like, a hand that would have most likely insured my victory. Realizing this presented a problem, he ignored the draw and began shuffling through the deck in search of a card he liked better. "Foul," I shouted! "You can't do that! You have to play the hand you were dealt." He ignored my exhortation and continued shuffling through the deck, soon finding a card more to his liking; he played it. "No! You can't do that!" Without a word, he tried another card. "No! You can't keep doing that, just looking for whatever and changing cards. You have to play what comes up! I know the rules and that's against the rules! That's cheating!" He realized he had met his match! He accepted he wasn't going to win- the argument or the game- so he mumbled something about being tired, folded and left the table.

Granted, most times I would have insisted the game be finished. I would have extolled the benefits of fair competition and good sportsmanship. I would have expounded on the premise civilizations rise and fall on the tides of integrity, competition, and achievement (defined as successful completion of tasks). Tonight, however, I won Candy Land by default against a four-year-old and I'm quite alright with that. Quite. Alright. I can put it away for now - in a deep corner of the dark cabinet or high on a shelf far away and out of sight. It's finally over and I won. I'll save the lecture for another time.

The Only Good Mouse Isn't

Getting older has its perks. It's expected you might forget your pants, dribble coffee down your front, or pee yourself occasionally. It's quite liberating and one could say I'm living the dream. Additionally, I find it interesting how maturity (or knowledge or experience) has altered my attitude and approach to certain things in life. I will resist the temptation to go into my customarily long monologue at this time and stay on point. You're welcome. Perhaps some other time.

As I was clearing some briars while enjoying the sunshine this afternoon, I was suddenly confronted by what I call a rodenta gross-maximus- commonly referred to as a mouse. I don't like mice. I have an irrational fear of mice and I know this on a conscious level. I don't know where/how I developed such a phobia to the creepy, disgusting, rodent. I only know I have no real fear of any other critter walking, slithering, swimming, crawling, or flying. Just mice. When I see a mouse my skin crawls. My reaction is a total visceral, psychological, and physiological mandate for flight. A fast-forwarded newsreel plays rapidly through my mind – visions of death by bubonic plague, trash piles teeming with rats and mice, marauding mice masses munching food reserves, and a malicious mouse army led by " Ben" gnawing through my bedroom walls to devour me in my sleep. And THAT'S before I lose rational thought. Those closest to me know this and expect I would have screamed like a girl upon my encounter today, ran in place before directing my jog to the truck, locking myself inside for protection as I convulsed in a full-body shudder, and vacating the location indefinitely. I did not. I stood my ground. I have 'matured'.

I may have matured but not to the extent of my dear friend, Dannah. I recall a time several years ago when the entire county was experiencing a particularly prolonged and destructive siege by these disgusting creatures. Homes, schools, and businesses were waging war by any means possible- and losing. I found it all very traumatic. Paranoia had me in its grip, making it difficult to eat or sleep or work without continually scanning my surroundings. And what was my dear friend doing as I existed in this phobic state, resembling a pathetic Chihuahua nervously shaking and shuddering through a thunderstorm? The blessed bleeding-heart tree-hugging hippie was sneaking around and releasing them back into the wild at every opportunity. She was even peeling them off sticky traps (I still can't venture to imagine that process). Perhaps that kind of maturity will only develop when I, too, reach a certain advanced age. Maybe I'll be just like her when I grow up. I can hope.

Unfortunately for the mouse I encountered today I have not yet attained such a state of benevolence. Instead of the customary 'flight' as the newsreel spun darkly through my mind, my response was 'fight'. Fight, I did! I reached out and bashed his dark, beady eyes and nasty buck-toothed face with the business end of my pruning loppers, flipping its graveyard dead body unceremoniously aside. SCORE! I did a victory lap around the tank dam. I did! And I felt great. I had finally faced my deepest, darkest fear head-on and won. I stood my ground. I stared into the disgusting, evil face of that devil on earth and laughed "Ha! Ha!"

Please, don't judge me harshly. I realize the nocturnal creeper was probably jolted from a sound sleep (dreaming of its midnight marauding). I realize it was lethargic and just sitting there on its hairy haunches (planning its strategic attack against me, like which leg to gnaw off first). I realize I'm much larger (which only means I can never enter his house through a hole no bigger than a dime and creep about, spreading nastiness and pestilence). However, the only guilt I feel is that of depriving some deserving snake or hawk or coyote of a little snack tonight! Vini, vidi, vici – rodenta grossmaximus – vini, vidi, vici!

WARNING: A mouse was tragically killed in the making of this story and may be disturbing to some readers. Sorry. (Uhmmm... I suppose I should have mentioned that in the beginning?)

Things Nasty Bumping in the Night

It was 1:00 in the morning and similar to trying to go to sleep in a cheap motel! You know? When there's a rhythmic SLAP! SLAP! SLAP! against the other side of the thin wall... SLAP! SLAP! SLAP! Pictures are shaking and light fixtures swaying and just when you think it will stop and you can go to sleep...SLAP! SLAP! SLAP! And you want to knock on the wall and yell but realize it would do no good so you pull the pillow over your head and try to ignore it. SLAP! SLAP! SLAP! It was like that!

I had already been up to investigate the source of the disturbance and found it to be loose sheet metal on a little gardening shed. The wind was howling, blowing at 20 mph with occasional hardier gusts, and I had concluded there was nothing to be done until daylight. I went back to bed. However- that incessant SLAP! SLAP! SLAP!

Then, I started to visualize that piece of metal being torn from the roof and blown into the carport. I could imagine the conversation the following morning as my daughter peeled that metal off her new car and assessed the scratches and dents. How would she react when I reported nonchalantly, "yeah, I heard that thing flopping in the wind and wondered if this might happen? But I was, you know, sleeping and stuff. Shame..." NO! I couldn't live out the rest of my life with that hanging over my head. I jumped out of bed and dressed, grabbing a penlight (yes, a penlight) on the way out the door.

I first retrieved the extension ladder. It's amazing how much lift-in-duced drag an aluminum ladder exhibits in conditions of high wind velocity; I almost went air-borne a few times. (Note to self: Check into this phenomenon next time it's windy and I have more time to ex-periment. Perhaps jumping from a roof with the ladder tied across my shoulders like wings...?). Anyway, I finally got the ladder to the shed and extended it a couple of rungs above the roof. Something was wrong. I turned on my penlight and discovered I had the ladder upside down. Silly me, but it WAS dark. I wrestled with the ladder some more in the wind, finally managing to flip it around, and tried again. It still wouldn't work. The wind was blowing the metal up with such force it was repelling the ladder, tossing it backwards from the shed. Even as I stepped on the bottom rung with a haydite block, the lighter top of the ladder would get violently pushed back. SLAP! SLAP! SLAP! *Sooooo... no. Just no. Even I ain't that dumb.*

Realizing my first attempt would not end well, I decided to slide the ladder atop the roof to weigh down the flopping metal. *Why didn't I think of this before?* I walked it around to the back of the shed (the shortest side) and gave it a big push upward. Third attempt, *Bulls eye!* I was feeling fairly accomplished...until the next gust lifted the roof, ladder and all! The ladder slid across the roof like fingernails on a chalkboard, adding a high-pitched, shrilling screech to the SLAP! SLAP! SLAP! in the darkness. *Urghhhhh!* It was sounding more and more like a cheap time on the other side of the tracks.

What to do now? I can't physically throw these blocks up in the dark and hope they don't come down on my head! That would be irresponsible! Then, I remembered Captain Jace (my son by another mother) had been working on a project and had been using a step ladder. Trusty penlight in hand I retrieved it from the other side of the house, observing its lift-drag was not nearly as significant as that of the extension ladder. (Note to self: Don't jump with the step ladder. It won't work.)

I set the ladder against the shed, realizing I now had a six-foot ladder and a ten-foot roof. Factoring in my height, I calculated if I climbed to the rung next to the top I would be high enough to set the blocks. Next, I had to calculate the correct distance from the edge. Too far away and I wouldn't be able to set the blocks on the roof. Too close, and the flopping sheet metal could mangle, possibly rip off, my arm or any sundry body parts which might be flopping around in the wind. After calculating and shifting the ladder a few times and checking the balance, I grabbed a haydite block, turned off the light and began my assent.

It was only as I stood at the top of the ladder, haydite block in hand, I realized I had forgotten to consider one tiny additional thing. The SLAP! SLAP! SLAP! of the metal echoing in the darkness like the chomping jaws of a ravenous, robotic crocodile reminded me this job needed much more than a few thoughtful calculations. I stood there atop the ladder in the darkness and realized I would need to calculate the rhythm of the wind. How could I know how long the jaws would stay closed and at rest? How could I know when the metal would be caught by the next gust of wind and its mighty jaws fly open again?

How could I know when it would come crashing back down, bearing razor sharp teeth primed to rip and tear into flesh?

I pondered my conundrum and shrugged. Nope. I couldn't outguess the whims of the wind and had to add a measure of HOPE and FAITH to the calculations. I waited for the SLAP! SLAP! SLAP! to stop and hurriedly tossed a block with the hope the timing would be right and faith the weight adequate to hold until I could get clear of the metal. It did. I placed three more blocks with no problems and nothing was heard but the howling of the wind. Like Tommy Boy, I had a plan! It's all good!

Now, to address the elephant in the room and defend against those who will reprimand me for failing to awaken others of the household to assist (or even perform) the task:

I considered it as an option. However, my belief is there will be plenty of opportunities in the future for my kids to get 1:00 a.m. wake up calls. Best case scenario: I'll ring my little bell and yell from the basement, "Hey! I need a drink of water!" or "I can't find my glasses!" or "where's my teeth?" or "I need my diaper changed!" Worst case scenario: My kids assured me when they were teenagers (after pointing out I would be in the third phase of Alzheimer's before anyone would detect a problem) that they would provide me the very best care in my golden years...THE VERY BEST CARE MY MONEY COULD BUY! Well, I've been thinking about the future and realize I may have saved enough for a weekly visit from Agatha Trunchbull. She will come in, raid the refrigerator, and slap me in the back of my head as she tells me to sit up straight and stop drooling! However, best or worst case...I'm protecting my options and banking my markers.

In the meantime, I may be found wandering around in the dark occasionally or driving a tractor or perhaps testing aerodynamic lift-to-drag ratios with a ladder on the roof! Please be assured I'll be calling when I really need something! So, get your sleep for now; you're gonna need it! There will be plenty of opportunities to express your love and devotion. I promise to tell you when it's time to reciprocate for all the sacrifices I have made on your behalf. The blood. The sweat. The tears.

The money. I will be certain to remind you I looked death in the eyes to give you the gifts of life! Know it! I hope this makes you feel better!

Things We Do for Love

Dad calls me every night to report "Kay, this is your Daddy. It's 8:32 and I'm sitting on the side of the bed, lights are off, and I'm ready to lay down and pull up the covers." I know it sounds like he got a recording but I actually answer and we say our 'goodnights' and converse briefly after this little ritual commentary. He does this EVERY night per my request so I don't have to go back down to his house to ensure he hasn't fallen before bed and will lay there all night. We all agree whatever happens beyond that point just happens…at least for now.

Last night (Christmas night) he reported for bed duty at the customary time. I was glad since everyone had left for the day, my kitchen was clean, and the house was nice and cozy and warm. I had just sat down with a cup of coffee when the phone rang at 9:30. It was him. "Kay, this is your Daddy. Something is banging and scratching and clawing under the house and sounds like it's trying to tear the siding off. It started right after I went to bed and I've been up three times. Can you come down with a gun and make it stop?" My mind protested, *Whut? Get all dressed and layered enough to go out there into the cold and dark to what?… what is it exactly he's asking me to do? Crawl on my belly under the dark house…in 25 degrees to go after God-Only-Knows-What is banging and clawing and scratching under there? Flickering lantern in one hand, knife clinched in my teeth, waiting for some red-eyed demon to drop from above and claw my jugular? Will he even remember I'm under there when the sun comes up in the morning? How long before I'm missed?* My mouth said, "sure, Dad, I'll be right there!"

I walked around the outside perimeter first to see if anything was digging or if something else could be banging on the house. He had mentioned the noise before, so I had previously closed any possible security breaches and checked for limbs or bushes or mops hitting against the house. The security check yielded nothing so I went inside. He was impatiently waiting for me. Fortunately, he did NOT expect me to go under the house to confront the demon. Instead, he wanted us to replicate the scene of the past few nights so I could hear the noise he had been hearing. To do this it would be necessary to fool the Entity into thinking Dad had gone to bed (this is when the critter wants to make itself known). Dad said we needed to turn off all the lights and sit quietly in the living room... and wait. So, I grabbed a cup of coffee and sat with him in the dark and silence for 30 minutes waiting for the BEAST to animate. When nothing happened after 30 minutes Dad said, "This is not very productive. I'm going to bed. " And he did. He grabbed his flashlight and walker and toddled off to bed...leaving me sitting there in the dark!

Boy oh boy, did I feel foolish! But not as foolish as sitting there for another hour...alone...in the dark... hoping to hear some monster-yet-to-be identified clawing its way into the living room. Or not as foolish as checking the perimeter once more at midnight in the freezing cold. And probably not as foolish as scavenging the frozen yard for materials to prop open an access door and provide an escape for the Creature from the Black Lagoon living under the house. And I'm thinking not as foolish as poking my head under the house, shining a flashlight around and hoping something didn't claw my face off. And most definitely not as foolish as mentally calculating exactly how wide an opening to leave- *too wide and I'll be inviting even more critters in from the cold and have a bigger problem...too small and it defeats the purpose.*

As I was on my knees out there- midnight, freezing, arguing with myself about the size of the gap in that stupid access door- it suddenly occurred to me that these are the times I will miss most. It's these times of inconvenience and discomfort offering the smallest amounts of happiness and peace to the man who has given me so much! My butt was freezing and my toes were certainly verging on frostbite. However, the realization provided an overwhelming, encompassing warmth against the cold. *Merry Christmas, old man... Sleep tight...and do NOT under any circumstances let the bedbugs BITE!*

This Blows

How does one spend a windy, overcast, and much-cooler-than-they-said-it-would-be Saturday in which the grandson (my playmate) is out of town?

1. Note the aforementioned weather conditions and sleep in later than usual
2. Waste entirely too much time on FB defending the position 'my time is very valuable'
3. Iron a patch on a nice pair of jeans I ruined with battery acid (Note to self: convert these jeans to work pants because they no longer look nice, even without the scorch marks
4. The wind reminds me to school myself in the art of making wind chimes
5. Go to workshop and gather whatever odds and ends I can scavenge to fashion wind chimes
6. Go in house and eat soup from the can as I watch an episode of Forensic Files (Note: weather hasn't improved)
7. Return to workshop and get entirely too engrossed in the project for too long
8. Note the sun is finally out but I'm too close to finishing to quit now
9. Finish the chimes (Note: the wind has finally stopped blowing)
10. Hang chimes anyway
11. Stand there and make them chime by slapping them with my hand...hard
12. Go check the skunk trap (Note: No skunk)
13. Move the trap
14. Return to workshop
15. Straighten the workshop (which means gathering every tool I own,

left scattered making chimes)

16. Go inside house and cut the always much-too-long laces on a pair of worn out tennis shoes to wear around the yard when I piddle (Note: I discovered laces having greater cotton to nylon ratio will ignite when melting a frayed end)
17. Put out fire (s)
18. Note: Think what a wonderful and productive day it's been thus far!
19. Note: Miss my grandson and our Saturday night date; wonder what to do next
20. Note: I still don't hear wind chimes! Maybe tomorrow.
21. Note: Consider the irony of making wind chimes when I absolutely detest the wind!
22. Eat tuna from a can as I watch an episode of Forensic Files.
23. Watch a few more episodes of Forensic Files, eating ice cream from the carton layered with caramel sauce and chocolate sauce and whipped topping, low-cal cherries thrown in for color.
24. Note: Hope Jonah comes home tomorrow
25. Return to FB with this list to prove my "my time is very valuable"!

Titanium Crystal

Mom had been moved home, on hospice, to die. She had passed many years battling a battery of serious conditions and illnesses, all with strength, grace, and humor. She took her last breath, brutally unexpected in timing and finality, sitting upright with a smile and words of thanksgiving on her lips.

***

A crystal – fragile, brittle, and time-worn.
I sit here holding your frail, transparent hand by the dim light.
You're so easily bruised and broken.
Life has chipped away at your edges; I see the fractures

Yet you continue to capture the least ray of light
And send back sunshine and all the colors of the rainbow.
How do you do that?
How do you give back more than you take?
We've tried so many times to fix your cracks, mend you -
But the supplies continue to dwindle.
How much more super glue and twine and duct tape ...?
What keeps your heart beating?
How do you glitter, though battered and torn and scarred?
Suddenly the wind, cold and brutal, crashes through the door and
I rush to hold you tight, desperate to shelter you -
No, hide you from its savage grasp.
I close my eyes and hear the crystal shatter within my embrace
And your breath fades, carried away on the wings of death.
I don't want to be alone in the dark.
I don't want to feel the dust sift through my fingers.
The torrent quickly passes and I realize only the broken fragments have been
Sifted and whisked away - like chaff on the breeze.
All that's beautiful remains with us – the spirit – your essence...
The brilliant crystal that will neither shatter nor fade.
You remain in your place of honor, esteemed – our treasure -
A precious gem reflecting light from darkness and shining on our lives.
Thank you, God. I understand.
...but I miss you, Mom... just the same....

To an Armadillo

I shredded an armadillo today. It wasn't with a fork in a 'Hey, kids, we're having tacos tonight!' way...it was in an unintentional tractor-shredder way. I was shredding a particularly overgrown portion of

212

acreage heavily choked by briars and bramble knitted tightly through the remains of small trees, long dead and fallen. Having pulled free as much of the dead wood as possible, I prepared to shred the small area of briars and move on to the next gnarly area in the same way. The land is too heavily overgrown with hidden rocks/stumps/holes underneath to responsibly drive through; I have to clear a small area of obstacles first, then back the shredder into the area previously prepared. I had started the tractor and made a few cuts when I heard the unmistakable THUD of something under the deck. I knew...just knew... it was something of flesh and bones and shuddered at the thought.

I immediately disengaged the blades and raised the deck as I drove a short distance, glancing the lacerated body over my shoulder. Poor guy. I jumped off the tractor and stood over his mangled body. After a respectful moment of remorse and horror... 'Why didn't you run, Raul de Armadillo? Hide? Move? You had to know I was coming your way; it's not like I could sneak up on you!' Having pinned blame for his untimely demise squarely on the dearly departed Raul, I picked him up by the tail and walked down the fence row a bit before unceremoniously tossing him over and into the field for the coyotes. 'Stupid armadillo,' I thought, 'you won't have the guts to do that again.' And turned to return to the work at hand, 'I'm sorry'.

My mind drifted and meandered down various trails for the remainder of the afternoon. I couldn't casually shrug off the fact I was the instrument of Raul's destruction. I admit I've shot a few varmints in my day after they refused other forms of encouragement to relocate. I've even shot a few armadillos if they continued to ignore my pleas to stop digging in the flowers and shrubs or under the house. As a general rule, however, I don't kill anything with malice or evil intent - even snakes or spiders. The exception to this would be the desire for total eradication from my sphere by any means possible - the disgusting scampering, gnawing, pooping, beady-eyed, and whisker-twitching rodent. I would shred them all and good riddance! I thought of the

Robert Burns poem 'To a Mouse' I read in High School British Lit. For the less nerdy, a farmer inadvertently plows through a mouse's home in the winter, destroying it and sending the little rodent scampering away in fear to a certain death with no food or shelter. The farmer lamented his part in the destruction; all living things, even the smallest creatures, are simply struggling to survive. I never understood the poet's wimpy brooding over a mouse. Perhaps if he had written "To an Armadillo" I could have related, because I found myself being pulled into a melancholy and philosophical funk as I worked.

I'm certain Raul didn't awaken this fine day expecting it to be his last hurrah. 'That's the way it usually happens, Raul. We never know when a crazy old woman with a shredder will appear out of nowhere destroying our Paradise or taking our life, metaphorically speaking. 'You never know,' as my Mom would say. That's why I tried to always tuck my kids into bed with a smile and send them off with an 'I love you' and a hug. I never wanted us to part with any tension or unhappiness between us. Is that too fatalistic an approach to daily life, to expect the best as you're also mindful of the worst? No, I think it's realistic and somewhat comforting. If the Great Shredder takes me today, I want those left behind to know those were my last words to them. And to this day, Raul, although the kids are grown with families of their own, we always exchange those words. My sister, too, and her family... We are all connected by the same philosophical dogma. "Depart on a high note because it may be all she wrote!"

To some, Raul, this is weird and unnecessary. To us, it is pragmatic and emotionally comforting. Maybe this approach began with my grandparents and that's why it runs so deep? It must have been planted and nourished from a belief that each new day is like a bronc; you always hope you can jump on, hold it by the mane, and ride it into the sunset. However, you also realize it has the potential to buck you off, kick you in the teeth, stomp you into the dirt...then trot off into the pasture with its head high and tail swishing. The grandparents raised families (including my parents) during the Great Depression. I'm thinking this was a life laden with hardships they couldn't have anticipated when they married. The maternal grandparents roamed in search of employment- picking cotton, trading and bartering their way across West Texas. The paternal grandparents scratched out their existence dryland farming, gardening, and raising chickens on the very same dirt on which I now find myself shredding. What they had in common was the knowledge each new day had the potential to bring complications unforeseen and undesired. Perhaps a job would no longer be available or the sky wouldn't rain. Either way, they must have lived each day with an optimistic hope for the best tempered with a touch of anticipation and preparation for the worst. Certainly, the children raised in this manner would adopt that approach to life. Not fatalistic. Simple reality.

Additionally, I doubt when my parents married that they could have anticipated the hardships soon scratching and gnawing at their door. Serious health issues shrouded my Mom and newborn brother, issues taking years to resolve in a manageable way. That same shroud draped over my Dad, the resulting financial and psychological woes determined to pull him under; each day was a fight to stay focused and afloat. I was born six years into this struggle and my sister two years later, and we lived it for an additional eight. We were unaware of the details at that time, sheltered from as much insecurity, stress, and poverty as was possible to provide. We were unaware of just how easy it would have been for my Dad to institutionalize my Mom and brother, put my sister and me into an orphanage, and walk away from it all. We were unaware how easy it would have been for my Mom to surrender her fight and fade away into her dark place. We were unaware of how much they both had to continue the struggle each day, holding on to the progress they made yesterday, fighting for a better today, and preparing for tomorrow's unknown battle.

We were aware, however, that we were loved and cared for. We knew that much when we had to occasionally stay with grandparents or uncles or family friends for extended times. We knew when we went to school. We knew when we were tucked in to sleep. We knew because they never failed to give a hug and say 'I love you' when they parted. They gave us that to hold on to, Raul, perhaps because it was all they had to give. They gave that until their last breath and I still cling to those hugs and I love yous.

My kids, too, had to learn too young how quickly life can pelt you with a load of lemons. In an ideal world, they would never have had to question a parent's devotion or have their world shaken, their hearts broken. They wouldn't have had a crash course in how to make lemonade and build a stand to serve it. They survived battered and torn, yet stronger with the realization that life can throw a curveball at any time; it's best to expect it and hope you can snag it, sidestep, or at least protect your face. All that can be done is control what's within our power, value what's most important daily, and keep hope alive for a better tomorrow.

So, Raul, I suppose that's why we continue as we always have – unashamedly ending phone/text conversations on a positive note with 'I love you' and personal hugs until we meet again. You never know. As Robert Burns continued the poem, ``the best laid schemes of mice and men go often askew and leave us nothing but grief and pain for promised joy". I know you can relate to those sentiments, Raul. I know I can. The farmer concluded his thoughts with how lucky the mouse was (the one whose house he had just destroyed) because all the mouse had to worry about was the present day. The farmer, however, had to look back to sad memories and forward into a fearful future. What a gloomy man, Raul! We wouldn't want to invite him to our New Year's Eve party, right? And talking to a mouse makes me think he may have been a tad wacky doodle.'

It was getting late and time for me to head to the house. I stopped briefly, 'I'm really sorry, Raul, for shredding you today and wish it hadn't happened; you deserved better. It wasn't a great day for us, was it? Somewhat traumatic. But I do have hopes tomorrow will be better. Well, for me anyway. Not so much for you...because you're dead and stuff. Sorry again'. And as I turned the truck toward home and rode into the sunset, 'I love you, Raul... Hugs'.

To Everything a Season

The grandson and I settled into the comfy recliner, giddily anticipating the rousing sights and sounds of Saturday morning cartoons on Nickelodeon. We were greeted, however, by a colorful frozen image on the screen and an irritating instrumental lilt. I initially assumed they were experiencing technical difficulties or perhaps a modern 'test of the emergency broadcast system'. Bummer. We'll wait. But upon closer evaluation, I realized the message was informing viewers Nick programming was suspended in honor of International Play Day. *Play Day?* It added, "We are going outside to play and so should you!" with a list of suggested outdoor activities. I admit I felt scolded and a bit of a sting, like a slap across the face. Who couldn't agree with their message or not support their intent? R*ight on, Nickelodeon! I hear ya! AMEN!* I considered my options and took drastic measures. I did what any loving, considerate and responsible Grammie would do- I immediately turned OFF the TV- then, accessed our inventory of Paw Patrol recordings, turned the TV ON, settled back, snuggled closer, and passed the chocolate milk! And it was awesome!

Perhaps I should feel guilty for my actions? Or lack of actions? I do not. Did I fail to mention we had just come inside, hot and sweaty... after almost two hours of yard work and playing? First, we played hide-and-seek. Then, tag. Followed by tag/hide-and- seek. Then, freeze/hide-and-seek/tag. Lastly, zombie/freeze/hide-and-seek/ tag. That means you hide from the zombies and when they find you, you get tagged but then you are frozen and can't get unfrozen unless the zombie hides and then yells 'Marco' and you yell 'Polo'. Then you unfreeze and you can be the zombie. Or something like that. So, sorry Nickelodeon and International Play Day. This Grammie had to sit down... and she liked it! And she will probably do it again...if that rascally zombie will just come back here and unfreeze me.

Tomatoes Gone Wild

I've heard several gardeners of some experience heaping lamentations over their tomato crop, or lack thereof. I actually planted two vines this year and have harvested exactly one and a half tasty tomatoes. Although the vines are still healthy and loaded with fruit only time will tell if the sweet talk, cajoling, weeding, timely watering, and loving caresses will have been enough to see a gratuitous return on my time and effort. I have, however, discovered something which may help us all as we anticipate planting a fall garden.

First, let me say I don't usually complain about things for which I volunteer (e.g. rising in the morning, wearing a bra, yard work) ...but these wild morning glories can eat my grits! They're a pain, especially when they multiply in the wrong places; the rain and temperature this spring seem to be exactly what they needed to pop up everywhere - uninvited and abundantly. I spend more time dealing with them than I'd like to admit, but it keeps the recurring nightmare at bay. You know... the one where the prolific vines creep under the doors and around the windows and down the chimney and up the pipes and through the ducts as I sleep, silently crawling along the floor and up the bed and walls before totally enveloping me in a fatal embrace and choking the life out of me ...only to be found in the morning with delicate purple flowers blooming out my ears and nose? Remember carnivorous Audrey II? The creepy trees in 'The Wizard of Oz'? The bean stalk leading straight to a mean giant? The mysterious pods in 'Invasion of the Body Snatchers'? Plants can run amok and get all crazy!

I was surveying my empire of dirt this morning and wandered into a basically neglected corner of the yard. I noticed a heaping mound of the tenacious morning glories and started pulling and yanking - kindly reprimanding and suggesting they go somewhere else and DIE DIE DIE! I was tearing and ripping and snipping when I suddenly stopped, glimpsing something through my rage as oddly familiar and out-of-place. *What? That looks like a tomato vine leaf.* I yanked some more morning glories away. *And that looks like tomato blooms!* After more carefully peeling away another layer of the dreaded weed vines I saw them... *Green tomatoes? Tomatoes!* And several of them, at least a number equaling the ones on my pampered vines! A volunteer tomato vine, most likely from a seed from last year... a seed lying dormant and surviving all the extreme elements this year has rested until conditions were right for it to present. *Whoa!*

I stood there a moment, considering how such a specimen found its way here. Discarded rotten tomato? Not likely. Perhaps carried here by a bird or animal? Maybe. Or possibly eaten and left here as a fertilizer 'deposit' -a deposit by a bird or animal, not ME! (I don't do that in the yard...YET). I considered the location and finally concluded the most likely scenario included tomatoes, water, and a kitchen sink. I won't say any more lest I attract the attention of the FEDS and have them all up in my business. Just know, it's truly remarkable to have it geminate and survive to this point - neglected, untended, and under a virtual blanket of morning glories. And if it survives my indelicate efforts to liberate it from the choking grasps of the Hedge Bindweeds I may have enough tomatoes for a BLT! Unfortunately, I'm betting I roughed it up too much and now the sun will beat it down the rest of the way. It was, after all, doing quite well without my interference.

If it thrives, we may need to reevaluate the loving care and attention given to our gardens. Perhaps we tend them to death with all our fertilizer and water and pampering. Maybe all we need is to toss random stuff in the yard and forget about it. That's my kind of gardening!

Turkey Should Come in a Can

I'm not a lot of things and a fine carver of meat could be counted amongst them. Every holiday I could easily convince anyone sitting at the table my platter of turkey and/or ham was the product of roadkill – looking like it was hit by an 18-wheeler, closely followed by a funeral procession and pack of Hell's Angels before I came along and scooped it up with a seed fork! I watch the commercials and see the magazine pics. I know what it's SUPPOSED to resemble. I carefully read the carving instructions and reference them throughout the process yet it never works out the same for me.

I've tried a variety of things over the years in an attempt to hone this particular skill. I tried an electric carving knife once but it looked like I graduated from the Leatherface School of Carving – the fine art of carving meat with a chainsaw. However, I don't think that fiasco was totally my fault. The stupid knife had two blades moving in different directions simultaneously and I never could figure out which blade I was supposed to be following. Forward or backward? Up or down? And they gyrated at break-neck speed; I couldn't keep up. Fail.

The next year I decided to slow it down and use ONE blade – ye olde manual, non-electric kind. I realized halfway through I probably should have taken the time to check for sharpness and perhaps hone a blade just a tad. My effort looked like I had invited Jose Cuervo to my carving party- like maybe he got there a little too early and maybe things got a little out of hand- like maybe we strung a turkey piñata from a tree and took turns blindly hacking at it with a baseball bat- like maybe what was plattered looked like limp piñata remains we scooped up from the ground! So, yeah, not one of my better efforts. For that, I blame Jose. Bad Jose. Bad.

My family has always said I should NOT be around sharp objects and will cautiously take it from me if they see I have one. But, for my next experiment in the art of cutlery I had no choice but to exercise great care and sharpen my knife properly. Covert operations in the late hours. I honed and honed, then honed some more; In time, that blade could split a hair. Truly. I know because I tried it. The result? Hannibal

Lecter would have been absolutely giddy at the sight of all my blood-dripping from the multiple cuts pooling in puddles on the floor and Helter Skelter on the wall and smeared on the countertop, drawers, and cabinet doors. Fortunately, I got the mess sopped up just before the family arrived. No one asked why I wore pink rubber gloves through dinner. I suppose they were distracted by the surgically precise pile of whittled flesh set before them on which to nosh... unsightly, yet tasty... especially with some 'fava beans and a fine chianti. `

Last year I decided I needed an arsenal of blades. And Zen...lots of Zen. I would let logic be my guide while supplementing the world view with my intuition and artistic soul. I would FEEL the turkey...BECOME the turkey...listen to it and become one with its rhythm. I'd let it speak to me and guide my hands. I gathered the blades and carefully arranged them side by side. Butcher knife, frozen food knife, paring knife, bread knife, cleaver, steak knife and butter knife. Then, I waited and listened. And waited. And listened some more. I finally heard the turkey whispering to me and started cutting.

I thought it was the turkey but I may have been mistaken. The last thing I remember was picking up the cleaver and chopping away in a frenzy as I hummed "Lizzie Borden took an axe and gave the turkey 40 whacks". At least 40, maybe 41? I was eventually jolted to my proper mind and surveyed the damage. Every knife in the arsenal had been used and left haphazardly about the kitchen. Except for one, plunged deeply into the door facing and still vibrating. Sadly, the turkey looked like crap. However, on a positive note, I must say I've never spent a more Zen holiday! I still pick up that cleaver occasionally and wallop on some random object. They're right... Zen can take you to your happy place! Happy, happy, HAPPY!

Which brings me to this year. My Son by Another Mother fetched the ham and brought it to me. He must have sensed how I struggle with the carving (he's very intuitive that way) because he provided me with a PRE-CUT spiral. *Pre-cut? Seriously? Who knew?* I'm sure he was thinking there's no way I could make a mess of that. One would think. I read the cooking instructions very carefully. I prepared it for the oven exactly as directed. I calculated the precise time, preheated the oven, and set the timer. I stood in front of the oven and removed it just as the buzzer sounded. I read through the carving instructions AGAIN while the ham cooled, submitting the schematic provided on the label to memory. I smiled as I gently lifted the hunk of meat to the cutting board, feeling confident victory was finally mine this year!

I soon realized this was not going to end well as anticipated. For one thing, the first step was to cut 'around the bone'. The picture shows a little round spot in the middle to be the bone. I located that little round spot and plunged the knife in per instructed...only to hit more bone hidden underneath the surface. So I moved over a little to a different spot and plunged the knife in again... only to hit bone again. And AGAIN. AND AGAIN! I admit I may have gone a little Norman Bates on that butt! "Don't panic," I thought. "You've got this," I thought. "No! Step away from the cleaver!" I thought.

I decided to approach the project from a different angle. I would slice the ham in a logical manner, remove the ham in chunks, and then simply separate the precut spirals! Which brought me to the second dilemma. The instructions also didn't mention how the slices would stick together when cooked nor how thin they would be. Seriously! Does anyone truly cut their ham in 1/16" slices? El Zorro? Freddy Krueger? Wolverine? (He can slice through my ham any time! Yummy!) Perhaps THEY can separate each slice without having them fall to pieces in the process. They. Not me. Is there an actual family out there carefully forking over a 1/16" slice of ham before passing the plate? Do the diners then slowly and deliberately cut and chew each bite? When asked if they would like seconds on the ham do they reply, "Oh, no...I couldn't possibly have another. I'm stuffed"? If I so desired I could have read a Good Housekeeping article on "How to Carve the Perfect Ham " through those slices. I didn't desire.

So, yeah... I got a little angry. And maybe I got a little carried away as I started hacking and slapping that ham in big honking chunks on the platter. Perhaps some may judge me harshly for not being able to dissect a pre-cut ham for proper platter presentation. But I know my family. And I know how we eat when we get together for that purpose. One foot on the floor. Basically, if it can't out-run us or out-talk us and goes fairly easily between the shoulders it's game on! It's going down! So, no one criticized my bad carving job-they never do- and that's just one of the things for which I give thanks every year at this time. They accept my shortcomings and failures and mistakes...and love me just the way I am. Or at least they keep their criticisms to themselves. How blessed I am. How grateful! But it doesn't mean I won't keep trying. Note to self: Next year, try wearing a frilly apron and high heels. It seems to work on the commercials.

Virgin No More

I was hacking through a particularly dense growth of briars and brambles today, lost in rambling thoughts and humming 'Master of Puppets'. Snipping and grubbing with sweat beading on my brow and trickling down my neck, I found myself thinking about my first time. First times are almost always the most special. It wasn't anything I had planned and wasn't emotionally prepared for what happened. I remembered how nervous and awkward I felt, unsure what to do with my hands or how to act. But afterwards, breathless and sweaty with heart pounding and ears ringing, I knew it had been the right thing to do. It was awesome! I was sorry when it was over, exhausted and worn, but knew I would most certainly be doing it again every chance I got. My first was truly an experience and a memory worth sharing!

My first was the Metallica Sanitarium Tour, 2003, Texas Stadium, Dallas. My kids knew I had an infatuation with Metallica; neither of them understood it, but they tolerated and accepted it. They scolded me often, though, "Mom, we are the only kids that have to tell our MOTHER to turn down the music! It's embarrassing." They knew I had never been to a concert before, never considered it something I would want to do. My son, however, scored two tickets for the concert and gifted me with the opportunity. He couldn't go (possibly embarrassed to be seen with his Mom?) but my daughter agreed, somewhat reluctantly, to go with me. I was almost fifty years old - an age when you have to consider if an activity is age-appropriate. Actually, the decision is usually based on two things: it's age appropriate if you really want to participate and 2) it's not age appropriate if your body isn't feeling up to the challenge and wants to take a nap. Anyway, of course I wanted to go.

Stephanie and I got up that Sunday morning and headed to the city. We wanted to get there early to ensure a good spot for viewing the concert and to see the featured bands opening for Metallica. It was going to be epic! After driving two hours and maneuvering through city traffic we finally saw it - the dome of Texas Stadium! Metallica! We parked the truck and entered the venue to stake out our place in the sun. Literally. High noon in the middle of a football field. In Texas. In August. It was awesome!

We were among the first to arrive and opted to get as close to the stage as possible. We staked a place at the barricade separating the mosh pit from the rest of the venue. It stretched the width of the field, made of cheaply constructed wooden panels in six foot sections and four feet high. It wasn't anything fancy but we called it home for the next several hours. The crowd slowly gathered throughout the afternoon and we watched as guards constantly turned concert-goers away from the mosh pit. They repeated time and time again how the pit required a special ticket for entry. A short argument would ensue but the hopeful encroachers would retreat, disappointed and mumbling as they left. This scenario repeated time after time all afternoon, the mosh pit wannabes becoming more aggressive and vocal as the day wore on into night.

We stood vigil at that barricade for six long hours, taking turns with bathroom and snack breaks or to stroll around and take in the sights. As the crowd grew larger and louder we guarded our place with due diligence, keeping at least one hand on the rickety barricade at all times. The stands and 'floor' began to fill with fans closer to my age, obviously die-hards coming only to see Metallica and having no interest in the younger, newer bands. We listened and watched - the stage, the crowd, the spectacle that was a Metallica concert. Band after band, hour after hour - and the stadium filled as the time slowly approached for my boys to take the stage. We were wearing down, for sure, but the anticipation and excitement kept me going strong. My daughter, however, relied on hard-headed determination to keep her standing there, refusing to give in to the heat, noise, and fatigue. She was a champ! My hero!

Suddenly, the lights dimmed and the strains of a most familiar tune filled the air. I recognized the music from a CD the kids had given me and knew what to expect. I was almost giddy. There was to be an extended, melodic introduction to build anticipation. The intro would slowly crescendo for a time before exploding into the loud, pulsing beats of Lars's drum, the electrifying riffs of Kirk's guitar, the throbbing rumble of Tru's bass, and James's powerful voice and presence. Foreplay was over; it was time to get down to business and drive it home!

I don't know what first made me feel something else in the air at that moment, something besides the obvious excitement and anticipation. Mother's intuition? What kids now describe as 'spidey sense'? Survival instinct? But something didn't feel right, something was off. I could feel the hair on my neck creeping and a tingle running up my spine. I could hear shuffling feet and muffled voices through the din, nothing specific enough to create alarm. But I was suddenly uncomfortable and certain we were in harm's way.

I instinctively shifted my stance to stand behind Stephanie, between her and the crowd. I grabbed the top rail of the barricade with my hands and wedged her between it and my body. I yelled in her ear, 'Grab the barricade tightly and don't let go of it. Hold on. Something's not right!' At that moment I began to feel the push of the crowd against me - pushing and pushing; pushing us forward against the barricade. We set our feet firmly, grasped the rail tightly, and started pushing ourselves back against the force. I heard shouting and rustling feet behind. Although I couldn't make out words or see anything, I just knew a significant push was coming as some overly anxious fans were determined to rush the mosh pit.

We held our ground and pushed back with all our strength, but our efforts were useless against the press of the crowd. The barricade very soon toppled forward and we were forced over with it. We lay there helpless, my daughter pinned beneath me and against the boards of the barricade. I could see rushing feet stepping around and over us, tromping across the fallen barricade on their way into the pit. The fear of injury or worse was very real. It's amazing how many thoughts flashed through my mind in that brief moment. Then, as quickly as it started it was over.

We struggled to our feet in the dimmed lighting, the musical intro just beginning its crescendo. Stephanie was terrified, tears streaking her face as I frantically checked her for injuries. A flustered guard joined us immediately, pulling us aside and checking for blood and broken bones to determine if we needed medical assistance. She assured us repeatedly she was fine, not injured, only shaken and needing a moment to compose. I watched guards escort a few dozen rebels from the mosh pit. Thankfully, it had not been an organized action by the masses but a half-hearted effort by a few. I assumed most of the younger disgruntled were too drunk or high to rush the pit and the older die-hards too tired to care. It was our lucky night, I suppose.

I suddenly realized we were actually IN the pit, knocked and pushed into the very pit which had been the source of such contention all day. I thought it a bit humorous and mentioned that observation to

Stephanie, in case she cared. She didn't. So, I reminded her Metallica would be taking the stage any second and we needed to go find another place to watch. She didn't care about that either. I was at a loss as to how I should proceed. What should I do? Where should we go? Our assigned angel in a guard's uniform returned and told us we were absolutely to stay in the mosh pit for the duration of the concert; it seemed they suddenly had some openings! What? Seriously?

I was ecstatic at the thought, ready to rock and roll! No harm, no foul! Steph, however, was still doubled over and breathing deeply, red-faced, but finally settling down. The crescendo was reaching a fevered pitch, the crowd yelling, the lights starting to flash and pan. I bent down and yelled in her face, "Are you going to be alright? I mean, you're not bleeding and there's no apparent bones sticking out. Metallica is coming on stage any second now. We've waited all day for this moment. Do we need to go? Or can you tough it out a while longer?" My daughter, bless her - she slumped down, back against the wall, and waved me away. "I just need a few more minutes to calm down and cool off. I'm going to stay over here by the wall. You go ahead."

So, I did. I left my daughter -traumatized, bruised, exhausted, and gasping for air- propped against a wall in Texas Stadium so I could watch Metallica take the stage and rock my world for the next two hours! Shouting! Devil horns! Rocking! Seeing the boys up close! First time AND doing it in the mosh pit! It was spectacular! So, perhaps it wasn't the most maternal thing to abandon her under the circumstances. Perhaps it was a bit selfish. Perhaps I got a little carried away in the excitement of the moment. In my defense, though, you don't always make the wisest choices the first time.

*FOOTNOTE: I am not a monster! Stephanie actually rallied rather quickly that night. She soon joined me on the mosh pit floor and we finished our long, hard day as it had begun - together. However, the trauma must have affected us both deeply and for quite a while afterwards.

Fifteen long years would pass with no mention of concerts. Then, 2018 and Pink and Beautiful Trauma World Tour! Ironic and poetic, don't you think - Beautiful Trauma? I took it as a sign to try the concert thing again! I love Pink! She loves Pink! American Airlines Center. Indoors and air conditioning. Chairs. Mostly females, mostly dressed in pink, mostly whispering quietly amongst themselves; feather boas, balloons, cotton candy, and white doves. Yes, please! I treated us to that most special happening, finally compensating her for the brutality she endured for me all those years before- the long hours standing in the heat, the noise, the drunken crowd - oh, and that pesky little mosh pit episode. Pink, as always, was AWESOME and FANTASTIC! I think all was finally forgiven.

And, no regrets the morning after! I'd do them all again. One at a time or all together! They are my affairs to remember!

Waiting for a Lift

I don't particularly like elevators. I don't like to be locked inside a confined space much like a water closet or be suspended in mid-air by a metal rope; or watch the doors closing on life as I know it, sealing both me and my fate inside; or the slight jolt at the beginning and end reminding me my safety is dependent upon electrical, digital, and mechanical components performing in unison; or the groaning sounds of the cables and pulleys as if gasping "too...heavy...can't...do...it"; or all the buttons, many with graphics I don't understand. I especially don't like the signs I do understand — like in case of a fire 'this' or in case of an emergency 'that'. And I usually count heads and estimate weight on the hoof before fully committing to participate in the elevator experience with a random group of germ-laden strangers. I usually take the stairs. I need exercise.

Recently, however, I was with someone at a hospital and opted to take the elevator. There were no others waiting and we were only going from the first floor to the basement. I considered it worth the risks: only one floor to fall, if stuck it would be with only one person, AND there was a fully staffed medical facility nearby. Also, I had accompanied him to the hospital for scheduled physical therapy due to a serious injury and considered it bad form to abandon him there. I pushed the 'down' button and waited. And waited. I checked the floor status of the elevators and waited some more. I didn't want to be one of those impatient people incessantly stabbing at the buttons and pacing, giving the appearance their time is more valuable than everyone else's. I calmly stood my ground and smiled, mentally enumerating the ranking of possible catastrophes causing the delay. Then, my mind started to wander:

Is there such a thing as an elevator control center? Where would it be? Is there like a Captain watching monitors and listening for alarms if something goes wrong? Maybe he would answer the elevator phone if I call. Or maybe there are hidden cameras; is that how they would know if the weight capacity is exceeded? I glanced around nonchalantly, looking for cameras and resisting the urge to scratch my butt. *No cameras but that's a nice graphic hanging there. I'm not sure what it is but the colors are nice.* I nodded casually to my friend and turned my attention back to the elevator. *So, how does an elevator know on which floor it stopped? What if it skips a floor? Do the light bulbs behind the buttons ever burn out? Are they hard to change? You probably have to take the elevator apart to change them if they do. That would be a cool job.*

And we waited; I started reading elevator signage. It was then I noticed the sign shared here. It was from Building Management. *Who is Building Management? Is that you, Captain Elevator?* It was basically a sign saying the elevator met all elevator requirements and inspections, including addresses and phone numbers to file complaints, etc. blah, blah, blah. It ended with a Braille message, a message I assumed repeated the same information- but for the visually impaired to read and pass time should they find themselves stranded and waiting for the elevator to appear.

Cool! Braille! Like most people, I'm sure, when I see Braille I pretend I'm blind and try to decipher the message. When I have to wait outside the bathroom at Whataburger I close my eyes and touch the sign, wondering if those bumps actually translate WOMEN or MEN. Maybe. Maybe not. Or maybe they're clandestine messages between foreign spies, exchanging plans or maps or formulas. I wonder why a blind person would ever be in the predicament of having to discern which door exactly is the bathroom door? Does no one offer to lead them to the correct door? Or do they lead them in the general direction and leave them to fend for themselves, saying," I got you this far. Now YOU figure it out!" *It's an odd place for Braille, I think. Almost as odd as on the ATM machine in the drive-through lane at the bank...driver's side. Weird.*

We continued waiting. *How would a blind person even know there are signs? Would someone tell them, 'hey...there's a sign here you might want to read. It's from Building Management and looks important.* Assuming they found the message and actually started reading it... how would they react when they got to the bottom where the sign has obvious, visible damage...those random cracks and creases among the raised dots of Braille? I'm thinking a blind person would quietly back away from the elevator and tap, tap, tap that white cane to the nearest stairwell! They would rather risk falling down a few steps than take the elevator as, obviously, *Captain Elevator has failed to maintain the sign declaring all 'is in fine working order' in fine working order.* Irony? I think so. *It's like being greeted by a cleaver wielding, three-fingered chef at the teppanyaki table at Benihana.* I wouldn't want to see that. It's a matter of trust.

PS: Fortunately, the elevator finally came just as I exhausted my thoughts and ways to occupy the time. I stepped aboard and am glad I wasn't plunged one floor into a fiery abyss. It's all good.

Welcome Home

Life is full of mysteries. I don't mean the little moments like "I KNOW where I parked the car so how did it get all the way over there?" or "I KNOW I never met that woman so how did she know my name?" or "I KNOW I put on underwear this morning so...?" I mean the deep dark mysteries leaving us mumbling incoherently as we walk away scratching our butts. Those mysteries. I present the following experience in the search for answers to a few questions; a puzzle wrapped in a mystery inside an enigma.

I recently returned from a winter vacation to Boston. I arrived at midnight after a four-hour flight, a quick trip over to Dallas for dinner with my son, and a three-hour drive home. I was tired and perhaps a little grumpy. Although I had left the house secured and under the care of a trusted house sitter (my daughter), I unlocked the sun porch door and entered cautiously; I was looking for anything amiss. The only light at this point of entry was the faint, eerie illumination of the outside security lamp, but I immediately saw reasons for concern – a flower pot lying broken on the floor and a skewed lampshade. I inhaled deeply. *Had someone entered through that window?* I stood frozen and silently surveyed the room, looking for a broken window or the sound of a squatter in the house. Hearing nothing, I exhaled and further examined the room, finding all windows locked and intact and only a few additional items in the room out of place. *Weird.* I hesitated, at a loss and a bit shaky. I knew my house sitter had checked on things and turned on the heater before my arrival; she would have noticed this mess. Right?

Determining this room was not the point of a nefarious entry, it was time to turn my attention to the remainder of the house. You know those murder mysteries you watch on TV? The ones where the lady walks into the dark house, slipping in bloody pools and tripping over bodies? And she grabs a flashlight with an obviously weak battery and starts creeping through the house with nothing but a rolled up newspaper for a weapon, periodically hitting the flashlight to coax a weak, flickering beam? And you whisper to the screen, "Do NOT go up those stairs, stupid! RUN! Call 9-1-1 and get out!" Then, you turn to the one watching with you and say with a superior sniff, "She is so stupid! I would NEVER...". Well, I did. I even had my Glock (tucked snuggly in its case and buried deep inside one of the bags...I don't remember which one...or maybe still in the truck) but opted to continue the journey alone. Why? I don't know. Bravery, I suppose? Yes, bravery.

Before ascending the three steps from the sunroom into the living room I peered into the darkness, allowing my eyes to adjust to the dimmer, much more subdued light. I hesitated and listened. Nothing. My eyes gradually adjusted and I could determine the outline of something on the living room floor – something out of place, something that shouldn't be there. I kept staring. Eventually, I made it out to be a body, possibly dead. *Whoa!* I admit I was more than spooked, peering into that room and seeing a lifeless body sprawled in the middle of the floor! I was quivering and gasping for each shallow breath, heart pounding, ears ringing. My knees weakened and I feared I was going to throw up, possibly faint. (But I stood my ground, just like the woman in the movies!) I was very thankful I had recognized it wasn't the body of a person; I wouldn't have reacted well to a dead human on my floor.

Perhaps I should leave and retrieve the 9mm before proceeding? I considered that option, but determined it was better to go in alone than to empty a clip into my living room floor. I crept closer, quietly looking for any sign the sleeping devil would arise and wreak additional havoc. *What is that? A cat? A skunk? A possum? Is it dead? Maybe it's just sleeping!* Closer and closer, cautiously and never taking my eyes off the critter. The body sprawled so peacefully began to slowly come into focus, taking the final form of a squirrel. *Of course! A squirrel! Why didn't I think of that?*

I stood over the body for a while, hesitating, thinking I should probably give it a little poke. Which brings me to my first question regarding this mystery: How much time is appropriate before giving a possibly dead/maybe alive squirrel a poke just to be sure? I started with a 'five' count. But reconsidered and gave it an additional 'five' for good measure. Completing a ten count, I slowly bent toward the body to look for signs of life. Seeing none, I finally had the courage to give it a little nudge with my foot. Then, I waited. I fully expected it to rouse, climb my legs and attack my face- clawing and scratching and gnawing with its razor sharp nails and teeth and pulling out patches of hair. *How would I explain returning from a vacation with those injuries? Would anyone believe me?* It's funny what goes through one's mind in these situations. Anyway, no crazed squirrel responded and I was left with its dead, stiff carcass in the middle of my house at 12:30 in the morning. And the mysteries of its clandestine entrance and subsequent death.

After determining it offered no more threat, I continued throughout the house looking for additional damage or clues. No open doors. No broken windows. No collapsed wall or exploded roof. *Maybe that silly house sitter thought leaving a dead squirrel would be a funny joke, a "gag gift", so to speak? Or maybe I made her mad?* However, I finally found a few signs indicating it had scampered along window sills looking for a place to exit. The damage was surprisingly minimal, not near the destruction one should expect from a crazed squirrel left to its own devices in an empty house for a few hours, possibly days. I felt fortunate, under the circumstances.

The next task was an examination of the body, so to speak. Donning gloves, I checked Rocky for any signs of disease, injury, poisoning, or trauma. My family would pose starvation as plausible; they would say they have often languished staring into that bare or oddly stocked pantry. Whatever. Anyway, I am not a squirrel expert or medic but I felt it would be irresponsible to not at least check. The only thing I determined, for sure, was Rocky did NOT succumb beneath the weight of an 18-wheeler or at the business end of a 10-gauge shotgun. That's all I knew and it would have to be enough; I was not going to dump a bag of dead squirrel at the vet's for an autopsy.

I was then faced with the immediate task of body disposal. That led to another question resulting from this situation: What do others do with the body of dead squirrels found lifeless in the middle of their living room floor? Bury it? Cremate it? Freeze it? Stuff it? I was curious about that as I grabbed Rocky by the tail, walked him down the county road, and tossed him over the neighbor's fence and into his pasture. Don't judge me too harshly; it was 2:00 in the morning and I was done with that squirrel. Finished.

I awoke rested the next morning, still puzzled and primed to do a bit of investigating. I determined Rocky entered through the chimney after I discovered the fireplace doors slightly ajar; I was satisfied with that answer. Armed with my best CSI flashlight, I fully expected to find little squirrel footprints in the ash and traces tracked out onto the hearth; I found nothing. Nothing. I thought perhaps its untimely and accelerated death would be traced to a little tray of poison kept hidden in the bowels of the kitchen cabinets. I uncovered the buried stash, shined the CSI flashlight and found it seemingly undisturbed. I was out of ideas, pending an autopsy. Maybe he died of a broken heart or loneliness?

The mysteries remain. Although my best efforts to solve the case with hard evidence were thwarted, I remain confident my assumptions are correct. *Rocky picked the wrong house and succumbed to starvation and loneliness!* My barren pantry and solitary lifestyle are not for faint-hearted or weak-spirited; it takes a special kind of squirrel to hang with me! He probably should have crashed the party house down the road!

NOTE: A final question came to mind as I considered the mysteries surrounding this unfortunate event: Would it be considered customary for a 'house sitter' to remove dead animal carcasses from the middle of the house left to their care BEFORE the owner returns? I thought 'yes'...but perhaps that was expecting too much? She assured me it was not left as a surprise or joke or twisted revenge. She assured me she had checked the house earlier in the day and it was not in the house, alive or dead. Still, I wonder. It was her first time to house sit for me... and the FIRST time I returned to a dead animal. That seems just a little too coincidental. Right? Another mystery.

What Would Doris Do?

I had been working meticulously and methodically to rid a small stretch of pasture of ALL GRASS BURRS. I do this in my spare time because, well, I don't knit, nap, or paint with watercolor. I ever so carefully bagged each plant, diligently watching for even a single burr to drop. Should one fall, I would kneel down and search until I found it. If I saw a plant with no burrs, I dug it anyway and left it to die. Unfortunately, I had abandoned the grass burr eradication project for a couple of weeks. It has been too hot in the afternoons and I had another project come up unexpectedly requiring my time and effort.

However, this cooler afternoon I felt compelled to give it one more push and try to finish. My concern was the remaining burrs getting dry and popping in all directions, effectively negating my previous efforts. I grabbed my shovel and hoe and started grubbing. I noticed many of the remaining burrs, with a few exceptions, were shorter and held perhaps only one or two burrs. These were nothing like the first plants I went out to remove... the three footers with multiple stalks, each loaded with like a bazillion burrs. But a burr is a burr and I started this afternoon with the same gusto and determination I had brought to the task previously.

After an hour of this activity, I noticed I was humming 'Que Sera, Sera'. What? I thought that odd as I really don't care for the song, certainly don't consider it a hoeing- burrs –down- south- on- the –plantation- blues kind of song. I could understand humming any variety of rock anthems or classic rock or old rock and roll, any of which are good for working. I could even imagine humming a pop or rap out in the field to the rhythm of the task. But 'Que Sera, Sera'? What's wrong with this picture? I consider it more of a song for Doris Day to sing dream-ily flitting around the house in a dress and apron, dusting furniture as cookies bake and waiting for the handsome astronaut to come for supper. Very strange.

As I continued thinking of that song and pondering the universe I no-ticed I was not being quite as diligent as I had been before. If one or two or three burrs popped off in the process, I wouldn't even stop to give it much thought. Certainly not pick it up. What're one or two burrs in the scheme of things? I seriously considered the possibility that I could never get them all, no matter how hard I tried. I rationalized my previous efforts had already saved the property a major problem later. And I can always use pre-emergent next spring...now that I know there will be a problem. Right? I suppose that's not cheating. I was suddenly totally off my rhythm and had lost my motivation. My mojo was gone and I blame Doris Day for that!

'Que sera, sera'.... Whatever will be, will be. Indeed! My grubbing mojo was totally shot down by a Doris Day song and thoughts of roman-tic comedies, glass bottom boats, and pillow talk. They just don't mix well with digging grass burrs in the sun, so I loaded the shovel and hoe to consider the job completed. Looking at the bags of burrs in the back of the truck, I wondered how many burrs Doris Day had ever grubbed. Huh, Doris? Did you ever sweat? Did you ever look anything but perfect? Did you ever NOT get the handsome hunk by the end of the movie, no matter how badly you screwed up? Maybe I'll see her one day and I'll ask her. However, I've heard she's a bit of a recluse and probably does weird things in her spare time. She scares me a little. Que sera, sera.

When Is It My Turn?

I hosted 17 for Easter this year. It's important to note I was not a Supermom capable of multi-tasking with ease and mastering all. I was never one of those, the employed Moms we all know able to work full-time and simultaneously prepare for a holiday - cook the full holiday meal from scratch while handcrafting engraved seating placards and all the fancy decorations with ribbons and bows – a mop in one hand and potter's wheel in the other, rocking the cradle with one foot while having an intelligible conversation on the phone tucked neatly under her chin – finishing all the details early and spending the day before the actual holiday getting her hair styled and a manicure.

My brain is more of the linear variety, one task at a time methodically marked off the list before progressing to the next. It's not the best way, unfortunately. Before retirement, it meant I did little to prepare for a holiday (even hosting) until the last bell sounded and the office doors were locked. Only then would the holiday prep list come out and I start the mad dash to the last minute before the first guests arrived. It wasn't pretty.

Retirement presented an opportunity to improve upon my holiday modus operandi. As I was hosting Easter festivities, I incorporated certain preps into my list of daily activities. Yard was done by mid-week, short enough to look nice and an appropriate amount of time to grow and accommodate hiding eggs. Check. The porch was deep cleaned and ready for table and chairs Thursday morning; the grill was uncovered and cleaned Thursday afternoon. Check and check.

It was going well and I felt I was developing an efficient and effective system. Although I would not be having my hair styled and a manicure Saturday, I knew I would NOT be greeting my Easter guests out of breath and wiping the remnants of flour off my sweaty face. It was all good!

Friday was my shopping day on the list, food and miscellaneous items from Walmart. Typically, pre-retirement, this would have been a last-minute-fight-the-crowd-rush-on-the-day-before-a-major-holiday sort of trip. And I would have pushed my cart down the crowded aisles and felt disdain at all the old retirees blocking my way as they read each and every label and took their sweet time. I would have smiled weakly and nodded, but be thinking: *WHY THE HECK ARE YOU HERE NOW, OLD LADY? You had all week to come and shop. All day, every day! And you just had to come today?? Now? When I work all week and have only a few precious hours to prepare for everything? Urghhhhh!* Well, not this year! I had it all planned and would be strolling my way through well-stocked and wide-open aisles. I was almost giddy at the prospect!

So, Friday morning I jumped in the truck and headed to town. I can NOT adequately describe my bewilderment upon turning the corner and seeing a packed parking lot! What? How was it even possible Walmart could have so many customers on a typical weekday. This would usually be my divine sign to keep the vehicle in motion and come back another time.

But this day, Friday, was actually on a list and trumped any inclination I had to balk and run. If I waited until the night the shelves would be empty, the aisles full of stock-people or blocked by box mountains. Or, the next day I would be in the 'working-mothers-with-kids-out-of-school zone, the very thing I was trying to avoid! *Fight, not flight* was the mantra as I entered the doors and grabbed a cart. Like Dorie, the fish... *just keep swimming...swimming...swimming.*

I kept my head down, pushing the cart through the crowded aisles and trying to maintain a low profile. As I stood two aisles in and read a label, I realized I was blocking passage for a cart behind me. I adjusted positions to allow her by... two younger school-aged children in tow. I looked around and noticed there were school-aged kids scattered everywhere throughout the store! *Huh? It's Friday! My day! Why is she here and shopping TODAY? And aren't those kids supposed to be in school?* She wearily jockeyed her cart and two kids by. She smiled weakly and nodded her head. But, I know what she was thinking... *Hey, old lady! WHY ARE YOU HERE NOW? You had all week to come and shop? All day, every day! And you're here NOW?? Now? When I work and have only a few precious hours to shop, cook, and prepare for everything? Urghhhhh!*

It was then I suddenly realized I have officially made the transition. I am now one of THEM- a label-reading, moseying retiree blocking the aisle at Walmart on a non-school day! I felt guilty. I felt old. I needed to sit down and breathe! I wanted to apologize! But to whom? First, I wanted to tell her (and all the others like her to follow), "I'm sorry! I'm new at this! I didn't realize school was out today and this was YOUR day! I understand." I also wanted to apologize to all retirees I ever met under similar circumstances...the ones who got that same irritated look from me when I was a harried working mother with only a few hours to prepare for a major holiday..." I'm sorry! I didn't consider you also have a life and things to do. I understand."

I now know being a retiree shopping at Walmart on a school holiday weekday is brutal! I already knew being a working mother shopping at Walmart on a school holiday weekday is brutal. Evidently, we are all equally miserable. Explains a lot. Who knew?

NOTE TO SELF: Request school calendars for all school districts within a 50-mile radius. Cross-reference any and all of their free days with major holidays. And my family birthdays. Also, any family/friend's special dates which may require shopping throughout the year. DO NOT LEAVE THE HOUSE ON THESE DAYS! "The only real mistake is the one from which we learn nothing". I won't encroach upon their time zone if they stay out of mine! Seems fair.

Whores Be Makin' Money Today

I awakened this morning, realizing the day to be one set aside as a Memorial to men and women having given all in service to our nation. After a moment of silence and words of gratitude, I turned on the TV for some news and was soon reminded why I get so irked on this and other 'solemn' holidays. The commercials were soon flooding the TV with the word 'SALE' casually (callously) tacked on the phrase 'Memorial Day', the commentator loudly and proudly barking it like a sideshow carny. I visualize him holding back the tent flap, gold tooth reflecting in the sunlight, as he entices the giddy masses into the darkness storing wares of toilet tissue, bed sheets, buns, and wieners.

The blatant commercialization of such occasions has always been a personal pet peeve, one to quickly catapult me atop the nearest soapbox. Paradoxically, commercialism and free speech are basic tenets of the American way and the first reasons to go to war. Interesting. So, they sacrificed their lives so WE can be oblivious and have the freedom to set up showrooms and display cases at the cemetery gates of fallen soldiers? Basically. Still, a little reverent respect would be appreciated. It's starting to look a lot like Christmas!

X-Men

(I happened to be visiting Boston in 2013 during the Marathon bombings and their immediate aftermath. It was an extremely scary time and I was greatly relieved the day law enforcement approved air travel out. These are my thoughts, expressed as I rocked my sleeping grandson upon my return).

***

I just don't know, Jonah. Sometimes Grammie looks at the world and fears we are quickly losing all redeeming value as a species. I wonder how long before we lose this battle due to our own selfishness, bigotry, greed, malice, and hatred? Especially hatred. I see all that's wrong and making it right seems so overwhelmingly insurmountable... like trying to rein a heartless, faceless mass of jagged edges and sharp teeth. How do we put down a monster capable of changing color, religion, politics, and ideology at any moment in time? I got a glimpse of the claws and fiery eyes and it's so easy to let hope waiver, lose faith in your tomorrow.

But then I see the gladiators step forward...every time. Every time. Every time a faceless, gutless monster unleashes his unprovoked attack on the innocents, the gladiators fearlessly run toward the jaws – forward toward the explosions or sounds of screaming and gunshots. Quite ordinary people, really, until they strip down to their superhero tights. They seem to come in all shapes and sizes and colors...all religions and political orientations and ideologies. They don't go to Gladiator/Hero school. They don't get together on Saturdays to practice running into the explosions and blood and shattering glass and limbs. They don't even know they have the right stuff inside or entertain the thought of needing it until they are called upon to offer their warmth or apply pressure here or drag a body there. These ordinary, often nameless people restore the faith and hope we could so easily allow to be stripped from us.

There will always be monsters lurking in the shadows and hiding behind misplaced allegiance and ideology. But we will also witness the goodness and heroics of humanity as it responds to the threats. We can still find hope in the knowledge there will always be a Schindler compiling a list or a Harriet Tubman blazing a trail or an anonymous accountant running back into a collapsing tower or a teacher stepping up to take a bullet. And as demonstrated yesterday at the Boston Marathon, there will be ordinary college students and cab drivers and insurance salesmen... all manner of ordinary people enjoying an ordinary day... called into duty unexpectedly to do extraordinary things- even if it means running toward the smoke and blood and screams. We have yet to pin a face to this latest evil terrorist, foreign or domestic. But we do have faces for the hope of the future. It's the faces of those around us willing to aid and comfort and protect and fight. It's ordinary people with the right stuff.

I believe the powers-that-be should stop playing political correctness games and administer justice, swift and absolute. Life is short enough and ain't nobody got time or space to share with the hatemongers (the skinheads, radicals, reactionaries jihadists, gang members). Justice swift and absolute. No psychoanalysis. No suicide watch. Zero tolerance. No second chances. No three strikes. No pass, no play. I know it sounds harsh but I don't want my grandchildren growing up prisoners in their own world...bars on the school windows, locks on the church doors, afraid to play outside, armed guards at ballgames and spelling bees and dance recitals. It's not right to be held prisoner in your own home, especially if you've committed no crimes. It's not right.

Jonah, the cowardly bullies (foreign and domestic) need to be afraid... be very afraid. I'm just one little old Grammie in Texas who's been angered by what they are stealing from my kids and grandkids. But, I'm not alone; we Baby Boomers are Legion! To those cowardly bullies, I send a warning: If you piss off enough of us gray panthers you'll be running and knocking on Homeland Security's door to let you in... crying like the little wimps you obviously are. "Don't make me angry. You wouldn't like me when I'm angry!" That's what David Banner says before changing into the Incredible Hulk. We may look unassuming but beneath the surface beats the hearts of warriors! We come armed with walking sticks and motorized wheelchairs and all manner of drugs and monitoring equipment. We can cut you down with just a sharp word or icy stare. We have thick skin, x-ray vision, and a full set of bionic teeth. We are often invisible to others as we live out our last days. We are experienced fighters and were completing brutal missions before you were even born. Most of all, we are not afraid to fight; we have nothing to lose and everything to gain YEAH! BOOM BABY!

I'll admit I'm angry and confused, disillusioned and a little scared. Charles Xavier (Professor X) said, "balance lies somewhere between rage and serenity." I suppose that's true. My hope, though, is you inherit a world more balanced - a world in which we've learned to harness the powers of anger and hatred as a tool to achieve peace. Actually, that's my hope for all of us - to find serenity and discover the beauty hidden beneath the briars, brambles, and rusted barbed wire choking the happiness from our lives. That requires we never give up. Never surrender. We may get a few scratches along the way, but one day we'll uncover the rose beneath needing only the sunshine and air to bloom. It will be a good day! Any day the pricks don't win is a good day! At least, that's what this old lady roaming on an old peanut farm in Texas always says.

I continued rocking, considering how those words would sound coming from Garth Brooks:

> "No matter where you're goin',
> Doesn't matter where you've been,
> Every day's a good day if it's a day the pricks don't win.

> Rocking and humming. Amen.

Conclusion

One day, Jonah, you'll notice the scratches and streaks of dried blood on my arms after I return from time spent in the briar patch. You'll be sympathetic and ask, "Do they hurt? Are you alright?" I'll reply, "Yeah, they sting. But only a little bit. They're just my battle scars and war wounds. I'm quite alright,". Days spent in the briar patch have demonstrated I'm not afraid- of hard work or things that sting and bite; things that scratch and poke; things that bear their teeth and hiss. I'm not turned back by blood, sweat, and tears. If it is obscuring my vision or an obstacle to my progress, I will remove it. If it's threatening something I love, I will cut it down. If it attempts to overrun and choke, I will shred it to pieces.

It's nothing. We all encounter briars, brambles, and stretches of rusty barbed wire in the path as we move through life - people, situations, and conditions effectively holding us back. But only if we allow it. Thorns of the pointed words and actions of others, ripping at us with the intent to discourage or cause us hurt and pain. Unexpected conditions or situations we encounter, those brambles threatening to slow us down or hold us back from our full potential. Unavoidable and unforeseen stretches of rusty barbed wire standing between us and where we want to be. It will require a lot of effort and won't be easy to reclaim our rightful territory. It will most definitely scratch and sting; there will be drops of blood and sweat. We must decide for ourselves if the work will be worth the benefits of proceeding. It's a choice.

The hardest briars and brambles to clear are the ones we've allowed to grow wild in our minds and hearts. Feelings of bitterness, anger, or hatred directed at others. Feelings of defeat, despair, grief, or worthlessness directed at ourselves. These are often the hardest to define, definitely the most difficult to rip from our lives. However, left to grow they will choke our spirit and invade every part of our lives. These must go. Always. It won't be easy because they tend to spread quickly and return again and again. However, the results will be worth the effort. It's important.

There is one thing we need to understand, something valuable I've learned from years of experience. Sometimes there will be a briar patch from which you can walk away. There is no need for confrontation, no need to expend our valuable resources to remove. Each battle needs to be evaluated on its own merit. Basically, if it's not in

244

our way, not bothering us or hurting us in any fashion, there is no need to spend our time and effort with it. It is not to be considered defeat, rather the smart thing to do. There is no shame in walking away from some fights.

After years warring against the briars, brambles, and barbed wire I gradually came to a realization. I discovered the fight has not been as much about removing ugliness as I had first thought; it's actually been more about revealing the beauty hidden beneath, beauty obscured by the harshness surrounding it. That perspective changed this battle from one of destruction and chaos into one of nurturing and order. It became a noble battle, one worth winning.

> *"No matter where you're goin',*
> *Doesn't matter where you've been-*
> *Every day's a good day if it's a day the pricks don't win.*
> *"You can dance in the moonlight as you wish upon a star*
> *Singin' any day the pricks don't win*
> *Is a good day where you are!'*

Perhaps Metallica would like my song better than Garth? Anyway, ROCK ON AND KEEP YER POWDER DRY!

CPSIA information can be obtained
at www.ICGtesting.com
Printed in the USA
BVHW032021100821
613997BV00037B/44

9 781977 243836